■■■■■■■■■■■■■■■■■■■■■■■■■

Classifying
Social Data

*New Applications
of Analytic Methods
for Social Science Research*

■■■■■■■■■■■■■■■■■■■■■■■■■

Herschel C. Hudson

and Associates

Classifying

Social Data

 Jossey-Bass Publishers

San Francisco • Washington • London • 1982

CLASSIFYING SOCIAL DATA
New Applications of Analytic Methods for Social Science Research
by Herschel C. Hudson and Associates

Copyright © 1982 by: Jossey-Bass Inc., Publishers
433 California Street
San Francisco, California 94104
&
Jossey-Bass Limited
28 Banner Street
London EC1Y 8QE

Library of Congress Cataloging in Publication Data
Main entry under title:

Classifying social data.

  Bibliography: p. 231
  Includes index.
  1. Social sciences—Classification—Statistical methods. 2. Social
sciences—Research. I. Hudson, Herschel C.
H61.2.C55   300'.12   79-92464
ISBN 0-87589-505-0   AACR2

Manufactured in the United States of America

JACKET DESIGN BY WILLI BAUM

FIRST EDITION

Code 8117

■■■■■■■■■■■■■■■■■■■■■■■■

The Jossey-Bass
Social and Behavioral
Science Series

Special Adviser
Methodology of Social and
Behavioral Research
DONALD W. FISKE
University of Chicago

■■■■■■■■■■■■■■■■■■■■■■■■

Preface

Clustering and related pattern recognition procedures have become bywords in the field of biology in both North America and Europe. Since the appearance of Sokal and Sneath's *Principles of Numerical Taxonomy* in 1963, the outburst of publications utilizing these techniques has exceeded all expectations. Pattern recognition procedures are also used to organize sensor data gathered by aircraft and satellites, thus providing additional theoretical and empirical returns to the scientist. It was during discussions of these innovations at annual meetings of biological and social scientists that this volume was first conceived; we marveled at the spectacular growth of classification procedures in the fields of biology and statistics, as contrasted to the comparatively minimal use of these methods in social science.

By and large, methodological problems in the social sciences involve highly technical issues surrounding the generation of classes of data and their incorporation in ongoing research. Most investigators are concerned with special classes or groups of data, whereas the lengthier publications, and there are several, tend to focus on more formalized aspects of statistical and mathematical procedure. None of these works is authored by a social scientist. To encourage the use of classification methods by students and practitioners in the social sciences, the chapters in this volume offer a more data-oriented approach, one that lies in the intermediate level and that encourages a closer look at specific operations and the classifications that follow from them.

The following chapters may be of special interest to the numerically oriented student who wishes to venture into the partitioning of data, to the regular user of factor analysis or multidimensional scaling, and to anyone who seeks to identify underlying relationships between or within groups of attributes, characteristics, variables, or persons. For a more advanced treatment, the reader may wish to consult Van Ryzin's *Classification and Clustering* (1977), which was written primarily by mathematicians and statisticians.

While few procedures are so central to the social and natural sciences as the generation and use of classifications, classification alone is seldom the end product of research. It constitutes but one of two phases in what Dewey (1938, p. 284) called the "fundamental division of labor in inquiry," or what Köbben (1970, p. 586), in a more limited sense, called "classifying plus explanation." In one phase, observations of existing things are obtained and ordered by means of descriptive statistics, analysis of factors, clusters, and networks, or by the existential propositions of logic. The classifications they produce are grounded in place and time, are labeled with common nouns, and are the things that hypotheses relate. The remaining phase is conceptual and concerns the relation of meanings ascribed by the practitioner to his classifications. These meanings are related to one another by hypotheses of the if, then variety and the relationship, either functionality or causality, is labeled by an abstract noun for it is now free of any reference to space or time. When viewed from the standpoint of form alone, an if, then hypothesis is the scientific equivalent of a universal proposition. Both relate classes of things, the hypothesis in a provisional sense, pending further operations, and the universal proposition in a logical sense. When classes of things are related in either sense, they may be treated as components of a system.

The chapters in this book focus on classification as a specialized activity and on some of the problems the practitioner might encounter. Since each chapter is based on the ongoing research of its author or authors, the range of topics was limited to the kinds of work in progress when the volume was planned. This limitation further underscores the need this volume was designed to address: the need to encourage broader use of classification procedures. Despite the focus on classification, several of the chapters may appear to have little affinity for one another; this illustrates the disjunctive nature of the options available to the practitioner. Reflecting the state of the field in another way, the entire volume indicates that, although advances in computer technology have made feasible analytic methods not available a decade or two ago, many basic problems remain to be solved.

Classification came of age early in the Western world. Near the beginning of Greek thought, it was used to reduce the many and diverse parts of nature to a manageable few. By the time of Aristotle, classification had achieved so central a place in the overall scheme of things that taxonomic systems, similar to those found in zoology, were regarded as the fullest development of science. For Aristotle, the fixed, unchanging species was the ultimate qualitative whole that gave meaning to unstable singular things, which grew, changed, and died. Only the species was a real scientific object. Rather than gathering data, the classifier began by observing the individual object (specimen) and recognizing it as the embodiment of an unchanging form or universal nature (species). Next, he noted its characteristics in order to formulate a definition of this universal nature. These observations did not yield something independent of an explanation, even for the time being. They never became data the classifier could accumulate or quantify. Rather than collect data, he collected individuals and his observations taken from them did little more than support the prevailing view of the nature of the form. Without data to analyze and, as a result, no method for treating exceptions, many scientists hold that past taxonomies of the natural sciences reflected little more than community-wide orientations. Some modern social scientists might view these systems as forerunners of ethnoscience, but not everyone would agree.

Once defined, species were ordered so as to reflect the manner in which they were bound together in nature; major and minor propositions denoted the including (generic) and included (specific) classifications. In the resulting taxonomy, each classification, or the segment of nature that it identified, was defined by a set of distinguishing characteristics. Species were related to one another only by the fact that they were included in the same broader classification; if a species were connected to some outside event, an environmental condition, for example, the relation was thought to be accidental to the independent and eternal nature of the species.

Modern methods for grouping social data tend to follow one of two somewhat related paths. On the one hand, classes of people (socioeconomic) or characteristics (matrilineal) are derived from mathematical or logical tradition, and are ordered by hypotheses. Classes, however widely they may differ in levels of technical treatment, cannot be observed since they are not bounded by some particular time or place. Components of a class may be observed under appropriate conditions, for they consist of singular things or events that are bounded. Although their numbers are indefinite, any one of them, when treated individually, may be termed a representative of a particular class.

The other path leads to studies of small human groups and of the social relations associated with them. Both groups and social relations are usually restricted in time and place. The components of a group are definite in number and are interrelated in some fashion, and, when treated individually, are often designated as members. When group studies are repeated, the replications, under appropriate conditions, may take on the characteristics of a sample, and the sample in turn may be used to estimate population parameters. At this point the two related paths converge, for a population is the statistical equivalent of a logical class.

In order to examine a range of classification procedures and their applications and to encourage their use by those who work with social data, a workshop on Classifying Social Data was held at Charleston, South Carolina, under the terms of a National Science Foundation grant to this editor. In attendance were almost 20 scientists from the fields of anthropology, biology, geology, mathematics, psychology, and sociology. By and large, the chapters of this book grew out of the workshop, although we subsequently added several chapters to broaden the coverage of specific areas.

The first six chapters illustrate cluster or factor analytic studies, the next four look more closely at specific topics with which the analyst may be concerned, and the final three examine social structures that obtain within groups and among subgroups. Approaches vary widely, as do the choices of method.

In the early chapters, Robert Kozelka, John Roberts, Melvin Williams, George Poole, Ronald May, and Herschel Hudson use traditional cluster analytic procedures to generate nonoverlapping classes of social or archeological data, but they differ in the manner in which these classes are employed. Pascale Rousseau and David Sankoff cluster by way of a maximum likelihood criterion, whereas Karl Schuessler and Robert Parker reexamine factor analysis as a classificatory tool.

In the opening chapter, Kozelka accompanies the reader through a cluster analysis procedure. Using typical and well-worked data that should be familiar to many readers, he examines the effects of the method on the data and cautions that, for the seasoned professional as well as the novice, the quality of data and the appropriateness of the method selected for use require constant attention. Kozelka's suggestions should prove especially useful to those who are new to clustering.

An ethnoscience approach with commercial applications is the focus of Roberts, Williams, and Poole. Their findings make explicit how residents of an urban ghetto visualize used automobiles. Statistical classifications of autos are supported by ethnographic reporting, and their bases are examined by means of multidimensional scaling. The findings suggest that autos are grouped and ranked in the community in much the same way that their owners are.

One task likely to be confronted by the social taxonomist is that of assigning an individual or characteristic of unknown affinity to an established set of classifications. May suggests that discriminant function analysis can be used to identify the appropriate taxon. He discusses the conditions under which assignment is warranted and illustrates his views with examples taken from archeological literature.

The exploratory classification of a large body of social data that are nearly continent-wide in distribution is Hudson's subject. After noting the unexpectedly large number of subclasses within his sample and the relatively small portion of overall variance explained by each of them, he surmises that social heterogeneity contained in broad geographic areas may work against major reductions of the original set of attributes.

Rousseau and Sankoff examine yet another mode of clustering, that of likelihood maximization. The program they describe follows from the pioneering work of Diday and Simon (1976) and provides for unconstrained as well as partially constrained analysis. Language data, taken from Montreal French, are used to illustrate the solutions.

Schuessler and Parker begin with the speculation that recent innovations in multivariate analysis might have diminished the role of the decision-making analyst over the past decade or so. Using data that mark a continuation of earlier studies by Driver and Schuessler (1957, 1968), they trace the steps of a factor analysis that they employ as a classificatory tool and find that the procedure is no less arbitrary and subjective today than before and that the need for judgment has not waned.

Recurrent problem areas constitute the general topic of chapters by James Lingoes, John Fox, Juan Mezzich, Roger Blashfield, Mark Aldenderfer, and Leslie Morey. Individual subjects range from a comparison of unordered configurations to the validation of clusters.

Lingoes describes a program that enables the investigator to compare two or more multidimensional data structures. Based on transformations of matrices, the program determines the kind and complexity of analysis required, and norms variates and partitions variance as needed, and quantifies similarities and differences between configurations. It also compares data structures to target configurations, thus enabling the social scientist, working in the exploratory stages from, for example, an ecological or an economic base, to identify associated characteristics from other bodies of data. Lingoes illustrates the kinds of data transformations contained in the program by means of diagrams of fish.

Fox considers some of the difficulties inherent in the first steps of cluster analysis. Rather than focusing on the many measures of similarity or distance that are available, he examines different sorts of social science data and discusses the measures of association appropriate to each. In particular, he finds a useful measure for assessing resemblance among aggregates as well as variables but notes discrepancies in all measures when they are employed to determine resemblance among individuals.

Mezzich examines the relative performance of ten of the most frequently used clustering procedures. Using four data bases from as many research fields, he measures resemblance among variables with three different coefficients and proceeds to cluster them. Each of the taxonomic procedures is evaluated according to four criteria, and the results are compared.

Blashfield, Aldenderfer, and Morey broach the elusive topic of adequacy of cluster solutions, an issue with which the social taxonomist must ultimately come to grips. They categorize a variety of proposed cluster validation procedures as statistical measures, manipulative procedures, and graphic displays. The authors provide a list of bibliographical suggestions but note the paucity of proven validation procedures.

The authors of the final three chapters look to the structure within classifications and to the ties that obtain among them. Methods range from the permutation and blocking of matrices (Arabie, Boorman, and Ennis) to algebraic topology (Doreian).

Arabie and Boorman examine the method of blockmodeling and matters of practical import to those engaged in its use. Then they look to the future to some of the challenges this area of mathematical analysis might face.

After summarizing recent work on the spatial and algebraic representations of group structure, Ennis uses both approaches to analyze the structure of group data originally obtained by Bales (1950, 1968). In particular, Ennis compares the results of multidimensional scaling and principal components analysis with those of the CONCOR algorithm described by Arabie and Boorman in the previous chapter. Overall, he finds similarities in the configurations produced by all these methods.

Doreian, employing algebraic topology, compares the patterns of connectivity obtained by Atkin's approach with those obtained by other methods. He notes that his results are in substantial agreement with most previous analyses and affirms that the concepts of topology have a substantial capacity for describing the structure of social relations.

No book is complete without recognition of those who made it possible. The workshop on Classifying Social Data was funded by the Mathematical Social Science Board, which in turn was financed by the National Science Foundation (Grant SOC76-10351). Administrative support for the board's activities is provided by the Center for

Advanced Study in the Behavioral Sciences at Palo Alto, California. I am indebted to the National Science Foundation, to the Mathematical Social Science Board, to its chairman Eugene Hammel, and to Preston Cutler, associate director of the Center, for their suggestions and encouragement.

John Roberts had the original idea for a workshop and, with the skill of a pro, guided me through the proposal and planning stages. Our meetings also benefited from the presence of Robert Sokal, Kimball Romney, and Roy D'Andrade, all of whom made useful suggestions. On behalf of us all, I wish to acknowledge the generous help of Karl Schuessler and Donald Fiske, who read the manuscript and provided many worthwhile suggestions for its refinement. Errors of omission, however, belong to me.

A special note of thanks is due Mary McAdory of the Medical University of South Carolina (MUSC) for her meticulous care in drawing the figures. Last minute alterations were executed by Nancy Trammel of MUSC. I also thank Doris Kennedy for her diligent typing of the manuscript. And finally, I am most grateful to the contributors to this volume, all of whom made useful suggestions to one another and to me and patiently endured my novice editorship.

October 1981   HERSCHEL C. HUDSON
                                                        Charleston, South Carolina

Contents

xvii

■■■■■■■■■■■■■■■■■■■■■■■■■

The Authors

■■■■■■■■■■■■■■■■■■■■■■■■■

MARK S. ALDENDERFER, adjunct professor of anthropology, State University of New York at Buffalo

PHIPPS ARABIE, professor of psychology, University of Illinois

ROGER K. BLASHFIELD, associate professor of psychology and psychiatry, University of Florida Medical School

SCOTT A. BOORMAN, professor of sociology, Yale University

PATRICK DOREIAN, professor of sociology, University of Pittsburgh

JAMES G. ENNIS, assistant professor of sociology, University of Plattsburgh, Plattsburgh, New York

JOHN FOX, associate professor of sociology, York University, Toronto, Canada

HERSCHEL C. HUDSON, associate professor of anthropology and sociology, The Citadel

ROBERT M. KOZELKA, professor of mathematics, Williams College

JAMES C. LINGOES, professor of psychology and research scientist, University of Michigan

RONALD W. MAY, engineering geologist, Thurber Consultants Ltd., Edmonton, Alberta

JUAN E. MEZZICH, associate professor of psychiatry, University of Pittsburgh Medical School

LESLIE C. MOREY, graduate student, Department of Clinical Psychology, University of Florida

ROBERT NASH PARKER, assistant professor of sociology, University of Akron

GEORGE C. POOLE, supervising pathologist's assistant, Magee-Women's Hospital, Pittsburgh, Pennsylvania

JOHN M. ROBERTS, professor of anthropology, University of Pittsburgh

PASCALE ROUSSEAU, professor of mathematics, University of Quebec at Montreal

DAVID SANKOFF, research assistant, Center of Applied Mathematical Research, University of Montreal

KARL F. SCHUESSLER, distinguished professor of sociology, Indiana University

MELVIN D. WILLIAMS, professor of anthropology, Purdue University

Classifying Social Data

New Applications
of Analytic Methods
for Social Science Research

How to Work Through a Clustering Problem

Robert M. Kozelka

The only way to make sure that one thoroughly understands any mathematical technique is to work through a sample problem. I propose the following:

The numbers in Table 1 are coefficients of agreement; the higher the number, the greater the agreement. The different letters stand for different tribes. I wish to group the tribes into clusters by using the agreement-coefficient values.

The trouble with a clustering problem, unless the data are artificially constructed, is that there is no correct answer in the back of the book. This example has been chosen from the literature, however, and at least one nonmathematical solution is available. In what follows, that solution and one other are exhibited. I will also offer some simple-minded but (I hope) germane comments on clustering in general.

Faced with analyzing a set of inexact or rough data, the community of mathematicians finds itself, like Gaul, divided three ways. The largest group refuses to have anything at all to do with such a problem. Another group uses the most delicate available technique in an effort to "get more out of" the data. The third group,

Table 1. Coefficients of Agreement Between Tribes

	A	B	C	D	E	F	G	H	I	J	K	L	M	N	O
A		67	59	56	72	79	76	41	21	44	61	66	61	57	38
B	67		49	61	26	74	54	37	38	32	60	47	48	54	55
C	59	49		65	68	59	72	01	00	77	45	70	73	64	66
D	56	61	65		81	45	77	-18	-29	79	24	84	74	92	64
E	72	26	68	81		32	71	-30	-39	93	09	89	90	90	62
F	79	74	59	45	32		55	45	32	35	64	49	46	39	53
G	76	54	72	77	71	55		23	-09	73	30	92	86	69	59
H	41	37	01	-18	-30	45	23		86	-31	43	-18	-24	-24	01
I	21	38	00	-29	-39	32	-09	86		-31	42	-29	-43	-29	-07
J	44	32	77	79	93	35	73	-31	-31		19	88	90	89	70
K	61	60	45	24	09	64	30	43	42	19		22	13	14	59
L	66	47	70	84	89	49	92	-18	-29	88	22		99	89	66
M	61	48	73	74	90	46	86	-24	-43	90	13	99		89	58
N	57	54	64	92	90	39	69	-24	-29	89	14	89	89		58
O	38	55	66	64	62	53	59	01	-07	70	59	66	58	58	

Source: Adapted from Clements, 1954.

holding that rough data contain only minimal information, uses only rough techniques and gets what it can "off the top." This chapter adopts this last position as a pedagogical device.

Although attribute (presence-absence) data are not inherently inexact, the absence of an attribute in field reports has long worried anthropologists. Was the attribute there and not reported, or was it really absent? In that sense, as many analysts have recognized, the traditional 2 × 2 table showing joint occurrence of an attribute between two classes is quite often an example of "rough" data.

The Data and Some Methodology

The data in Table 1 are taken from Clements (1954). The letters in the margins represent Indian tribes, and the numbers are derived from presence or absence of attributes from the California Culture Element Distribution Series. (The order of the tribes has been randomized from Clements' table. Identifications appear at the end of this chapter, in Table 4, for interested anthropologists.) The raw data, taken from Driver and Kroeber (1932), are usually condensed into a standard 2 × 2 table.

Of the indices that have been proposed to measure similarity in such a table, some are familiar and some can only be described as arcane. An extensive list may be found in Goodman and Kruskal (1959). One of the common indices is:

$$\chi^2 = \frac{N\,(ad - bc)^2}{(a + b)\,(a + c)\,(b + d)\,(c + d)} \tag{1}$$

Since χ^2 is regularly used to test the statistical independence of two tribes, and large values indicate extreme dependence, this is a natural index. $\chi^2 = 0$ shows statistical independence, but large values do not distinguish between the extreme relationships

a	0
0	d

and

0	b
c	0

Furthermore, the upper limit of χ^2 depends on N.

A commonly used modification is

$$\phi = \frac{ad - bc}{\sqrt{(a + b)(a + c)(b + d)(c + d)}} \tag{2}$$

This equation may be most easily constructed by applying the formula for product-moment correlation to the 2 × 2 table. $\phi^2 = \chi^2/N$ is called Mean Square Contingency.

Pearson's coefficient of contingency

$$C = \sqrt{\frac{\phi^2}{1 + \phi^2}} \quad = \quad \sqrt{\frac{\chi^2}{N + \chi^2}} \tag{3}$$

is an obvious attempt to eliminate the dependence of χ^2 on N. Aside from that, it has little to recommend it mathematically.

Yule's coefficient of colligation

$$Y = \frac{\sqrt{ad} - \sqrt{bc}}{\sqrt{ad} + \sqrt{bc}} \tag{4}$$

appears to have nothing at all to recommend it, but see below.

Two coefficients constructed by Driver and Kroeber (1932) are worth mentioning. The arithmetic mean

$$\frac{1}{2} \left[\frac{a}{a + b} + \frac{a}{a + c} \right]$$

is the average of the empirical probabilities of the joint occurrence of a trait in the two tribes. The index

$$\frac{a}{\sqrt{(a + b)\ (a + c)}}$$

is the corresponding geometric mean.

Many of the indices constructed have never proved useful because it is difficult or impossible to relate them to a meaningful corresponding population index. Goodman and Kruskal (1954) have attacked the problem from this point of view: Given a population configuration, what index is useful to compute, and what is the appropriate sample estimate of this index? They offer various choices, depending on the nature of the categories: nominal, ordinal, and so forth. Thus it turns out, for example, that the coefficient Y of

(4) can be derived from the sample estimate of the proportion of error reduction in prediction that can be anticipated if some conditional information is given. The appearance of Y itself depends on an invariance property of the data and on a suitable algebraic transformation.

For data in which order is meaningful, Goodman and Kruskal (1954) recommend

$$\Gamma = \frac{P_c - P_d}{P_c + P_d} \tag{5}$$

where P_c (P_d) is the probability that two randomly chosen observations (X_i, Y_j) and $(X_{i'}, Y_{j'})$ from the population will be concordant or discordant:

$$P_c = Pr \left\{ (X_i < X_{i'}, \text{ and } Y_j < Y_{j'},) \text{ or } (X_i > X_{i'}, \text{ and } Y_j > Y_{j'},) \right\}$$

and

$$P_d = Pr \left\{ \text{the orderings are in opposite directions} \right\}$$

In a 2×2 table (present = 1, absent = 0), the maximum likelihood estimates of P_c and P_d give the estimator

$$\hat{\Gamma} = G = \frac{ad - bc}{ad + bc} \tag{6}$$

Goodman and Kruskal (1963) have determined the sampling distribution of G to be asymptotically normal for any number of categories. For the 2×2 case, their G has traditionally been called Q (sometimes Q_2) in the literature and is the similarity index used by Clements (1954). Clements remarks, however, "Although I have been guilty of using Q or Q_2 myself and in the latter part of this paper have employed illustrative data based on it, I now have no doubt that r_{hk} or *phi* [same thing] is the proper coefficient to use in the fourfold classification of 'presence or absence' data. . . . If r_{hk} [$= \phi$] coefficients had been available, they would have worked just as well in the procedural techniques" (p. 182).

Clements's clustering procedure, regardless of the choice of index, is as follows: For a given cluster, take the average of the index values between all pairs of tribes within the cluster and compare it to the average of the index values between all pairs of tribes which have one member in the cluster and one outside of the cluster. (This comparison of *within* scores to *between* scores is common to many methods of clustering. In analysis of variance, and elsewhere, the scores are sums of squares.) The ratio of these two averages Clements calls (following Holzinger and Harman, 1941) a *B*-coefficient:

$$B = \frac{\text{average within index value}}{\text{average in/out index value}} \qquad (7)$$

Then tribes are added to the given cluster as long as the *B*-ratio is increased "or remains practically unchanged" (Clements, 1954, p. 192). The computations are given in Table 2.

Having finished one cluster, we start over again with the remaining tribes and continue in this fashion until the data are exhausted. The computations can easily be performed on a hand calculator.

Two Results

Multiplying the values of Q by 100 for convenience and starting with the most similar pair (L, M: 99), the table shows the two clusters (*L, M, E, J, N, D, G, C, O, A, F, B*) and (*I, H, K*). The procedure does not vary with the choice of initial pairs. This clustering cannot be reconstructed from Clements's paper, since he stops the procedure after Tribe *O* in the first cluster and then starts again to find the two other clusters (*A, F, B, K*) and (*I, H*). He remarks that these clusters agree with those arrived at by Driver and Kroeber (1932). He also proceeds to cross-check the clustering by looking at the similarity of tribe profiles and at group mean Q values. These cross-checks need not concern us.

With all due respect to the hand calculator (and computer) industries, this example has been chosen to illustrate the fact that, when possible, it is often worthwhile to "let the data speak for themselves." Let's think about what we would expect a properly clustered matrix of similarity scores to look like: Tribes within a cluster should have high index values with each other and low index values with outside tribes. That is, we would expect the matrix to be partitioned into blocks, with the blocks on the diagonal showing

Table 2. Computations for Clements's Clustering Procedure

Cluster	c	Σ within scores	# within: $c(c-1)/2$	Σ in/out	# in/out: $c(15-c)$	B-coefficient
L,M	2	99	1	1376	26	1.87
+E	3	278	3	1732	36	1.93
+J	4	549	6	1917	44	2.10
+N	5	906	10	1954	50	2.32
+D	6	1316	15	1889	54	2.51
+G	7	1784	21	1781	56	2.67
+C	8	2273	28	1571	56	2.89
+O	9	2776	36	1267	54	3.29
+A	10	3305	45	1007	50	3.66
+F	11	3797	55	730	44	4.15
+B	12	4364	66	298	36	7.94
+K	13	4784	78	-37	26	< 0
I,H	2	86	1	-37	26	-60.5
+K	3	171	3	298	36	6.89

Source: Adapted from Clements, 1954.

large index values and the off-diagonal blocks showing small values. Also, if we arrange the blocks (clusters), we might expect that the off-diagonal index values would decrease as we get farther from the diagonal. For the matrix given, one may produce just such an arrangement by starting with the pair of tribes (*L, M*) having the highest index value (99), adding the tribe (*G*) having the highest index value (92) with any tribe already in the cluster, and so continuing. With one or two interchanges for cosmetic reasons, this produces Table 3.

The clustered matrix is exhibited in three different type fonts to emphasize the clustering: boldface for index values ≥ 60, roman for index values between 50 and 60, italic for non-negative values less than 50, and simple dashes for negative values. Notice that the tribes are clustered in accordance with Driver and Kroeber's (1932) and Clements's (1954) (incorrect) results. The diagonal blocks consist primarily of boldface values, and the off-diagonal blocks primarily of lesser values, decreasing (but not regularly) from the diagonal. Only Tribe *O*'s position seems to be in some doubt. Clements reports that Kroeber finds Tribe *O* "barely within the culture type" (1954, p. 198).

Having performed such an "eyeball" survey, one may then properly apply profiles, statistical tests of hypotheses, or other appropriate tests of whether the clustering is suitable. "Suitable for what?" the reader may ask. My feeling is that the suitability of the clustering is a nonmathematical question. Do the clusters make sense by anthropological standards (as per Kroeber here)? Presumably the researcher is doing the clustering for some nonmathematical purpose appropriate to the subject matter. The validity of the cluster results must surely be related to that purpose.

The Back of the Book

The following natural question has no answer: Which of the clusterings of Table 1 is "correct"? Unless some nonmathematical basis for clustering can be postulated, the question is meaningless. We may, at best, talk of "externally consistent" clustering results that agree with, say, the geographical clustering shown by Hudson (see Chapter Four). Or we may investigate "internal consistency" by comparing the clusters that result from various methods. (Mezzich,

	L	M	E	J	N	D	G	C	O	A	F	B	K	H	I
L		99	89	88	89	84	92	70	66	66	49	47	22	—	—
M	99		90	90	89	74	86	73	58	61	46	48	13	—	—
E	89	90		93	90	81	71	68	62	72	32	26	09	—	—
J	88	90	93		89	79	73	77	70	44	35	32	19	—	—
N	89	89	90	89		92	69	64	58	57	39	54	14	—	—
D	84	74	81	79	92		77	65	64	56	45	61	24	—	—
G	92	86	71	73	69	77		72	59	76	55	54	30	23	—
C	70	73	68	77	64	65	72		66	59	59	49	45	01	00
O	66	58	62	70	58	64	59	66		38	53	55	59	01	—
A	66	61	72	44	57	56	76	59	38		79	67	61	41	21
F	49	46	32	35	39	45	55	59	53	79		74	64	45	32
B	47	48	26	32	54	61	54	49	55	67	74		60	37	38
K	22	13	09	19	14	24	30	45	59	61	64	60		43	42
H	—	—	—	—	—	—	23	01	01	41	45	37	43		86
I	—	—	—	—	—	—	—	00	—	21	32	38	42	86	

Boldface (≥60)   Roman (50,60)   Italic (0,50)   — (negative)

Source: Based on data compiled by Clements, 1954.

in Chapter Nine, makes a comparison of this kind.) We may also talk about "useful" clustering methods; *useful*, like *consistent*, has two different interpretations. The method itself may be useful because of the ease or speed with which it may be applied. Or the *results* of the method may be useful, by drawing our attention to some features of the subject matter that had not been previously remarked (see D'Andrade, 1978).

All too frequently, the "best" clustering method is considered to be the method most commonly accepted. Probably the best-known such methods based on a matrix of similarity scores are Principal Components/Factor Analysis. These require, among other things, index values down the diagonal: 100s for Principal Components, "communalities" for Factor Analysis. Both involve the mathematical idea of solving simultaneous linear equations and minimizing sums of squares. The latter requirement may be reduced to sums of cross-products and hence leads naturally to the matrix of *product-moment* correlations. It is not clear how mathematically viable these methods are when the similarity indices do not constitute such correlations. There is more to Factor Analysis than this, but my mathematical reservations are also more extensive than this.

Another set of well-known clustering methods is the hierarchical techniques best known from the works of Sokal and others (for example, Sokal and Sneath, 1963). How far these and other ideas may be subsumed under the general rubric of multidimensional scaling (see Shepard, Romney, and Nerlove, 1972) depends on how one chooses to "cluster" the multitude of clustering algorithms. Many of these operate on a matrix whose indices are "distances," where small values indicate agreement. Mathematical conversion methods for changing similarity data to distances, and vice versa, are readily available. The reader is invited to use some of these methods on the matrix given and to compare both the resulting clusters and the computational effort involved.

Statisticians have managed to accumulate an appreciable body of accepted theory regarding "uniformly most powerful" tests of hypotheses and "admissible" decision rules and procedures. No corresponding ideas appeared at the workshop on which this book is based, nor have I seen them reported elsewhere. Indeed, even in the one-dimensional case, new and interesting clustering schemes are still being proposed. Furthermore, the possible criteria for such a theory of clustering do not seem to be universally accepted. Mathematical properties of the various methods are still under debate (for example, invariance under linear transformations of the data; see Chapter Eight), as are the various coefficients of similarity and their properties (see Chapter Six).

One way to avoid the latter problem is to work directly from the original incidence matrix of presences and absences, which is required for Lingoes's matrix multiplications (see Chapter Seven). For the example presented here, one must go to Driver and Kroeber (1932) for the original data from which they computed Table 1. One trouble with learning by doing in this way is that one learns first how quickly the computations become so extensive as to obscure what one is really trying to learn. For those who simply want a feel for the ideas involved, using only Tribes A, F, B, K, H, and I and a small number of traits (but which ones is not clear) should be satisfactory. Even that will probably require some computer time.

A final note on this example: It was not chosen solely because of its anthropological interest nor because the data were typical of much social science research. In a way, it is atypical—as this chapter has tried to demonstrate, an appropriate clustering is readily apparent, so apparent, in fact, that it would be surprising if a different clustering method led to appreciably different results. The choice was pedagogical, in that readers trying various methods on this example should focus on understanding what the method does and not worry about the results. If the results look very much different from those we have already produced, you probably made a mistake in applying the method. Try again!

Whatever methods you tried on the example, keep in mind the three groups of mathematicians mentioned in the introduction. Unless you belong to the first group yourself, there is nothing to be done about its members. Since you considered the problem, in which of the other two groups do you belong, or to which would you like your mathematical consultant to belong? For these data, those who skim "off the top" will find that this chapter follows their preferred behavior. On the other hand, those who want to get at the "fine structure" of the clustering have ample opportunity to do so. The same remarks may be made about Fisher's iris data (see May, Chapter

Table 4. Tribal Identifications

Letter	Tribe	Letter	Tribe
A	Van Duzen	I	Coast Yuki
B	Chimariko	J	Yurok 2
C	Tolowa	K	Mattole
D	Karok 1	L	Hupa 1
E	Yurok 1	M	Hupa 2
F	Sinkyone 1	N	Karok 2
G	Chilula	O	Wiyot
H	Kato		

Source: Adapted from Clements, 1954.

Three); they have been worked over extensively, and the resulting clusters continually reappear.

When you have finished, which methods do you find appealing? Why? Do mathematical properties of the method concern you? Is speed or cost of computation important? If you are fortunate enough (a value judgment on my part) to be, or to have access to, a mathematician in one of the last two clusters, remember to ask questions about the quality of the data and the appropriateness of the method before the analysis starts. In any case, mathematicians and social scientists alike will do well to remember Driver's comment, "Statistical results can never be better than the data" (1932, p. 255).

Used Car Domain: an Ethnographic Application of Clustering and Multidimensional Scaling

John M. Roberts
Melvin D. Williams
George C. Poole

The automobile is the symbol of an instrumental and expressive cultural complex that is salient throughout the United States but that may have even greater salience in the black culture of Pittsburgh, Pennsylvania. Here urban black males classify used automobiles in a way that has ethnographic interest in part because it is a key to understanding a rich area of expressive life and in part because it has

Note: Since this research was unfunded, the authors are particularly grateful to the University of Pittsburgh Computer Center for providing computing services without charge. The authors are indebted to Roy G.

some of the features of high-concordance linguistic codes (Roberts, 1965; Roberts, Strand, and Burmeister, 1971; Kozelka and Roberts, 1971). This used-car classification, however, is essentially implicit in that it is unlikely that any single respondent could fully describe it, but with techniques such as hierarchical clustering, multidimensional scaling, and ordinal scaling, it has been made explicit and useful for the ethnographer of urban black culture. To some degree this conversion of the implicit into the explicit is the subject of this exploratory and preliminary study.

Anthropological interest in high-concordance linguistic codes such as numbers, day names, month names, kin terms, letter names, and other codes controlled by the fully participating members of a culture is supported by their pervasive role in all communication and understanding. While no participant in a culture can possibly know all of the information stored in that cultural system, he must control the high-concordance codes that constitute a standardized framework for informational processing.

In all cultures, however, there are other linguistic codes that fail to match the extremely high levels of concordance characteristic of the high-concordance codes but that nevertheless display impressive levels of concordance, particularly in specific localities and for shorter periods of time. Perhaps such codes could be termed intermediate-concordance codes. In the United States, for example, the verbal identification system for the automobiles commonly found on the streets and highways constitutes such a code. In practice, linguistic identification is often strengthened by photographs of actual automobiles, yet identification can be based on the linguistic code alone. The properties of this intermediate-level concordance code are the concern of this report. We shall focus upon the used-car code shared by adult males of all ages living in St. Clair Village, an isolated black residential area in metropolitan Pittsburgh.

The expressive side of the automobile complex in a low-income area like St. Clair Village has a distinctive character, since

D'Andrade, who inspired this research and who generously permitted the use of his clustering program before the publication describing his U-statistic appeared. In addition the authors appreciate the help they received from Garry E. Chick, Richard G. Condon, Robert Harris, Richard B. Scaglion, and Allen L. Tan.

many of the middle-class expressive options are not available to the residents. The automobile has become one of the few expensive luxuries that extend to poor black urban areas. Even here the residents are convinced that "you got have your ride." It is doubtful that anyone who did not understand this code could understand the expressive life of this residential area.

The background for this study is found in two separate areas of research. The first involves a general consideration of expressive culture (Roberts and others, 1956; Roberts, Kozelka, and Arth, 1956; Roberts, Thompson, and Sutton-Smith, 1966; Roberts and Wicke, 1971; Hutchinson and Roberts, 1972; Roberts, Hutchinson, and Carlson, 1972; Roberts and Kundrat, 1978; Roberts, Hutchinson, and Hanscom, n.d.). The second area concerns the descriptions of urban black culture in the Northeast (Clark, 1967; Henderson, 1967; Liebow, 1967; Hannerz, 1969; Williams, 1974; Williams, 1981; Williams, n.d.; Roberts and Jones, n.d.). Space does not permit the full development of this background, but it should be noted that both junior authors have a deep knowledge of black culture in Pittsburgh and have had field experience in black communities.

In this paper we describe clustering and multidimensional scaling solutions as illustrations of the complexities of expressive travel and of expressive self-testing in driving. The work on self-testing (Roberts, Thompson, and Sutton-Smith, 1966; Roberts and Wicke, 1971; Hutchinson and Roberts, 1972; Roberts, Hutchinson, and Carlson, 1972; Roberts, Hutchinson, and Hanscom, n.d.; Roberts and Kundrat, 1978) suggests that high self-testing drivers like to drive faster, to pass other cars, and to take curves rapidly and in general enjoy driving a car more than low self-testing drivers do. Low self-testing drivers tend to display judgmental accentuation in that they overestimate the dangers of the road, the significance of signs, the severity of accidents, and like phenomena. High self-testers accept high self-testing in others, while low self-testers find it stressful. This study suggests that some automobiles have different meanings for high self-testers than they do for low self-testers in the urban black male population; that is, the used-car domain is partitioned differently within these two groups. It also suggests that there are differences between self-testers who like rural driving and those who like urban, although some individuals are clearly high self-testers in both environments.

The Ethnographic Setting

St. Clair Village is a federal housing project that lies on elevated ground approximately 10 miles south of the city of Pittsburgh and is bordered by three white neighborhoods: Carrick, Arlington, and Mount Oliver Borough. The Village lies approximately five miles from major shopping districts, and poor public transportation makes it difficult for many inhabitants to commute elsewhere. The Village is residential except for the large drive-in complex where a shopping center once flourished. The shopping center was closed in 1968 because of high crime rates and vandalism. Only one business remains, the neighborhood tavern. The neighborhood is composed of uniform, red brick, three-story dwellings interspersed with single units. Most buildings are in disrepair; many are boarded up and vacant. Debris litters the area. Abandoned vehicles often sit next to the operable used cars that occupy most of the curb space in the neighborhood. St. Clair Village is another federal slum (Rainwater, 1974) already scheduled for the wrecker's ball. The steep and winding roads that lead to this hilly location are just another indicator of its isolation. St. Clair Village was originally built in the 1950s as an integrated project designed to house individuals living under poverty conditions in Pittsburgh and to provide them with facilities for a better life. Now it has lost its integrated character and any hope for a better life that it may once have offered.

Everyone in St. Clair Village knows that subsistence resources are very scarce. You may pay 10 dollars for a cabaret ticket without provoking comment, but no one is surprised when you are "out of" sugar, bread, or bologna. You can borrow clothes, disposable diapers, cigarettes, and food here without stigma. In this social context, the used car is a major expressive and instrumental asset.

The poor black male in St. Clair Village, who is denied the substance of power and status, accepts the expressive symbols instead—stereos, liquor, "rolls" (of money), razors, switchblades, "Saturday night specials," and used cars. These adaptive mechanisms help him to maintain self-esteem and to secure necessary social membership, as well as to mitigate disruptive economic differentiation in the context of his already unstable economic and residential confinement (Abrahams, 1962; Williams, 1975, p. 112).

Like other Americans, these blacks treasure the car as symbol and servant. Indeed, among the poor, the automobile may be more of a symbol than a servant since the vehicles they possess sometimes demand more service than they provide. The car, though, is one of the few resources to which poor black Americans have almost unrestricted access, by means of complex and expensive time-payment plans or by bartering for junk that dealers are anxious to convert into small amounts of cash. The used car is important to this section of the population.

The Research

The research design was simple and appropriate to the exploratory, unfunded nature of this work. Other exploratory studies with related methodologies have been published (see, for example, Roberts and Chick, 1979; Roberts, Golder, and Chick, 1980; and Roberts and Nattrass, 1980), and others are in preparation or in press.

Since there were no resources available for a fuller survey of the automobiles owned and operated in St. Clair Village, a list of 60 different automobiles was compiled by simply visiting the Village in June 1977 and listing the year, model, make, and type of the first 60 different automobiles seen on the streets (see Figure 1). Although this list does not constitute a representative sample, each automobile listed was familiar to those residents of St. Clair Village who were later interviewed.

Make, model, year, and type of each automobile were typed on a card. Later in 1977, each of 60 black male respondents was asked to sort the shuffled deck of cards into piles, each of which included the cards for cars he regarded as similar. The respondents were told that they should have more than one pile and fewer than 60 piles, but otherwise there were no restraints. For each respondent, this sorting produced a 60 × 60 similarity matrix of 1's and 0's in which entries indicate how an automobile is grouped with regard to each of the others. Next, the 60 matrices were added to produce a composite matrix where entries now show the number of times each automobile is grouped with the others. This aggregate similarity matrix, generated by the U-statistic hierarchical clustering procedure of D'Andrade (1978), was then clustered by means of that procedure. Based upon the nonparametric measure of association as defined by the Mann-Whitney test, the U-statistic begins by combining closest pairs from a list of the original units and continues by joining pairs of classifications whose elements are jointly less distant from one another than those of any other pair. The U-statistic technique has been found to be more accurate in recovering the structure of error-perturbed data than either the single-link or complete-link method (D'Andrade, 1978).

The clustering solution was examined by informed judges familiar with urban black culture in Pittsburgh. These judges concluded that the clustering was ethnographically valid. The same judges also aided in naming the clusters.

The fact that the hierarchical clustering solution seems to make sense ethnographically suggests that both the entire group and the major subclusters represent underlying semantic domains. The similarity matrices, then, for the entire list as well as for the three main subclusters, were subjected to multidimensional scaling (the KYST program; see Kruskal, Young, and Seery, 1973). Once the dimensions of the clusters were determined, the positions of the automobiles along each dimension were identified. Cards for three groups of selected cars as determined by the three main subclusters were then given to a different set of 27 male respondents from St. Clair Village, who ranked the automobiles in three ways: the degree to which they would like to own them, the degree to which they considered the cars "big time," and the degree to which they recognized them as "family man" cars. Each of these respondents was also asked six questions designed to rank him on a scale of high to low self-testing drivers. The associations between the self-testing driving scale and the three scales described above were also considered.

The two sets of respondents used in the clustering and in the scaling were not chosen on the basis of an acceptable sampling design, but each respondent was a resident of St. Clair Village. At the exploratory level, the respondents can be considered representative of black males in this residential area.

The Results

The U-statistic hierarchical clustering solution for the 60 St. Clair Village automobiles is presented in Figure 1. These automo-

Figure 1. *U*-Statistic Hierarchical Clustering Solution for 60 St. Clair Village Automobiles

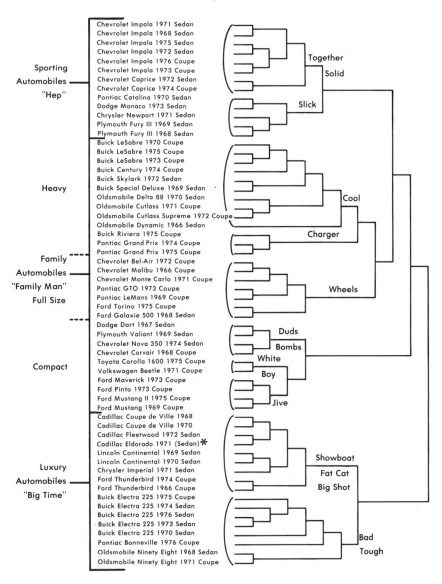

*This automobile was erroneously listed as a sedan. It should have been listed as a coupe.

biles were clustered on the basis of information on make, model, year, and type.

The 60 black male respondents grouped the automobiles into three major clusters, and these in turn were divided into subclusters. The three major clusters were: (1) sporting automobiles, or "hep" cars, (2) family automobiles, or "family man" cars, and (3) luxury automobiles, or "big time" cars. All of these major clusters appear to be subdivided on the basis of make, but the family automobile group could also be described as subdivided into heavy, full-size, and compact cars.

The major clusters warrant only brief ethnograpic description. Certainly the perceptions of used cars by blacks in St. Clair Village suggest complex images for the categories of luxury, family, and sporting. The terminologies used here are based on ethnographic experience but not on direct sociolinguistic research.

For the family man car, interior size may not be as important as a newer model. This car symbolizes the "straight guy" who is not "running a game" on anyone, but who is "legit" (legitimate). He is trying to make a living the traditional way through hard labor. He has a family, but he is not concerned that they all be transportable simultaneously. His car provides dependable transportation to work and to play. It is a symbol of his success in keeping body and soul together within an ecological niche where such a feat is admirable. It serves his family as well, but he can periodically use it to escape them. It is the car of the guy "who breaks his back to make ends meet," who has no angles, who has his "ass up front." The family man in St. Clair Village has the image often associated with the blue-collar worker in the mainstream culture. He is respected but not admired. If he is successful, he moves out of the Village.

The luxury car in St. Clair Village is the car that the family man cannot afford. It requires "angles" to "keep up the payment." Those who drive it give the impression that they may have a job but that they definitely have a "hustle." It is a big time car because it is big and big-shots drive it. Big time cars never get old; they just fade away in rust and disrepair. Big cars that are not luxury cars, like the 1968 Ford Galaxie 500 (the "top of the line" in that year), are often associated with big time guys merely because big size is a pervasive cognitive domain. People in St. Clair Village seldom ask "What year?" after you tell them what kind of car you drive. The luxury car is owned by the guy who beats the system. He has income with no visible means, or more income than those visible means supply. His car is a symbol of his hustle success, even though he may not always have a hustle or success. He may have bought the car in good times but refused to be a "has been." The luxury car in St. Clair Village, as in mainstream America, projects the image of wealth, ability, and status. But in the Village the image is illusory unless you wear the special ghetto-specific lenses that allow you to participate in this ceremonial expressive behavior. Anyone who can really afford a luxury car can also afford to live elsewhere.

The sporting car lies between the family and luxury cars. Owning it is akin to being a political moderate, a choice between the radical big time and the conservative "regular," "straight," "family man," or "jive turkey." The sports cars are "hep," "cool," "nice," "alright rides." They are big enough although they are not big time. The sporting car is a sophisticated car in the ghetto, although it is not something to "write home about." The sporting car and the luxury car are both acceptable for customizing into "superfly," or "souped-up" cars. The sporting car is not a "jive" car but a good "ride" for those, especially the young, who are highly sensitive to expressive symbols.

In Figure 1 the titles for subclusters are congruent with ghetto-specific cognitive maps (the names were again provided by informed judges). "Together" cars are "solid." They are not indicative of "guys on the move" (changing their life), as are "slick" cars. Slick cars are subtle evidence that one is about to "go" or "move" into the family or luxury driving categories. "Cool" cars reflect the unassertive family man who appears to be settled into his way of life. Cool is unperturbed, "rolls with the punches," accepts its fate, and is "breezy." Cool cars are in contrast to "chargers," which represent the assertive and even aggressive family man who has designs upon the "hep" or big time life-styles. "Wheels" are innocuous utility cars for basic transportation, and all except the GTO represent little flair for the ghetto male. "Duds" are cars that the hep and big time guys "wouldn't be caught dead in." They are "bombs," and if you associate yourself with them it has to be done with disdain, as you might wear a cheap shoe. You cut your corns out, walk on the collapsed rear portion, make them "slides," but you never recognize them as shoes. So the hep or big time guy may drive one of these "wrecks," but he is likely to paint *Ouch* in bold letters on the severely damaged portions of the car.

"White boy" cars are cars that belong to an out-group. "Jive" cars border upon being duds. They are tolerable but are hardly noticed as meaningful expressive items and are sometimes the objects of ridicule. "Show boats" are the "fat cat" and "big shot" cars, but a guy living in St. Clair Village is a picture of incongruity if he drives a show boat. So the "bad" cars have the highest expressive value in the Village. Bad cars are the poor man's "hog" (Cadillac), especially the "deuce and a quarter" (Buick Electra 225) or the 98; they compete fiercely for the expressive value of show boats.

The overall clustering solution suggests that the used car fits in a well-defined semantic domain for men in St. Clair Village. The multidimensional scaling solution (KYST) for the similarity matrix produced by the sorting task also provided some insight into that domain. Table 1 gives the data for this solution, and Figure 2 plots the first two dimensions. The numbers in Figure 2 refer to the numbers of automobiles in Table 1.

There appear to be three main dimensions for the total group of used cars, if not four. The three-dimensional solution is easier to interpret, although its stress value of .105 is somewhat higher than that of the four-dimensional solution (.073).

The first dimension reflects the relative prestige of the cars in the eyes of the respondents. Such variables as cost and condition figure in these placements, but apparently no individual variable can account for the overall assessment. Prestige is a composite of both general variables and variables that are specific to the ghetto.

The second dimension is that of feasibility. Figure 2 shows the curious characteristic of this dimension. The automobiles in the upper half of Figure 2 are not "feasible" from the viewpoint of the average respondent. Those at the right, ranging from the Ford Thunderbird to the Chrysler Newport, are not feasible because of their cost, while those at the left, ranging from the Volkswagen Beetle to the Pontiac GTO, are not feasible because of the degree to which people in the community reject them.

Table 1. Three-Dimensional Scaling Solution for the 60 St. Clair
Village Automobiles (KYST)

Automobile	I Prestige	II Feasibility	III Expressiveness
1. Cadillac Eldorado 1971 Sedan*	1.069	.451	−.017
2. Cadillac Fleetwood 1972 Sedan	1.056	.427	.020
3. Lincoln Continental 1970 Sedan	1.020	.747	.071
4. Cadillac Coupe de Ville 1970	1.008	.461	.208
5. Lincoln Continental 1969 Sedan	1.005	.745	.019
6. Cadillac Coupe de Ville 1968	.992	.470	.118
7. Buick Electra 225 1975 Coupe	.960	−.104	.182
8. Buick Electra 225 1973 Sedan	.941	−.099	.217
9. Buick Electra 225 1974 Sedan	.922	−.104	.281
10. Buick Electra 225 1976 Sedan	.914	−.164	.170
11. Buick Electra 225 1970 Sedan	.911	−.101	.128
12. Chrysler Imperial 1971 Sedan	.895	.662	−.344
13. Ford Thunderbird 1974 Coupe	.787	.805	.257
14. Pontiac Bonneville 1976 Coupe	.771	.230	.367
15. Oldsmobile 98 1968 Sedan	.728	−.343	−.127
16. Oldsmobile 98 1971 Coupe	.692	−.291	−.160
17. Ford Thunderbird 1966 Coupe	.683	.847	.175
18. Chrysler Newport 1971 Sedan	.537	.032	−.830
19. Buick Riviera 1975 Coupe	.463	−.262	.716
20. Chevrolet Impala 1972 Sedan	.379	−.406	−.498

*This automobile was erroneously listed as a sedan. It should have been listed as a coupe.

Table 1 (continued)

Automobile	I Prestige	II Feasibility	III Expressiveness
21. Chevrolet Impala 1976 Coupe	.372	−.481	−.363
22. Chevrolet Impala 1975 Sedan	.340	−.475	−.465
23. Chevrolet Impala 1973 Coupe	.321	−.486	−.424
24. Chevrolet Impala 1968 Sedan	.274	−.401	−.558
25. Plymouth Fury III 1969 Sedan	.248	−.071	−.887
26. Pontiac Grand Prix 1975 Coupe	.214	−.094	.790
27. Plymouth Fury III 1968 Sedan	.210	−.058	−.938
28. Chevrolet Impala 1971 Sedan	.190	−.495	−.495
29. Pontiac Grand Prix 1974 Coupe	.178	−.146	.862
30. Buick Le Sabre 1970 Coupe	−.134	−.812	.249
31. Buick Le Sabre 1975 Coupe	−.137	−.783	.293
32. Buick Le Sabre 1973 Coupe	−.137	−.757	.237
33. Buick Century 1974 Coupe	−.258	−.606	.529
34. Chevrolet Caprice 1974 Coupe	−.283	−.787	−.204
35. Oldsmobile Delta 88 1970 Sedan	−.291	−.562	.125
36. Chevrolet Caprice 1974 Coupe	−.308	−.796	−.088
37. Oldsmobile Dynamic 1966 Sedan	−.377	−.490	−.560
38. Buick Special Deluxe 1969 Sedan	−.396	−.698	.530
39. Pontiac Catalina 1970 Sedan	−.487	−.534	−.293
40. Dodge Monaco 1973 Sedan	−.500	−.268	−.700
41. Buick Skylark 1972 Sedan	−.509	−.571	.404
42. Oldsmobile Cutlass 1971 Coupe	−.564	−.350	.309

Table 1 (continued)

Automobile	I Prestige	II Feasibility	III Expressiveness
43. Pontiac GTO 1973 Coupe	−.579	.163	.775
44. Chevrolet Monte Carlo 1970 Coupe	−.687	−.584	.306
45. Toyota Corolla 1600 1975 Coupe	−.702	1.262	.183
46. Oldsmobile Cutlass Supreme 1972 Coupe	−.707	−.403	.402
47. Chevrolet Bel-Air 1972 Coupe	−.757	−.505	.114
48. Ford Torino 1975 Coupe	−.760	−.326	−.267
49. Volkswagen Beetle 1971 Coupe	−.765	1.282	−.001
50. Ford Pinto 1973 Coupe	−.778	1.139	.128
51. Pontiac Le Mans 1969 Coupe	−.820	−.129	.421
52. Dodge Dart 1967 Sedan	−.822	.671	−.655
53. Chevrolet Nova 350 1974 Sedan	−.857	.303	−.109
54. Ford Galaxie 500 1968 Sedan	−.874	−.018	−.641
55. Ford Mustang II 1975 Coupe	−.894	.766	.199
56. Plymouth Valiant 1969 Sedan	−.894	.768	−.563
57. Ford Maverick 1973 Coupe	−.918	.901	.112
58. Chevrolet Corvair 1968 Coupe	−.943	.782	−.246
59. Chevrolet Malibu 1966 Coupe	−.953	−.074	.265
60. Ford Mustang 1969 Coupe	−.985	.717	.269

The third dimension is that of expressiveness. Those cars on the positive end of the scale have a dashing quality and those on the negative end are stodgy.

For the dimensions of the large subclusters, the multidimensional scaling of the sporting car cluster produced a two-dimensional solution that appears to be degenerate. Consideration, therefore, will be restricted to the family car and luxury car clusters.

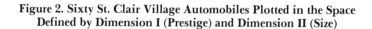

Figure 2. Sixty St. Clair Village Automobiles Plotted in the Space
Defined by Dimension I (Prestige) and Dimension II (Size)

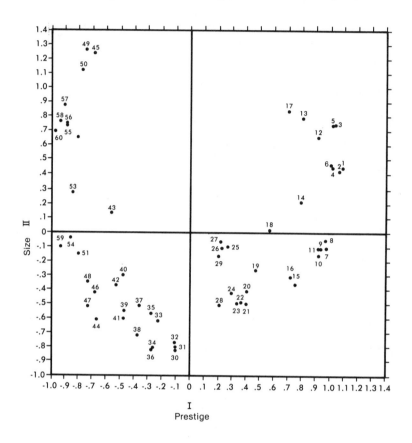

For the family automobile cluster, the three-dimensional solution (stress = .082) provided three interpretable dimensions: (I) size,
(II) style, and (III) conservatism. This solution is given in Table 2,
and the three-dimensional representation is given in Figure 3.

The multidimensional scaling for the luxury automobile cluster also produced three interpretable dimensions (stress = .028): (I)
popularity, (II) size, and (III) age. This solution is given in Table 3,
and the three-dimensional representation is given in Figure 4.

Although the clusters and their dimensions figure in the
general cognitive domain of the used automobile for St. Clair Village

Table 2. Three-Dimensional Scaling Solution for the St. Clair Village
Automobiles in the "Family Automobile" Cluster (KYST)

Automobile	I Size	II Style	III Preference
1. Buick Riviera 1975 Coupe	1.113	.828	−.023
2. Buick Le Sabre 1975 Coupe	1.011	−.131	.137
3. Buick Le Sabre 1970 Coupe	1.010	−.234	.063
4. Buick Le Sabre 1973 Coupe	.976	−.169	.244
5. Buick Century 1974 Coupe	.850	−.061	−.010
6. Buick Special Deluxe 1969 Sedan	.831	−.404	−.135
7. Pontiac Grand Prix 1974 Coupe	.753	.941	.192
8. Pontiac Grand Prix 1975 Coupe	.663	.989	.144
9. Buick Skylark 1972 Sedan	.624	−.115	−.243
10. Oldsmobile Delta 88 1970 Sedan	.606	−.406	.134
11. Chevrolet Monte Carlo 1971 Coupe	.495	.224	−.490
12. Oldsmobile Dynamic 1966 Sedan	.423	−.961	.021
13. Oldsmobile Cutlass Supreme 1972 Coupe	.360	−.193	−.159
14. Oldsmobile Cutlass 1971 Coupe	.354	−.338	−.272
15. Chevrolet Bel-Air 1972 Coupe	.315	−.041	−.564
16. Ford Torino 1975 Coupe	.279	−.118	.784
17. Pontiac Le Mans 1969 Coupe	.062	.018	−.125
18. Pontiac GTO 1973 Coupe	− .000	.582	.197
19. Chevrolet Malibu 1966 Coupe	− .096	−.148	−.558
20. Ford Galaxie 500 1968 Sedan	− .140	−.617	.778
21. Chevrolet Nova 350 1974 Sedan	− .533	−.114	−.485
22. Ford Mustang 1969 Coupe	− .831	−.054	.474
23. Ford Mustang II 1975 Coupe	− .859	−.029	.350
24. Dodge Dart 1967 Sedan	− .967	−.630	−.255

Table 2 (continued)

| | I | II | III |
Automobile	Size	Style	Preference
25. Chevrolet Corvair 1968 Coupe	− .993	.153	−.593
26. Ford Maverick 1973 Coupe	−1.057	.094	.330
27. Plymouth Valiant 1969 Sedan	−1.079	−.556	−.214
28. Ford Pinto 1973 Coupe	−1.306	.232	.428
29. Toyota Corolla 1600 1975 Coupe	−1.395	.512	−.017
30. Volkswagen Beetle 1971 Coupe	−1.465	.451	−.136

Figure 3. Three-Dimensional Representation for Interpoint Distances for 30 "Family" Automobiles

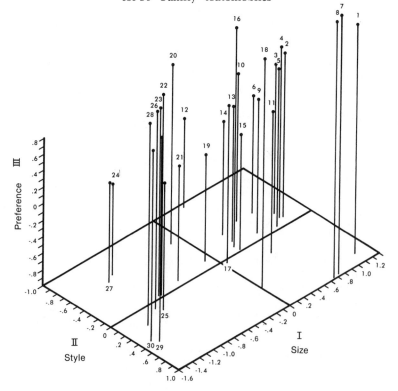

Table 3. Three-Dimensional Scaling Solution for 17 St. Clair Village
Automobiles in the Luxury Automobile Cluster (KYST)

Automobile	*I* *Popularity*	*II* *Size*	*III* *Age*
1. Oldsmobile 98 1968 Sedan	1.484	− .148	−.144
2. Oldsmobile 98 1971 Coupe	1.232	.307	−.702
3. Buick Electra 225 1976 Sedan	.770	− .009	.295
4. Buick Electra 225 1975 Coupe	.727	.227	.123
5. Buick Electra 225 1970 Sedan	.706	− .514	.075
6. Buick Electra 225 1973 Sedan	.697	− .011	.333
7. Buick Electra 225 1974 Sedan	.677	− .056	.354
8. Pontiac Bonneville 1976 Coupe	.162	.492	.603
9. Cadillac Fleetwood 1972 Sedan	− .441	− .551	−.178
10. Cadillac Coupe de Ville 1968	− .492	− .135	−.784
11. Cadillac Coupe de Ville 1970	− .493	.027	−.354
12. Cadillac Eldorado 1971 Sedan	− .520	− .553	−.256
13. Ford Thunderbird 1966 Coupe	− .712	1.065	−.189
14. Ford Thunderbird 1974 Coupe	− .867	.648	.166
15. Chrysler Imperial 1971 Sedan	− .929	− .595	.493
16. Lincoln Continental 1976 Sedan	− .992	− .088	.122
17. Lincoln Continental 1969 Sedan	−1.011	− .107	.043

blacks, it was felt that a more detailed consideration of attitudes toward specific automobiles would be enlightening. Eight of the 60 automobiles were selected on the basis of their place in the clusters and on the dimensions of the total group, as well as on the basis of attitudes expressed in the course of ethnographic interviews. Sim-

Figure 4. Three-Dimensional Representation for Interpoint Distances
for 17 "Luxury" Automobiles

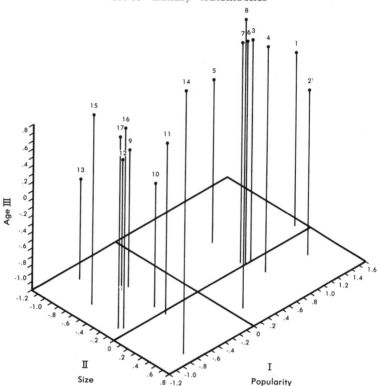

ilarly, eight were selected specifically for the family group and seven
specifically for the luxury group, although some automobiles in
these groups also appeared in the total group. These automobiles are
listed in Table 4.

Sixty-one informants were asked to scale the cars in the general
group, family group, and luxury group on the basis of preference;
they were asked, in other words, "Which would you most like to
own?" The automobile they most wanted to own was given a value of
one. They were also asked to rank the cars in terms of big time cars and
also as family man cars. These rankings are presented in Table 4.
The same table gives the rankings in terms of the dimensional values
presented earlier, but this is only to indicate that the cars were well-
distributed through the multidimensional scaling.

Identification	Preference Rank Average	Big Time Rank Average	Family Rank Average	Dimensions		
				Prestige Rank	Feasibility Rank	Expressive Rank
General Group:						
Pontiac Grand Prix 1974 Coupe	1. (2.56)	2. (2.5)	5. (4.4)	3.	2.	1.
Cadillac Fleetwood 1972 Sedan	2. (3.07)	1. (1.6)	4. (3.9)	1.	5.	5.
Buick Le Sabre 1970 Coupe	3. (3.39)	3. (3.6)	2. (3.5)	4.	1.	3.
Ford Galaxie 500 1968 Sedan	4. (4.80)	4. (4.1)	2. (3.5)	6.	4.	7.
Ford Mustang 1969 Coupe	5. (5.13)	6. (6.2)	7. (5.8)	8.	6.	2.
Ford Pinto 1973 Coupe	6. (5.15)	7. (6.4)	6. (5.2)	5.	8.	4.
Plymouth Fury III 1968 Sedan	7. (5.44)	5. (4.8)	2. (3.5)	2.	3.	8.
Chevrolet Corvair 1968 Coupe	8. (6.46)	8. (6.8)	8. (6.1)	7.	7.	6.
Family Group:				*Size*	*Style*	*Preference*
Buick Riviera 1975 Coupe	1. (2.23)	1. (2.1)	5. (4.2)	1.	2.	7.
Pontiac Grand Prix 1975 Coupe	2. (2.68)	2. (2.2)	6. (4.5)	3.	1.	3.
Buick Century 1974 Coupe	3. (3.90)	3. (3.9)	2. (4.0)	2.	5.	5.
Ford Torino 1975 Coupe	4. (4.25)	4. (4.7)	4. (4.1)	5.	6.	1.
Ford Galaxie 500 1968 Sedan	5. (5.28)	6. (4.9)	1. (3.4)	6.	7.	2.
Toyota Corolla 1600 1975 Coupe	6. (5.32)	7. (6.3)	7. (5.4)	8.	3.	6.
Oldsmobile Dynamic 1966 Sedan	7. (5.61)	5. (4.8)	3. (4.02)	4.	8.	4.
Chevrolet Corvair 1968 Coupe	8. (6.78)	8. (6.9)	8. (6.5)	7.	4.	8.
Luxury Group:				*Popularity*	*Size*	*Age*
Pontiac Bonneville 1976 Coupe	1. (2.98)	5. (3.8)	1.5 (3.4)	2.	2.	1.
Lincoln Continental 1970 Sedan	2. (3.10)	1. (2.3)	1.5 (3.4)	6.	3.	3.
Chrysler Imperial 1971 Sedan	3. (3.62)	4. (3.7)	3. (3.3)	5.	7.	2.
Lincoln Continental 1969 Sedan	4. (3.89)	2. (3.3)	5. (4.0)	7.	4.	4.
Cadillac Coupe de Ville 1968	5. (4.44)	3. (3.5)	6. (4.8)	3.	5.	7.
Ford Thunderbird 1966 Coupe	6. (5.00)	7. (5.7)	7. (5.4)	4.	1.	6.
Oldsmobile 98 1968 Sedan	7. (5.03)	6. (5.6)	4. (3.6)	1.	6.	5.

For the general group and for the family group, there was a significant rank order correlation between the preference scale and the big time scale (tau = .786, $p < .01$, two-tailed in the first case, and tau = .857, $p < .002$, two-tailed in the second). This relationship did not hold for the luxury group. For the first two groups, however, the automobiles the respondents wanted to own were also the automobiles they thought were big time cars.

In contrast, there were no significant associations between the preference and family man scales for the general and family groups, but there was such an association for the luxury group (tau = .675, $p < .05$, two-tailed). Here the respondents seemed to be thinking in terms of the family man.

Other associations have some interest. For the family group, there was an association between preference and the size dimension (tau = .607, $p < .05$, two-tailed) and between the big time scale and the size dimension (tau = .786, $p < .01$, two-tailed). In the luxury group, there was an association between the family man scale and the age dimension (tau = .675, $p < .05$, two-tailed).

The foregoing discussion has treated the respondents as one group, as representatives of the black subculture in St. Clair Village. The respondents, however, differed in their self-testing driving attitudes as measured by their answers to six questions. These results illustrate the complexity of the domain.

For each of six questions, each respondent circled a number on the following scale to reflect his feeling toward the activity: "Unhappy −3 −2 −1 0 +1 +2 +3 Happy." The questions were:

1. In the country, how well do you like to drive an automobile at relatively high speeds on two-lane roads?
2. In the city, how well do you like to start fast, that is, burn rubber, after a stop?
3. In the country, how well do you like to pass cars while driving at relatively high speeds on two-lane roads?
4. In the city, how well do you like to take corners at relatively high speeds?
5. In the country, how well do you like to take curves at relatively high speeds?
6. In the city, how well do you like to drive through intersections at relatively high speeds?

The raw responses given in Table 5 show that high self-testing attitudes were more likely to be displayed in the country than in the

Table 5. Responses to Six Self-Testing Driving Questions

A. *Raw Responses*			*Unhappy*			*Happy*		
	N	− 3	− 2	− 1	0	+ 1	+ 2	+ 3
Country:								
High Speed	61	12	6	14	4	14	9	2
Pass	61	22	8	4	11	12	4	0
Curve	61	25	13	10	5	5	1	2
City:								
Intersection	61	32	11	3	8	5	2	0
Corner	61	36	10	7	4	2	1	1
Start	61	39	5	5	8	4	0	0

B. *Goodman-Kruskal Coefficients of Ordinal Association for the Variables*

	Pass	Curve	Intersection	Start	Corner
Speed	.423[c]	.518[c]	.472[c]	.246	.297[a]
Pass		.513[c]	.530[c]	.539[c]	.416[b]
Curve			.618[c]	.488[b]	.476[b]
Intersection				.750[c]	.689[c]
Start					.764[c]

[a] Tau B   .05
[b] Tau B   .01
[c] Tau B   .001

city. The six self-testing scales, however, were highly correlated, although each measures a slightly different driving attribute. Incidentally, ongoing studies have shown that the attitudes expressed verbally in response to such questions are associated with actual driving styles on curves and bridge approaches (see Roberts, Hutchinson, and Hanscom, n.d.).

The ordinal scales presented in Table 5 have some interesting associations. The gamma is used as a measure of association rather than the tau b or tau c because it can be more readily compared with other coefficients of association. This statistic is described in *SSPS: Statistical Package for the Social Sciences* (2nd ed., Nie and others, 1975, pp. 227–228), and its values are given in Table 6 below. The negative associations reflect the preferences or attributed preferences of high self-testers, and the positive associations reflect those of the low self-testers. Self-testing attitudes are associated with attitudes toward specific used cars.

Table 6. Self-Testing Associations with Preferential Attitudes Toward Automobiles

	Country			City		
	Speed	Pass	Curve	Intersection	Corner	Start
Respondents' Personal Preference Scales:						
General Group:						
Pontiac Grand Prix 1974 Coupe	-.309[c]	-.147	.040	-.111	-.321[b]	-.184
Ford Galaxie 500 1968 Sedan	.185	.060	-.030	.307[a]	.175	.190
Family Group:						
Pontiac Grand Prix 1974 Coupe	-.260[b]	-.214	.062	-.281[a]	-.201	-.181
Buick Century 1974 Coupe	-.123	-.090	.051	.150	.381[c]	.287[a]
Ford Galaxie 500 1968 Sedan	.302[c]	.153	.120	.255[a]	.186	-.052
Chevrolet Corvair 1968 Coupe	.017	.198	.028	.037	.097	.401[b]
Luxury Group:						
Oldsmobile 98 1968 Sedan	-.114	-.263[b]	.272[b]	-.016	-.030	-.022
Lincoln Continental 1968 Sedan	.043	.251[a]	.026	.106	.089	.435[d]
Attributed "Big Time" Preference:						
General Group:						
Pontiac Grand Prix 1974 Coupe	.153	-.049	.156	-.213	-.160	-.386[b]
Cadillac Fleetwood 1972 Sedan	-.420	-.295	.163	-.419[a]	-.466[a]	-.248
Ford Galaxie 500 1968 Sedan	.238	.138	.123	.467[d]	.322[b]	.253

Family Group:

Oldsmobile Dynamic 1966 Sedan	.164	.140	.022	.330[c]	.115	.138
Toyota Corolla 1600 1975 Coupe	-.144	-.362[d]	-.045	-.163	-.097	-.265[a]
Ford Torino 1975 Coupe	.167	-.233[a]	-.022	-.387[d]	-.114	-.219
Chevrolet Corvair 1968 Coupe	.004	.242[a]	.068	.029	.263	.497[c]

Luxury Group:

Oldsmobile 98 1968 Sedan	.231[a]	.019	-.077	.105	.149	.366[b]
Lincoln Continental 1970 Sedan	-.048	.190	-.017	.071	.322[b]	.466[d]

Attributed "Family Man" Preference:

General Group:

Ford Mustang 1969 Coupe	.030	.323[c]	-.040	.135	.060	.236

Family Group:

Buick Century 1974 Coupe	-.238[b]	-.007	-.175	.017	-.278	-.128
Ford Torino 1975 Coupe	-.147	.030	.021	-.170	-.316[b]	-.117
Chevrolet Corvair 1968 Coupe	.228[a]	.288[b]	.152	.278[a]	.126	.358[b]

Luxury Group:

Chrysler Imperial 1971 Sedan	-.140	.007	-.348[d]	-.150	-.117	-.095

[a] p < .10 two-tailed
[b] p < .05 two-tailed
[c] p < .02 two-tailed
[d] p < .01 two-tailed

It would be a mistake, however, to over-analyze these data, since the 61 respondents were simply an off-the-street sample. Although it is possible to aggregate the self-testing scales through the use of Z scores, it is probably more informative ethnographically to deal with the associations given in Table 6. In this connection, a few ethnographic comments are in order.

The Pontiac Grand Prix 1974 Coupe is a "charger" in St. Clair Village. It is considered "fast," and, as we would expect, the high self-tester who likes to drive at high speeds in the country and around corners in the city seems to prefer this automobile. But the Buick Century 1974 Coupe is a "cool" car, and we are not surprised to find that the low self-tester who does not like fast starts or speeding around city corners prefers it. The Ford Galaxie 500 1968 is only "wheels" (basic transportation) and is preferred by the low self-tester who is not attracted by speed in the country or the city. The Chevrolet Corvair 1968 Coupe is a "dud" and as we would expect is preferred by low self-testers who do not like fast starts. Meanwhile, the Oldsmobile 98 1968 Sedan, a "bad" car with a famous "passing gear," is preferred by the high self-tester who likes to pass and take curves in country driving. A "show boat" car is to be seen, not heard ("screeching tires," "burning rubber"), so the large Lincoln Continental 1968 Sedan is preferred by the low self-tester who likes not fast starts but a slow parade where he can be seen.

Among the respondents who chose big time cars, the Pontiac Grand Prix 1974 Coupe is again preferred by those high self-testers who like to start fast. The Cadillac Fleetwood 1972 Sedan, noted for its weight and smooth highway performance, is selected by those high self-testers who like to drive fast in the country. The Ford 500 1968 Sedan, a consistent choice of low self-testers, is selected by those who do not like to drive through city intersections at high speeds. The Oldsmobile Dynamic 1966 Sedan is selected by the low self-testers who do not like to pass on country roads. This is another example of a "cool" car preferred by the low self-tester. The fact that a Toyota Corolla 1975 Coupe is considered to be a "white boy" car is consistent with its selection by the high self-tester who likes to pass in the country. We would assume that only a high self-tester would purchase and drive this car in St. Clair Village. After all, it is daring to be different.

Although the self-testing variable is only one of a series of variables pertinent to a consideration of used cars, the foregoing interpretations illustrate that it is possible to go beyond clustering and multidimensional solutions. The used car domain is truly complex.

Discussion

Unlike most of the chapters in this volume, this study has not been designed as a contribution to methodology. Instead it applies descriptive techniques to an interesting ethnographic context. We suggest that most ethnographic field studies could profit from the early application of such techniques, but the value of this particular study in subsequent research has yet to be demonstrated. We also argue that this exploratory study was cost-effective in that the results amply warranted the investment of time and energy, but it is difficult to obtain cost-effectiveness data on other studies for comparative purposes. In the end, then, the ethnographic significance of this study must be its justification.

In a sense, this report on a used car domain is only a snapshot view of a semantic or cultural domain that is constantly changing. A similar study executed a year later would be different, because the universe of used cars changes as new models are added and as economic factors change, yet in all probability the general characteristics of the domain are relatively stable. These cars represent more than a transportation system: They are symbolic of an entire social system and are grouped and ranked in much the same way that their owners are grouped and ranked. Entering field workers who knew this domain would have an advantage even if their concern lay in some other area of culture.

The study produced an integrated code or taxonomy. Any black male found on the streets of St. Clair Village knows elements in this code and is also able to arrange them in some way. Still, exploratory work with informed judges showed that no single individual could produce the code in all of its complexity without substantial help from the elicitors. The elements of the code are explicit, but its detailed structure seems to be implicit in the culture. The procedures used here have made the implicit explicit.

It is remarkable how expressive and essentially nonutilitarian the used car domain can be. This is particularly evident when the names of clusters are considered or when the related self-testing attitudes, themselves expressive, are mapped into the domain. This system is an expressive system, inasmuch as it reveals a great deal about expressive life in this neighborhood.

There is nothing simple about the used car domain, and this study has only begun to reveal its intricacies. As Kapsis (1978) points out, there is a dearth of data about the subcultural nature of black neighborhoods in America. The study of expressive codes like the used car code offers a potential illumination of distinctive features among black ghetto populations. Most scholars would agree that these populations are not monolithic, but few have succeeded in analyzing the nature of the diversity (see Blackwell, 1975; Green, 1970; Hannerz, 1969; Johnson and Sanday, 1971; Kapsis, 1978; Lewis, 1971; Rodman, 1963, 1971, 1977; Williams, 1981; Young, 1970). Furthermore, we believe that approaches like ours will facilitate the "more structural approach to urban neighborhoods" for which Kapsis (1978, p. 1151) pleads. Of course, our work is exploratory, but we intend to pursue these directions until we exhaust their usefulness. At the very least, this study shows that simple stereotypes about blacks' car preferences cannot be defended. Personal preferences, "big time" and "family man" preferences, and the self-testing data make it clear that this is a complex cultural system.

Moreover, though the statistical proof is lacking, the self-testing data give the impression that the distribution of low and high self-testers is different in the black community than it is in the general white population. Each form of self-testing may indicate a different response to individual and social stress. Future research will deal with this problem.

In summary, it was possible on a small-scale, exploratory basis to collect data that sustained an interesting mapping of the used car domain for an urban black neighborhood. Both the clustering solutions and the multidimensional solutions have intrinsic ethnographic interest. The ordinal scaling in terms of personal and assigned preferences and in terms of the self-testing variable added depth to the formulation and suggested new directions for research. When the expressive life of the urban black is examined in greater depth, this study will prove to be a valuable base line for such work.

Discriminant Analysis in Cluster Analysis

■■■■■■■■■■■■■■■■■■■■■■■

Ronald W. May

Classification as a procedure is distinguishable from identification. Following the biological usage of this terminology (Sneath and Sokal, 1973), classification orders objects into groups on the basis of their relationships and, in the case of numerical taxonomy, on the basis of phenetic similarity. *Cluster analysis* designates the numerical methods designed to establish a numerical taxonomy. Once a classification has been constructed, it often becomes necessary to assign unknown individuals to the correct classes or groups. The process of assignment is essentially one of identification and can be performed quantitatively by a procedure known as *discriminant analysis.*

Theoretical treatments of cluster analysis are found in Clifford and Stephenson (1975), Hartigan (1975a), Duran and Odell (1974), Anderberg (1973), and Sneath and Sokal (1973). Classification problems in the broadest sense involve either variables or objects (cases, individuals, and so forth). The classification of variables delineated as *R*-mode analysis can be handled by cluster analysis but is more commonly handled by principal components or common factor analysis (Mulaik, 1972; Rummel, 1970; Harman, 1967). When the problem involves objects, or *Q*-mode analysis, groups or clusters are constructed on the basis of mutual similarity. Hartigan (1975a), for example, defines a cluster as a set of similar objects. Anderberg (1973) describes the clustering procedure as one of finding natural groups. Sneath and Sokal (1973) outline a series of eight criteria for determining what a cluster is. However, they purposely leave the definition of cluster somewhat vague when they state that it is a set of objects in an n-dimensional space which exhibits a distribution neither too regular nor too random. Obviously, there is no airtight definition of a cluster. Almost invariably, definitions result from a recursive interaction between the data analyst and the analytical rendering of the data. In all fairness, however, criteria based on statistical methodology can be utilized to assess the value of a cluster analysis result (Hartigan, 1975a) by determining whether or not statistically distinct clusters are present.

Lachenbruch (1975a) opines that discriminant analysis is concerned with identification of an unknown. Basically, the problem is to assign an individual to one of two or more groups, using a procedure that attempts to minimize the error rate. It would also seem appropriate, in the context of cluster analysis, to include the techniques for the assessment of between-group differences usually ascribed to MANOVA procedures (Cooley and Lohnes, 1971). Because discriminant analysis implicitly assumes that the initial data are classified correctly and that the groups are statistically discernible a priori, a test of this assumption would seem to be warranted, particularly when discriminant analysis is used in tandem with cluster analysis.

In discriminant analysis, which is predicated on identification and assignment of unknowns, the usual problems are (Lachenbruch, 1975a): (1) the performance of the assignment rule, (2) the validity of assumptions inherent in the methodology, and (3) the selection of variables to be utilized in the assignment rule. A fourth problem, related to the MANOVA aspects, should perhaps be the first to be considered: Are there significant differences between the group centroids? If not, then perhaps the assignment rule will not perform satisfactorily. Further division into more clusters should be considered.

Discriminant Analysis

Conceptual aspects of the procedure to be discussed here have been presented by such authors as Demirmen (1969) and Hung and Dubes (1970). Hartigan (1975a) suggests that discriminant analysis may best determine the combination of variables that best distinguishes the clusters. Sneath and Sokal (1973) provide an illustration of this approach for biological data. It must be recognized, of course, that for any particular set of data, different clustering algorithms can produce groups with different memberships. Discriminant analysis provides an objective means of evaluating the results of a clustering procedure.

The details of theory and applications of discriminant analysis are well documented (Lachenbruch, 1975a; Cacoullos, 1973; Cooley and Lohnes, 1971; and Rao, 1952). A number of computer programs are also readily available (see those of Dixon, 1971; Nie and others, 1975; and Cooley and Lohnes, 1971). The interested researcher should therefore have no problem utilizing the technique.

The usual application of discriminant analysis is an assignment problem or a decision theory problem. Basically, an object or individual of unknown affinity must be assigned to one of a number of previously defined groups. The implicit assumption is, of course, that the unknown does in fact belong to one of the known groups. It is also assumed that the initial data or training set, as it is sometimes called, can be classified correctly into disjoint groups.

Linear Discriminant Functions. Analytically, the problem can be stated in the following fashion: Consider a series of groups G_1, $G_2, \ldots, G_k$ and an $r \times 1$ observation vector x. The individual whose attributes are described by x is to be classified into one of the G_k. For the sake of illustration, consider the situation in which $k = 2$ groups are involved. This is the classical problem originally considered by Fisher (1936). In this approach, a linear combination of the variables measured is constructed so as to maximize the ratio of the difference of the means of the linear combination to its variance. Following the notation of Lachenbruch (1975a), let the required linear combination be $y = \lambda'x$. The mean of y in G_1 is $\lambda'\bar{x}_1$, and in G_2 it is $\lambda'\bar{x}_2$; its variance is $\lambda'S\lambda$ in both groups, since the method assumes equality of covariance matrices. The λ is chosen in such a way as to maximize the function

$$f = \frac{(\lambda'\bar{x}_1 - \lambda'\bar{x}_2)^2}{\lambda'S\lambda} \tag{1}$$

Differentiating f with respect to λ and setting $\partial f/\partial \lambda = 0$ gives the result

$$\bar{x}_1 - \bar{x}_2 = S\lambda \frac{(\lambda'\bar{x}_1 - \lambda'\bar{x}_2)^2}{\lambda'S\lambda} \tag{2}$$

This leads to the following assignment rule:

Assign the unknown to G_1 if the linear combination $y = \lambda'x = (\bar{x}_1 - \bar{x}_2)' S^{-1}x$ is closer to $y_1 = (\bar{x}_1 - \bar{x}_2)' S^{-1}\bar{x}_1$ than to y_2; otherwise, assign the unknown to G_2. The quantity

$$\bar{y}_1 - \bar{y}_2 = (\bar{x}_1 - \bar{x}_2)' S^{-1}(\bar{x}_1 - \bar{x}_2) \tag{3}$$

is Mahalanobis's D^2 and can be used to test the significance of differences between the two groups. In particular,

$$F = \frac{n_1 n_2 (n_1 + n_2 - m - 1)}{(n_1 + n_2)\ (n_1 + n_2 - 2)m} D^2 \tag{4}$$

where n_1 and n_2 are the number of cases in G_1 and G_2 respectively and m, the number of variables in the linear combination, is an F variate with m and $(n_1 + n_2 - m - 1)$ degrees of freedom.

Generalization to More Than Two Groups. The generalization of the two-group problem to the multi-group problem has been discussed by Lachenbruch (1973), who compares two approaches: The first he calls the *multiple discriminant function* (MDF) *method*, and the second, the *eigenvector* (EV) *method*. The first procedure essentially involves a rule that maximizes the average probability of correct classification under the assumption that the population (represented by the K-groups $G_1, G_2, \ldots, G_k$) density functions $f(x)$ are known. Under the assumption that covariance matrices are normal and equal, this rule is equivalent to assigning the unknown x to some G_i if

$$(x - \tfrac{1}{2}\bar{x}_i)' S^{-1}x_i = \max_j\ (x - \tfrac{1}{2}x_j)' S^{-1}\bar{x}_j \tag{5}$$

The other procedure is a generalization of Fisher's two-group problem to k-groups. If B is the between-groups mean square and cross-product matrix and W is the within-groups mean square and cross-product matrix, then the linear combinations are the eigenvectors of $W^{-1}B$, and there are at most $\min(k - 1, m)$ nontrivial eigenvectors where k is the number of groups and m the number of variables. In this situation, the optimal assignment rule when using r eigenvectors is to assign the unknown x to a group G_i if

$$\sum_{\ell=1}^{r} (\lambda'_\ell (x - \bar{x}_i))^2 = \min_{j} \sum_{\ell=1}^{r} (\lambda'_\ell (x - \bar{x}_j))^2 \tag{6}$$

or

$$(y - \tfrac{1}{2}\nu_i)' \nu_i = \max_{j} (y - \tfrac{1}{2}\nu_j)' \nu_j \tag{7}$$

where

$$y' = (\lambda'_1 x, \lambda'_2 x, \ldots, \lambda'_r x) \tag{8}$$

and

$$\nu'_i = (\lambda'_1 \bar{x}_1, \ldots, \lambda'_r \bar{x}_i) \tag{9}$$

In his assessment of these two approaches, Lachenbruch notes the following:

1. The EV procedure performs much better on collinear mean vectors than on simplex configurations.
2. Increasing sample size decreases the apparent probability of correct classification.
3. Increasing the number of groups reduces the apparent probability of correct classification because there are more chances for erroneous assignment.
4. Increasing the number of variables increases the probability of correct classification. This reflects the fact that a set of data can be fit more exactly with more variables.

The more usual procedure is the eigenvector procedure, which has the advantage of being a canonical vector method. If the means are collinear, a single vector may be sufficient for discrimination; plotting of the canonical vectors may prove useful in analyzing the structure of the data; and the eigenvalues can be used to test hypotheses of equality of mean vectors in the form of the Wilks Lambda criterion (Cooley and Lohnes, 1971).

$$\Lambda_{\ell+1} = \prod_{i=\ell+1}^{r} 1/(1 + \lambda_i) \qquad (10)$$

After accepting the first k functions, $\Lambda_z + 1$ can be utilized in a χ^2 test for the significance of the discrimination afforded by the remaining r-2 functions. The quantity,

$$-(N - (r+k)/2 - 1) \log_e \Lambda_{z+1} \qquad (11)$$

is a χ^2 statistic where N is the number of samples in all populations, r is the number of discriminant functions, and $(r-\ell)$ $(k-\ell-1)$ the degrees of freedom.

   Normality and Equality of Covariance Matrices. When the data do not permit the assumption of either normality or equality of covariance matrices, then the linear combination approach does not constitute an optimal assignment procedure. A number of studies have been concerned with the behavior of discriminant functions when the basic assumptions of normality and equality are not satisfied (see Krzanowski, 1977; Lachenbruch, 1975a; Lachenbruch, Sneeringer, and Revo, 1973; Michaelis, 1973; Marks and Dunn, 1974; Gilbert, 1969; and Han, 1968). Unequal covariance matrices constitute a major problem which is perhaps more common than others. Whereas non-normality may often be handled by a suitable transformation (Lachenbruch, Sneeringer, and Revo, 1973), covariance matrix inequality may not. To this end, Anderson and Bahadur (1972) have considered the two-group case when the covariance matrices are unequal. Dempster (1964) has proposed a test for the equality of covariance matrices in the two-group case. Marks and Dunn (1974), assuming unknown parameters, have studied the performance of the Fisher linear discriminant function, the best linear discriminant function (Clunies-Ross and Riffenburgh, 1960), and the quadratic discriminant function. When the differences between covariance matrices are small, then the equality assumption probably makes little difference. However, these authors recommend the use of the quadratic discriminant function even when the differences between covariance matrices are not large. The method appears to be robust to contamination.

   Choice of Variables. Another question that arises in discriminant analysis concerns the selection of variables. Specifically, which variables provide the best discrimination between groups? For lack of a more precise definition, a set of variables will be considered to be the best discriminating set if it includes the smallest number of variables that also provides the minimum probability of misclassification. The problem of variable selection has not been thoroughly investigated. Weiner and Dunn (1966) compared four methods of variable selection and found that stepwise selection, where at each step the variable that contributes most to a reduction in the residual sum of squares is entered, and Studentized t differences in means were more effective than the simple random selection of a subset. They also suggest that the selection of a subset of variables may suitably be based on the largest standardized discriminant coefficients, although this method resulted in a larger number of misclassifications.

Rao (1970) provides a significance test for the coefficients of a discriminant function that leads to selection of a subset of variables. Eisenbeis, Gilbert, and Avery (1973) suggest that different selection methods could quite differently assess the relative importance of an individual variable and suggest that no hierarchy of variables should be reported without reference to the selection criterion being utilized. As to the problem of selecting an optimal subset, they state that the choice will depend on whether it is desirable to maximize differences between group means or to provide the best classification results. Although their results favor the use of an exhaustive approach over the stepwise approach, the choice of an optimal subset is still largely subjective. Urbakh (1971) offers a criterion for estimating the loss of discriminating power when a variate is omitted. He also proposes a criterion based on Mahalanobis's D^2 to determine whether a variable may safely be omitted from the analysis. Cleveland and Lachenbruch (1974) provide an approach for the two-group case based on the amount of overlap. Lachenbruch (1975b) suggests that a variable selection could be based on estimated distance between populations. McKay (1976) proposes a simultaneous test procedure for reducing the number of variables required in the two-group discrimination problem. He develops a method to find all variable subsets whose discriminating powers are not significantly different from the original set of variables.

Qualitative Data. The majority of discriminant problems in the physical sciences involve quantitative data. In the social sciences, and to some extent the medical and physical sciences, a number of problems involve categorical data. Examples include medical diagnosis based on presence or absence of a symptom and biological taxonomy studies using dichotomous variables. The problems and methodology inherent in basing discriminant analysis on qualitative data are presented by Lachenbruch (1975a), J. A. Anderson (1975, 1973, 1972), Gilbert (1968), Day and Kerridge (1967), Cox (1966), Cochran and Hopkins (1961), Linhart (1959), and Johnson (1950). Current research centers around the use of the logistic approach that utilizes a maximum likelihood estimate of the discriminant function coefficients (see J. A. Anderson, 1973, 1972). In the earlier paper (1972), Anderson presents the necessary equations for a solution using a Newton-Raphson procedure for k-populations. Gilbert utilized dichotomous Bernoulli variables in a study of the performance of four different discriminant procedures: Fisher's linear discriminant function, two functions based on a logistic model, and a function based on mutual independence of the variables. Her study, limited to the case of six variables, suggested very little difference among the four procedures when the probability of misclassification was used as a criterion for judging the outcomes. Gilbert suggests that, because of the difficulties encountered in estimation in the logistic model for large numbers of variables, Fisher's linear discriminant function may be more desirable. This desirability is enhanced by the possibility of combining discrete and continuous variables. Lachenbruch (1975a), in discussing the approach of Cox (1966), Walker and Duncan (1967), and Day and Kerridge (1967), notes also that linear discriminant analysis is robust for Bernoulli variables. This fact may explain why in Gilbert's study there was little difference between the logistic and the linear discriminant function approaches. Krzanowski (1975) treats the problem of discrimination with mixed binary and continuous variables. This area of discriminant analysis methodology is one for further research.

Application

To provide examples that readers can test on their own and to compare the results of discriminant analysis with those obtained by the original workers, this method will be illustrated using data from the literature. Fisher (1936) compared a large number of samples of his iris data over a few variables. The other two examples are taken from the archeological literature: The first involves a small number of samples and a large number of variables, and the second was somewhat artificially constructed to include a small number of samples and a few variables.

Cluster analysis and discriminant analysis have been used in archeology and anthropology for some time (Hodson, Kendall, and Tauter, 1971; Hymes, 1965). In particular, these techniques have been used in archeology to study the general problem of sources of raw material (Hammond, Harbottle, and Gazard, 1976; Bieba and others, 1976; Harbottle, 1975; Prag and others, 1974; and Ward, 1974), and in anthropology to study both cultural aspects (Johnson and Johnson, 1975; Kay, 1975) and physical aspects (Stringer, 1974; and Rightmore, 1970). The examples illustrate the utility of combining both methods rather than relying solely on one or the other.

Problems. Any procedure involves a few operational constraints. For example, using discriminant analysis on four or five clusters based upon 50 samples is questionable because the small group sizes may render untenable the assumption of equality of covariance matrices. Even when a very large number of objects are clustered, a large number of clusters may mean that the number of individuals in each group is very small. In these situations, therefore, a certain amount of caution must be exercised in the interpretation of results. Cochran (1964), Lachenbruch (1968), and Lachenbruch and Mickey (1968) discuss the problem of error rate and its relation to sample size and number of parameters. For small samples, discriminant analysis may be a reasonable approach in initial phases of data analysis if one is not overly concerned with minimal error rates. For more than five clusters, however, it may be appropriate to consider an approach in which the groups are examined two at a time.

Most discriminant analysis is based on less than 20, more often less than 10, variables. Cluster analysis is, however, often performed on a larger number of variables. One may in such cases use principal components, retaining those sufficient to account for a significant percentage of the variance. Further work in this area is desirable.

Fisher Iris Data. In his initial discussion of the methodology for linear discriminant analysis, Fisher (1936) considers four variables for each of three species of iris. Sepal length and width and petal length and width are provided for each of 50 individuals of the species

Iris setosa, Iris versicolor, and *Iris virginica.* Fisher generates a discriminant function for assigning an individual to the first two species and uses this to suggest affinities for the third species. For the sake of illustration, however, we will assume that the initial data matrix consists of four measurements on each of 100 individuals and that the only a priori information we can have suggests the possible existence of two species.

Single-linkage clustering (Figure 1) based on a distance matrix (Wishart, 1975) produced two groups. That these do in actual fact correspond to the two species *I. setosa* and *I. versicolor* is not relevant to this particular example. Using the SPSS package (Nie and others, 1975) and the "minimum-residual" criterion, which seeks the variable while minimizing residual unexplained variation, a stepwise linear discriminant analysis was performed. This provided the first set of linear discriminant function coefficients shown in Table 1. The results are thus comparable to those obtained by Fisher, but the stepwise procedure demonstrates that the variable sepal length is redundant insofar as it does not contribute significantly to discrimination between the two groups. Fisher also provides similar information for a third group, *I. virginica.* Clustering (Figure 2) reveals that this species groups with *I. versicolor.* A discriminant analysis using *I. setosa* as one group and *I. versicolor* and *I. virginica* as the other group provided the second set of discriminant function coefficients that appear in Table 1. The results compare favorably with those of Fisher (1936), Kendall (1966), and Friedman and Rubin (1967).

Table 1. Discriminant Function Coefficients for Fisher Iris Data

Variable	I. setosa vs. I. versicolor	I. setosa vs. I. versicolor and I. virginica
Sepal width	0.3765	−0.1738
Petal length	−0.3749	−0.5104
Petal width	−0.6078	0.5658
Constant	0.3834	0.4496

Figure 1. Dendrogram from Single-Linkage Clustering of Fisher's Iris
Data Using Only the Two Species *I. Setosa* and *I. Versicolor*
as the Unknown Group

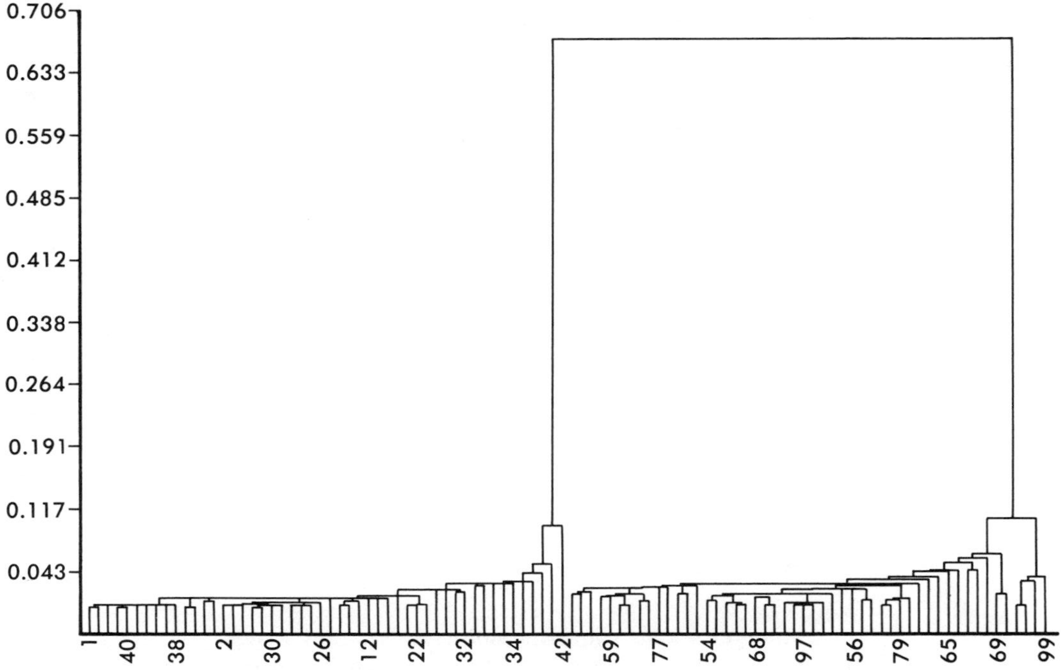

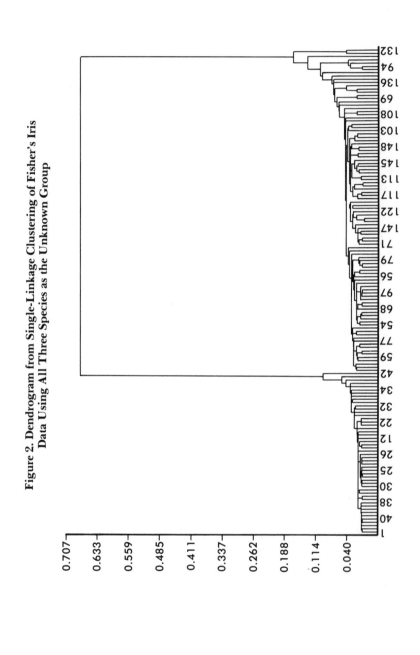

Figure 2. Dendrogram from Single-Linkage Clustering of Fisher's Iris Data Using All Three Species as the Unknown Group

Inscribed Stirrup Jars. Catling and Millett (1965) present a detailed description of 25 clay pots found at Thebes. The stirrup jars were analyzed for nine elements: Mg, Ca, Al, Fe, Na, Ti, Cr, Mn, and Ni. In particular, the authors were interested in where the jars were manufactured, since this has bearing on the problem of relations between Greece and Crete in the period of about 1400–1200 B.C. From a strictly empirical point of view, this example is also somewhat artificial in that rudimentary inspection of the data reveals the existence of two groups on the basis of Ca content alone. If we number the jars from 1 to 25, two distinct major groups, jars 1 to 12 and jars 13 to 25, result from single-linkage clustering of the distance matrix (Figure 3). The latter can be further divided into two subgroups, 13 through 18 plus 25, and 19 through 24. This result compares favorably with the authors' graphical treatment of the data, except in the case of jars 24 and 25. Catling and Millett conclude from their treatment of the data that these jars do not appear to be related to any of the others. Since it is not the purpose of this chapter to focus on the archeological aspects of these differences, the interested reader is referred to the original article for a complete discussion. For the two major groups found in the cluster analysis, a discriminant analysis using the minimum residual criterion provided the coefficients given in Table 2.

To illustrate the type of approach that may be useful in the initial stages of data analysis, the two major subgroups (jars 13 through 18 and 25, and jars 19 through 24) were subjected to a discriminant analysis. The coefficients are given in Table 3. Although the samples are relatively small, the results are at least suggestive. In this latter analysis, Ca and Na are still part of the discriminant function; Ti has disappeared; and Mg, Cr, Mn, and Ni have been added. Differences between jars 13 through 18 and jars 19 through 23 are also noted by the authors. The latter have higher nickel and magnesium concentrations than the former.

Bronze Age Material. Brown and Blin-Stoyle (1959) present a series of chemical analyses of material from the Middle (Group I) and Late (Group II) Bronze Age in Britain. Thirty of these, 15 from each group, were selected as a sample, as shown in Table 4. This selection was based on the availability of a more or less complete chemical analysis, particularly for the elements lead, arsenic, and antimony.

Figure 3. Dendrogram from Single-Linkage Clustering of Inscribed
Stirrup Jars

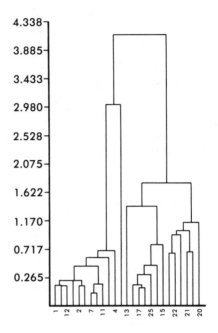

Table 2. Discriminant Function Coefficients for Stirrup Jars

Variable	Coefficient
Ca	0.1479
Na	-0.5598
Ti	-1.6924
Constant	0.5190

Single-linkage cluster analysis based on distance using the three
variables provided results as shown in Figure 4 and summarized in
Table 5. All of the Group I bronzes and one of the Group II bronzes
were clustered into what will be called Group A. Group B consists of
13 Group II bronzes. One of the Group II bronzes was not clustered

Table 3. Discriminant Function Coefficients for Jar Subgroups

Variable	Coefficient
Mg	−1.2390
Ca	0.3200
Na	0.1879
Cr	17.5578
Mn	−2.7749
Ni	166.2992
Constant	−3.2294

Table 4. Serial Numbers of 30 Selected British Middle and Late Bronze Age Materials

Group I	Group II
1	23
4	24
8	29
10	30
11	40
12	41
13	45
14	46
15	47
16	70
18	71
21	72
53	97
58	100
64	101

into a specific group and was omitted from subsequent consideration. Discriminant analysis using the stepwise criterion discussed previously produced the results shown in Table 6. As in the previous example, any detailed discussion of the results must consider the small sample size and archeological aspects that are beyond the scope of this chapter. This example does, however, suggest that this

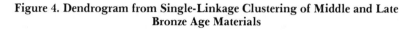

Figure 4. Dendrogram from Single-Linkage Clustering of Middle and Late Bronze Age Materials

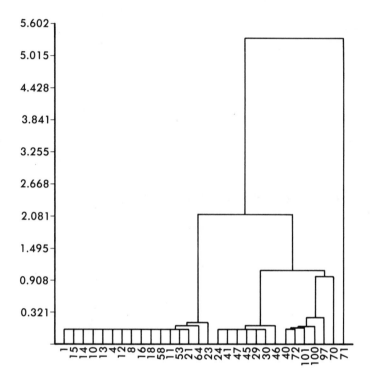

approach may provide some insight into the data even when samples are small and variables few.

Conclusion

Both cluster analysis and discriminant analysis have been applied individually to a wide variety of problems in the physical and social sciences, with reasonable success. The procedure discussed here, which uses discriminant analysis to analyze the results of clustering, has been found useful in the initial, more or less exploratory phases of data analysis. It would be, however, somewhat remiss to end this discussion without a caveat. All too often these techniques are

Table 5. Serial Numbers of Samples Used in Discriminant Analysis
Based on Clustering

| Cluster Group A | | Cluster Group B | |
Bronze Group I	Bronze Group II	Bronze Group I	Bronze Group II
1	23	24	
4		29	
8		30	
10		40	
11		41	
12		45 < 46	
13		47 < 70	
14		72	
15		97 < 100	
16		101	
18			
21			
53			
58			
64			

Note: Sample No. 71 is not included in this analysis.

Table 6. Discriminant Function Coefficients for British Middle and
Late Bronze Age Materials

Variable	Coefficient
Lead	.2707
Arsenic	−1.7786
Antimony	1.1650
Constant	−0.4043

regarded as a panacea for all that ails our data. Computers with relatively sophisticated multivariate statistical analysis packages "on tap" are readily available. There is thus the potential for a rather cavalier attitude toward the analysis of data sets. In most applications of cluster analysis, it is not at all obvious in advance where things are going. It is therefore necessary to pay special attention to the three C's—care in the collection of data; caution in the use of analytical procedures; and control, particularly self-control, in the interpretation of results.

Cluster and Factor Analysis of Cultural Data from Continuous Geographical Areas

■■■■■■■■■■■■■■■■■■■■■■■■■

Herschel C. Hudson

In many ways this chapter follows from previous studies that begin with large collections of cultural data assembled from continuous geographical areas and proceed by numerical means to reduce them to smaller numbers of classifications. Driver (1962) notes that it was Franz Boas, among anthropologists, who launched the first of these studies with his comparison of folktales on the Northwest Coast in 1894. By 1911, Jan Czekanowski of the European Kulturkreise school was clustering items of material culture obtained from African ethnic units. When he mapped the results of his R-mode approach (correlation over units), Czekanowski was able to describe two areal units, a tropical forest culture and a Sudan–East African culture. These numerical procedures later found their way to America by way of the University of California at Berkeley where, from 1926 until the outbreak of World War II, they were used to construct a number of regional classifications. Ehrich and Henderson (1968) and Driver (1962, 1970) review many of them.

Of more immediate concern to the work described here is a paper by Driver and others (1972), which was the first to determine culture classifications for the entire continent by statistical methods. Using data obtained from Murdock's *Ethnographic Atlas* (1967) and corrected through January 1971 from issues of *Ethnology*, the authors intercorrelated 273 North American native ethnic units (*Q*-mode, over traits) in terms of the proportion of 279 shared social and cultural traits. Coefficients were then clustered by a centroid clustering program developed by Joseph Jorgensen (1969), and the resulting tree diagram was interpreted at levels that produced 7, 9, 10, 35, and 55 groups, excluding singletons. These groupings were selected so as to compare with Kroeber's (1939) seven culture areas and levels of intensity, the Voegelins' (1966) nine language phyla, Murdock's (1967) 10 culture areas and his 35 culture provinces, and the Voegelins' 55 language families.

This was followed by a similar analysis of the Driver-Massey (1957) sample of native North American material culture. Driver and Coffin (1975) analyzed correlations among 392 culture traits (*R*-mode) and 245 tribes (*Q*-mode). The tribes were selected to match the North American part of Murdock's sample. Groupings obtained from both analyses were compared with the genetic language classifications of the Voegelins and with the physical types of Georg Neumann (1952).

Anticipating the theme of the present chapter, Smith and Crano (1977) again turned to the Murdock sample and to 27 installments of addenda and corrigenda appearing in *Ethnology*. With the assistance of Jack Sawyer and Robert LeVine, they rated the components of 22 Murdock columns on Guttman-type scales where ratings ranged from zero to as high as 100, and they claimed high inter-rater reliability. Eleven of 25 dichotomous variables were discarded because they lacked an underlying metric representation; components of the remaining 14 were ordered although each lacked one or more properties of a metric scale. Among the 54 variables that remained, intercorrelations (*R*-mode) were computed over a worldwide sample of 863 societies and for each of six regional subsamples. Once ordered, the 54 by 54 matrix of coefficients taken from the larger

sample was clustered visually by marking off nonoverlapping trian-
gular sections along the diagonal. A cutoff point that appears to be at
a correlation of $r = .40$ yielded 11 clusters and eight singletons. The
eight residual variables were then combined to produce a ninth
classification, and the nine groups were subjected to a multiple group
factor analysis so as to compare with the clusters.

The major thrust of Smith and Crano, however, lay in their
factor analyses of one worldwide and six regional samples. This part
of their paper also built upon several prior studies, which we pause
here to summarize.

Cultural data were first factored when Schuessler and Driver
(1956), in a Q-mode study, produced an areal classification of 16
primitive societies. By 1960, Prothro reduced the 29 variables of
Whiting and Child (1953) to three dimensions of permissiveness,
while in 1962 Gouldner and Peterson factored Simmons's (1945)
cross-cultural data. The latter consist of four-point ratings on 58
cultural characteristics for 55 ethnic units that range in level of
development from the Polar Eskimos, Tasmanians, and Yahgans to
the Aztecs, Norsemen, and Ashanti. In the same year, Hickman (1962)
showed that 12 characteristics that followed from Redfield's (1941)
folk-urban continuum produced two factors that he identified as
size-complexity and relative isolation. In more rapid order there
followed the factoring of English kinship terms by Romney and
D'Andrade (1964), semantic comparisons of factors across languages
by Osgood (1964), and the reduction of 19 characteristics of alcohol-
ism to four major classes by Bacon, Barry, and Child (1965).

In the factor analyses of Spiro (1965), Sawyer and LeVine
(1966), Driver and Schuessler (1968), and Smith and Crano (1977),
attention is once again focused upon worldwide culture distributions. Three of these works treat data contained in Murdock's "World
Ethnographic Sample" (1957), while Smith and Crano turn to his
Ethnographic Atlas (1967). Spiro's R-mode analysis examines social
structure and social institutions over Murdock's six cultural areas.
His judgmental selection of 10 societies from each of these areas is
reexamined by Chaney (1966). More exhaustive are the studies of
Sawyer and LeVine, Driver and Schuessler, and Smith and Crano,
who incorporate cluster analysis as well. The first two authors begin
with the 210 categories reported over 565 societies, which Murdock

had grouped to 30 variables in the 1957 sample. Using a judgmental approach, Sawyer and LeVine scale the categories of each variable where possible. This results in four-point scales for seven variables, three-point scales for 13, and dichotomies for the remaining 10. Driver and Schuessler dichotomize their data by opposing the most frequently reported category of each of the 30 variables against remaining categories. Then they factor analyze (R-mode) correlation coefficients among the 30 variables of both studies and interpret the factors over worldwide and regional samples.

The factor analysis of Smith and Crano begins with the inter-correlations among 54 variables they have previously clustered. Fourteen factors with characteristic roots of $\lambda \geqslant 1.00$ are produced by principal axis procedures. Since the construction of the variates of Sawyer and LeVine and Smith and Crano are very similar, the latter authors suggest that their gain of four factors reflects the wider coverage of the *Ethnographic Atlas* as compared to the "World Ethnographic Sample."

In this chapter I explore the dimensionality of cultural and social characteristics of the North American Indian by means of cluster and factor analysis and compare the results with those of similar analyses.

Cultural Characteristics and Correlations

Work began with 279 attributes recorded over the 273 ethnic units of the 1972 Driver and others study. Driver worked with a data deck obtained from Murdock (1967) and brought it up to date by consulting issues of *Ethnology* through January 1971. The manner in which Driver reduced the 57 primary items (column headings with capital letters) to 49 and converted the component attributes to dichotomies is described in full (pp. 313–314). Subsequent to 1972, Driver removed 33 Great Basin ethnic units from the sample to correct for over-representation in that area and added five Mayan units to increase the number of complex societies. Table 1 lists the remaining 245 units. A further look at the data revealed that 49 of the 279 attributes used in the earlier study were not reported by any of the revised set of 245 units. Again the set was reduced, leaving the 230 dichotomous cultural and social attributes listed in the figures. My

Table 1. The 245 Ethnic Units of the Sample

1. Nabesna	48. Tsimshian	95. Coast Yuki
2. Tareumiut	49. Haisla	96. Huchnom
3. Copper Eskimo	50. Bellacoola	97. Northern Pomo
4. Kaska	51. Alkatcho Carrier	98. Eastern Pomo
5. Naskapi	52. Nootka	99. Southern Pomo
6. Nunivak	53. Klahuse	100. Wappo
7. Attawapiskat	54. Squamish	101. Lake Miwok
8. Ingalik	55. Comox	102. Patwin
9. Aleut	56. Lummi	103. Monachi
10. Chugach	57. Klallam	104. Lake Yokut
11. Nunamiut	58. Puyallup	105. Wukchumni
12. Baffinland	59. Quileute	106. Salinan
13. Polar Eskimo	60. Chinook	107. Kawaiisu
14. Dogrib	61. Tillamook	108. Chumash
15. Satudene	62. Coos	109. Gabrielino
16. Slave	63. Tlingit	110. Serrano
17. Chilcotin	64. Bellabella	111. Cahuilla
18. Carrier	65. Makah	112. Cupeno
19. Kutchin	66. Quinault	113. Luiseno
20. Caribou Eskimo	67. Cowichan	114. Kiliwa
21. Iglulik	68. Stalo	115. Tenino
22. Labrador Eskimo	69. Alsea	116. Southern Ute
23. Angmagsalik	70. Siuslaw	117. Havasupai
24. Greenlander	71. Takelma	118. Sanpoil
25. Tanaina	72. Tututni	119. Hukundika
26. Tahltan	73. Shasta	120. Washo
27. Sekani	74. Chimariko	121. Kutenai
28. Beaver	75. Karok	122. Lillooet
29. Chipewyan	76. Hupa	123. Thompson
30. Eastern Cree	77. Wiyot	124. Shuswap
31. Montagnais	78. Lassik	125. Flathead
32. Northern Saulteaux	79. Mattole	126. Kalispel
33. Pekangekum	80. Sinkyone	127. Coeur D'Alene
34. Nipigon	81. Nomlaki	128. Sinkaietk
35. Chippewa	82. Tubatulabal	129. Wenatchi
36. Rainy River Ojibwa	83. Yokuts	130. Klikitat
37. Katikitegon	84. Atsugewi	131. Wishram
38. Eastern Ojibwa	85. Miwok	132. Umatilla
39. Ottawa	86. Diegueno	133. Nez Perce
40. Micmac	87. Yuki	134. Wadadokado
41. Potawatomi	88. Klamath	135. Kidutokado
42. Haida	89. Modoc	136. Kuyuidokado
43. Twana	90. Achomawi	137. Eastern Mono
44. Kwakiutl	91. Yana	138. Panamint
45. Yurok	92. Maidu	139. Spring Valley Shoshoni
46. Eyak	93. Nisenan	140. White Knife Shoshoni
47. Tolowa	94. Wintu	

Table 1 (continued)

141. Bohogue	176. Omaha	211. Acoma
142. Agaiduka	177. Miami	212. Laguna
143. Gosiute	178. Wichita	213. Mescalero
144. Shivwits	179. Pawnee	214. Jicarilla
145. Kaibab	180. Fox	215. Western Apache
146. Chemehuevi	181. Hasinai	216. Hopi
147. San Juan Paiute	182. Menomini	217. Cocopa
148. Uintah	183. Iowa	218. Kamia
149. Uncompahgre	184. Oto	219. Mohave
150. Wind River	185. Ponca	220. Yuma
151. Walapai	186. Shawnee	221. Keweyipaya
152. Yavapai	187. Caddo	222. Lipan Apache
153. Tolkepaya	188. Huron	223. Sia
154. Gros Ventre	189. Seminole	224. Tarahumara
155. Kiowa-Apache	190. Creek	225. Papago
156. Comanche	191. Penobscot	226. Huichol
157. Crow	192. Cherokee	227. Seri
158. Cheyenne	193. Delaware	228. Chichimec
159. Mandan	194. Natchez	229. Pima
160. Sarsi	195. Timucua	230. Yaqui
161. Teton	196. Catawba	231. Chinantec
162. Arapaho	197. Iroquois	232. Aztec
163. Arikara	198. Yuchi	233. Popoluca
164. Assiniboin	199. Choctaw	234. Totonac
165. Blackfoot	200. Chiricahua Apache	235. Mazateco
166. Blood	201. Navaho	236. Huave
167. Bungi	202. Zuni	237. Mixe
168. Hidatsa	203. Maricopa	238. Tarasco
169. Karankawa	204. Taos	239. Tlaxcalans
170. Kiowa	205. Cochiti	240. Zapotec
171. Piegan	206. Jemez	241. Chorti
172. Plains Cree	207. Picuris	242. Yucatec Maya
173. Santee	208. Isleta	243. Mam
174. Ojibwa	209. Tewa	244. Lacandon
175. Winnebago	210. Santa Ana	245. Quiche

purpose here is to compare 230 cultural traits reported over 245 North American ethnic units.

In preparation for an *R*-mode analysis, the 230 attributes were intercorrelated using the phi coefficient. This resulted in a matrix of 26,335 coefficients. The phi coefficient was adopted in order to render the results more comparable to those of Driver and others (1972). In addition, phi values can be factor analyzed, whereas some other measures of association cannot.

Only Driver and Schuessler (1968) and Coffin (1973) have provided frequency distributions of R-mode coefficients. The latter study derives from a survey of material culture over North America (Driver and Massey, 1957), which Coffin expands and clusters. His sample of ethnic units is identical to that of the present study, as is his use of the phi coefficient.

In order to compare distributions, interval tallies of coefficients were converted to percentages in the present study. The R-mode coefficients tend to be distributed with a mean just in excess of zero, a mode to the negative side of zero, and a small but noticeable positive skewness. The interquartile range (middle 50 percent) is defined within the two most central intervals ($-.10$ to $.10$) of all three distributions, whereas four central intervals ($-.20$ to $.20$) encompass between 80 percent and 93 percent of the coefficients. This leaves 20 percent or less of all three distributions for the remaining 80 percent of the intervals. Clearly these R-mode distributions are leptokurtic or more peaked than normal, although the Driver-Schuessler data are less so than the others.

Accumulations in the low negative range are due in part to the skewed dichotomies in many of the 2 by 2 tables, which impose reduced upper limits upon intertrait correlations. The Driver-Schuessler distribution is of interest when compared to the present study, for it shows less skewness and a broader distribution about the mean. These effects were anticipated by Driver and Schuessler when their variates were constructed.

For the present work, I begin with the data set used by Driver and others (1972) for their Q-mode cluster analysis of North American native ethnic units. Coefficients of correlation (phi) are computed among 230 cultural and social attributes over 245 tribes, all in binary form. The resulting 230 by 230 matrix of coefficients is clustered in hierarchical fashion and factored using the method of principal components. These analyses differ from previous ones in that others have transformed each of the Murdock columns, either by scaling or dichotomizing, before proceeding with analysis. While this transformation preserves the conceptual integrity of the Murdock column, the dimensional uniformity that is thereby imposed upon within-column variability tends to reduce the individual identities of many component characteristics. By contrast, the Driver data used here focus upon the component attributes of the columns and treat each as if it were an independent variable, thus preserving the full identity that each might bring to a matrix of correlation coefficients.

Cluster Analysis

I cluster analyze the matrix using a hierarchical program originally devised by Jorgensen (1969) at the University of Michigan and later adapted for use with the Q-mode work of Driver at Indiana University. Jorgensen's program begins by forming first pairs. Then it tests candidate classifications by forming geometric or spatial averages of the combined subgroupings and selects those that average out at the lowest values. This sequence is repeated until only one inclusive classification remains. Lance and Williams (1967) call this a centroid technique.

While clustering is performed by computer, the determination of clusters and their boundaries depends upon outside criteria. For these, I turn to the pattern concept (Cattell and others, 1966) that begins by noting the first pairs on the 230-attribute tree diagram and listing the units that jointly report both attributes. As the clusters grow, in hierarchical fashion, the list of units jointly reporting the set diminishes until a limit of reporting is reached. A cluster, then, is defined here as a set of attributes whose last bridge on a tree diagram marks the limit of its capacity to jointly support a geographical representation. On the tree diagrams, a single cluster appears as a set of connected solid lines, while broken lines identify the remaining structure of the macrocluster. Single lines that join broken lines in the upper regions indicate independent characteristics. This method produced 50 clusters, which are grouped to form the eight macroclusters in Figures 1 through 8.

When measured by correlational affinity (see scale on right of figures), Macrocluster I is the least related to the remainder of the total sample. Its placement at the beginning of the ordered matrix and its separation from the following attributes by three singletons both tend to confirm this minimal association. The first set of four clusters tends to center upon the Northwest Coast; the later clusters, however, are more broadly based.

Figure 1. Macrocluster I, Clusters 1–7

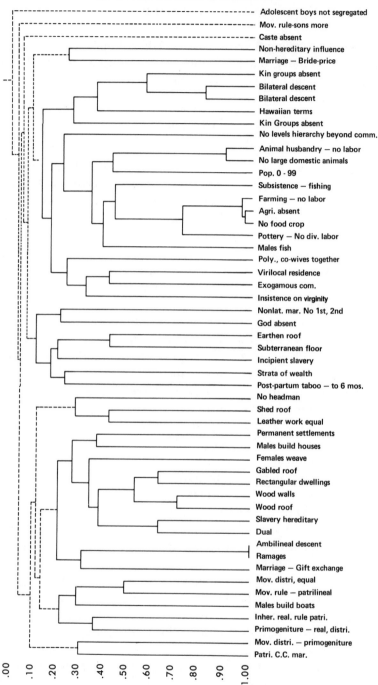

Source: Based on data provided by G. P. Murdock.
*The scale on the right indicates the level of correlation between traits or groups of traits.
Note: A cluster can be identified by a bridge (solid horizontal line) that has no other solid-line bridge above it. (Thus, above, Cluster 1 includes the first two traits, Cluster 2 includes the next five traits.) The clusters mentioned in the text can be identified by counting from the left.

Figure 2. Macrocluster II, Clusters, 8–11

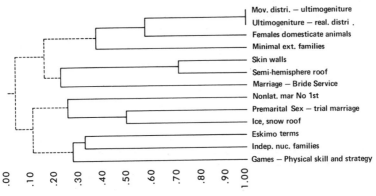

Source: Based on data provided by G. P. Murdock.

Figure 3. Macrocluster III, Clusters 12–19

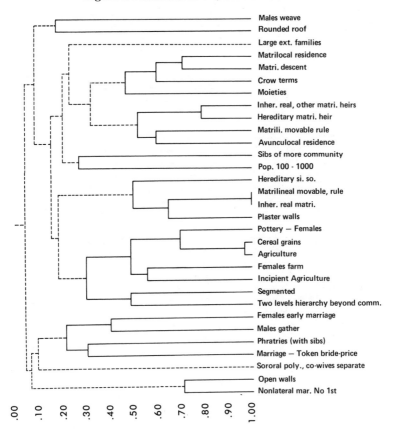

Source: Based on data provided by G. P. Murdock.

Figure 4. Macrocluster IV, Clusters 20–29

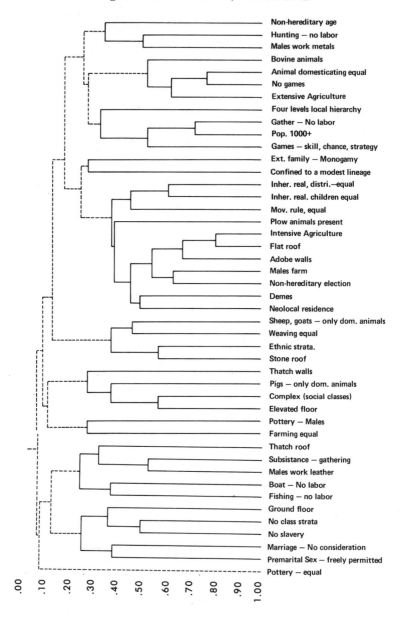

Source: Based on data provided by G. P. Murdock.

Figure 5. Macrocluster V, Clusters 30-32

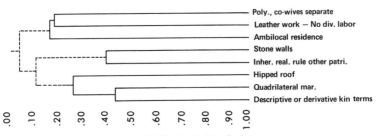

Poly., co-wives separate
Leather work — No div. labor
Ambilocal residence
Stone walls
Inher. real. rule other patri.
Hipped roof
Quadrilateral mar.
Descriptive or derivative kin terms

.00 .10 .20 .30 .40 .50 .60 .70 .80 .90 1.00

Source: Based on data provided by G. P. Murdock.

Figure 6. Macrocluster VI, Clusters 33-42

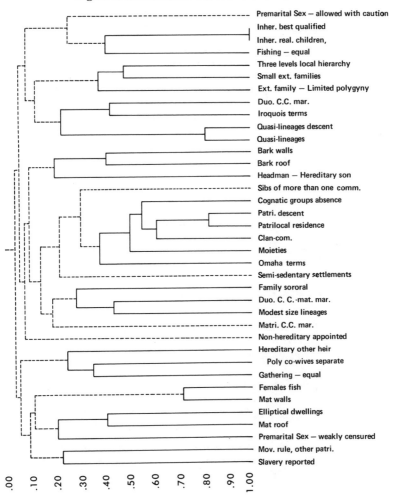

Premarital Sex — allowed with caution
Inher. best qualified
Inher. real. children,
Fishing — equal
Three levels local hierarchy
Small ext. families
Ext. family — Limited polygyny
Duo. C.C. mar.
Iroquois terms
Quasi-lineages descent
Quasi-lineages
Bark walls
Bark roof
Headman — Hereditary son
Sibs of more than one comm.
Cognatic groups absence
Patri. descent
Patrilocal residence
Clan-com.
Moieties
Omaha terms
Semi-sedentary settlements
Family sororal
Duo. C. C.-mat. mar.
Modest size lineages
Matri. C.C. mar.
Non-hereditary appointed
Hereditary other heir
Poly co-wives separate
Gathering — equal
Females fish
Mat walls
Elliptical dwellings
Mat roof
Premarital Sex — weakly censured
Mov. rule, other patri.
Slavery reported

.00 .10 .20 .30 .40 .50 .60 .70 .80 .90 1.00

Source: Based on data provided by G. P. Murdock.

Figure 7. Macrocluster VII, Clusters 43–48

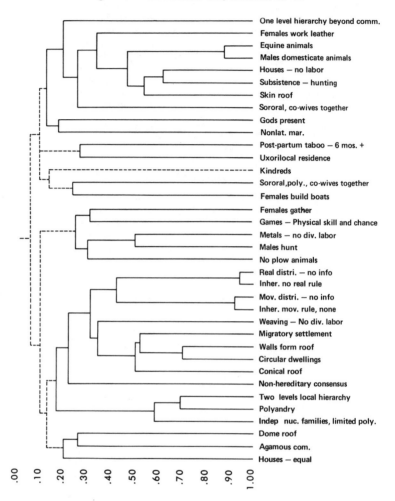

One level hierarchy beyond comm.
Females work leather
Equine animals
Males domesticate animals
Houses — no labor
Subsistence — hunting
Skin roof
Sororal, co-wives together
Gods present
Nonlat. mar.
Post-partum taboo — 6 mos. +
Uxorilocal residence
Kindreds
Sororal,poly., co-wives together
Females build boats
Females gather
Games — Physical skill and chance
Metals — no div. labor
Males hunt
No plow animals
Real distri. — no info
Inher. no real rule
Mov. distri. — no info
Inher. mov. rule, none
Weaving — No div. labor
Migratory settlement
Walls form roof
Circular dwellings
Conical roof
Non-hereditary consensus
Two levels local hierarchy
Polyandry
Indep nuc. families, limited poly.
Dome roof
Agamous com.
Houses — equal

.00 .10 .20 .30 .40 .50 .60 .70 .80 .90 1.00

Source: Based on data provided by G. P. Murdock.

Figure 8. Macrocluster VIII, Clusters 49-50

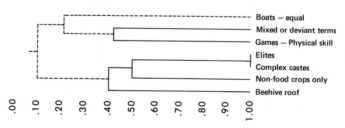

Boats — equal
Mixed or deviant terms
Games — Physical skill
Elites
Complex castes
Non-food crops only
Beehive roof

.00 .10 .20 .30 .40 .50 .60 .70 .80 .90 1.00

Source: Based on data provided by G. P. Murdock.

Macrocluster I groups seven clusters with attributes that obtain largely in western North America. Five of these clusters variously focus upon the Northwest Coast from Alaska to California as they divide the area into as many individual effects. The most distinguishing features of these subareas consist of attributes that form first bridges in each of the clusters. The subareas consist of: (1) a sweep over the Northwest Coast that centers upon wooden plank dwellings, (2) an interior sweep that lies adjacent to the former and centers upon subterranean floors and earthen roofs, (3) the Tlingit with their patrilineal cross-cousin form of marriage, (4) the Coastal Salish with their shed roofs and joint working of skins, and (5) coastal Oregon and California, which center on the use of wealth in acquiring a bride or the office of headman.

Four clusters join to form the second macrocluster. The 13 attributes they assemble are only minimally reported over North America, and the clusters they produce tend to describe unique effects in isolated areas.

The somewhat loose grouping of Macrocluster III treats matri-oriented activities. In the central region, a bridge joins two main effects at a correlation of $\phi = .15$. Cluster 14 provides the only extensive treatment of horticulture in the ordered matrix. Its placement within a context of matri-oriented attributes reflects the fact that females are more engaged in agricultural pursuits than are males.

The domestication of corn first appeared south of the Rio Grande River. Cluster 14 describes its northerly diffusion as it locates in the Southwest and then, avoiding the lower Basin and California areas, veers to the east and northeast until it reaches the Atlantic Coast or a latitude where temperature or rainfall impede its movement. Although it is not a necessary accompaniment, the manufacture of pottery has long been associated with agriculture. Where agriculture is reported north of the Rio Grande River, pottery is largely a female occupation. To the south, pottery was often only one of many specialized occupations practiced by males. On the Northwest Coast and neighboring areas, the pottery manufacturing units did not practice agriculture.

The most highly developed form of agriculture consists of the use and re-use of the same tracts of land, often with the aid of some fertilizing agent. This form, known as intensive agriculture, is reported in a nearly continuous area from the Southwest to the Aztecs. Extensive agriculture is more likely to be found in tropical areas, where rapidly growing native vegetation requires a frequent slashing or burning of virgin areas for planting. This form is widely reported by the Mayan units and by others from about central Mexico south. The incipient form is the least advanced and consists of garden-like plots that require a minimum of planning. Cluster 14 indicates that as agriculture spread eastward across North America, it was the incipient form that spearheaded the move and females who not only tended the crops but also manufactured the pottery necessary to store the yield. These conditions obtained in almost all of the units east of the Mississippi River; farming west of the Mississippi was usually advanced beyond the incipient form. Cluster 14 also indicates that the most frequent pattern of community organization consisted of segmented clans without local exogamy. This locates for the most part among Iroquoian-speaking peoples.

Cluster 15 treats matrilineal inheritance rules for real and movable property and includes the office of headman whose heir also is the occupant's sister's son. These infrequent rules are jointly reported by only the Timucua, as are dwelling walls of wattle and daub. As the absence of attributes that treat the distribution of real and movable property suggests, we cannot always determine if practices and social prescriptions reflect one another.

The second major effect centers upon Clusters 17 and 18. The former, as above, specifies rules of inheritance for real and movable property and for the office of headman where the heirs are consistently matrilineal. Avuncular residence is also included in the cluster. Once again, these prescriptive attributes are jointly reported by only a few units, although the distances that separate them suggest an element of functional cohesion between the real property rule and the succession of headmen. As in the case of the inheritance rules of Cluster 15, observed distribution practices do not cluster here.

Cluster 18 focuses upon descent and residence, two social characteristics that play active roles in the evolutionary development of social structure. Like the inheritance attributes of Cluster 17, these attributes locate in the Northwest, the Southwest, and the Northeast, although there are more units reporting. Cluster 18 also locates on the Plains and in the Southeast.

Matrilocal residence is reported only in the presence of matrilineal descent; their joint occurrences are widely scattered. Matrilineal descent is additionally observed in 16 units that report other residence patterns. While this study was not designed to probe deeply into these matters, I note a pronounced tendency for female-oriented inheritance rules, descent, and residence to occur among farming peoples where the female is more engaged in agriculture and in pottery manufacture than is the male. But the suggestion that matrilocality rests on a permanent homesite does not hold for the Northwest. The Kaska and the Alkatcho Carrier, the only two Northwest units reporting matrilocal residence, are situated east of the Coast Mountains in settlements described as migratory. Matrilocal residence among these people means living with in-laws who neither farm nor manufacture pottery but repeatedly move to tracts of land they do not claim to own and do not view as a potential inheritance.

Matrilineal descent is reported continuously over the middle to upper Northwest Coast, but in the absence of matrilocality. This more widespread distribution rests upon male-dominated subsistence activities like hunting, in the interior, and fishing, in the tidal waters of the Pacific. The chief occupation of the female is weaving, an activity that has no territorial import and no direct relation to subsistence activities. The rather exceptional pattern that emerges is one of matrilocality where locality is not important and of matrilineage where pivotal members play secondary roles in major subsistence activities. Only the Kaska in the Northwest, the Creeks and the Choctaw in the Southeast, and the Hidatsa on the Plains report moieties (division of the tribe into two functional groupings).

At first reading, the large assembly of Macrocluster IV suggests an evolutionary interpretation. Beginning to the right of the tree diagram, the macrocluster grows in a stepwise hierarchical fashion throughout. Clusters at the left list an absence of class strata, slavery, and fishing but include subsistence gathering. At the right, one finds large cities, extensive agriculture, domesticated cattle, and metallurgy. All of the clusters that occur between these extremes treat agriculturalists or animal husbandmen of one sort or another, and for this reason researchers look beyond evolution for an explanation. The tendency for clusters that treat agriculture, domesticated animals, and metallurgy to locate, almost in isolation, below the Rio

Grande River was not anticipated. Macrocluster IV identifies a range of attributes that are unique to Mesoamerica and owe their origins to Spanish influences.

Macrocluster V is the smallest of the macroclusters. It groups only three clusters and a total of nine attributes. Located between the subsistence-oriented Macrocluster IV and the patrilineal Macrocluster VI, it marks a transition between these two major groupings. Following the pattern of the former, Macrocluster V consists of several isolated effects. The first two are located in Mexico, the remaining one in California. Anticipating Macrocluster VI, there is the first appearance of patrilineal rules of inheritance.

Macrocluster VI comprises 10 clusters and five singletons for a total of 38 attributes. Its wide range of events is more expressive of patrilineage than of any other phenomenon. Many clusters, especially in the central region, are loosely held together and are divided by more singletons than occur in any other macrocluster. This suggests that patrilineage, in its varied forms, does not present itself as a coherent structure over North America. The tree diagram separates the macrocluster into three subunits with bridges at correlational magnitudes that fall below the .05 level of significance.

As a unit, Macrocluster VI centers upon patri-oriented descent and residence, just as Macrocluster III centers upon matri-oriented descent and residence. The largest lineage-oriented groups of each are moieties that list Omaha or Crow kinship terms for cousins as appropriate. Lineages which make up these moieties reside in more than one community and, because of this, are called sibs. Both macroclusters indicate that moieties are the prevalent mode of community organization.

The patrilineal Macrocluster VI also diverges from the pattern of Macrocluster III. Where the latter clusters avuncular residence and inheritance rules for other matrilineal heirs, Macrocluster IV offers no alternative. Matrisibs cluster in larger settlements of 100 to 1,000 inhabitants, whereas patrisibs tend to cluster in smaller settlements. At times this kinship grouping does not develop beyond the lineage, especially when it is found in small and impermanent patri-oriented settlements.

Patrilineal rules of inheritance tend to occur outside of Macrocluster VI and, where they occur, they tend to cluster with characteristics that describe distribution practices. Matrilineal rules of inheritance form distinct clusters in Macrocluster III, where they appear in the absence of distribution practices. I infer from this that matrilineal residence, descent, and inheritance prescriptions cohere in nearly functional fashion but that patrilineal attributes, while occasionally functional as in the case of Cluster 2, are prone to distribute in a more fragmented fashion and to cluster with other attributes of the sample.

Lastly, in Macrocluster VI, males are not grouped with their occupations or subsistence activities as are females in the matrilineal set. This suggests that male-oriented occupations are more independent of kinship structures than are female occupations.

Thirty-six attributes variously grouped by six clusters make up the seventh macrocluster. Together they describe many of the features of simpler societies throughout North America. The tree diagram divides the macrocluster into two principal subclusters, which contain three clusters each. Cluster 45 of the first subcluster provides a framework for the total macrocluster by describing hunting as a male-oriented activity that takes place in the absence of metalworking. This pair is reported by almost every social unit of the sample, whether hunting is practiced to provide a major source of subsistence or to supplement the diet of extensive or intensive farmers. Cluster 45 also cites gathering by females, thus identifying the most frequent division of labor between males and females in North America. The Nabesna and Huichol report gathering by males, but no unit of the sample reports hunting by females. Beyond Cluster 45, Macrocluster VII treats units that rely primarily upon hunting and gathering for subsistence. The attributes of the first subcluster probably assumed their present configuration after the Spanish introduced the horse.

Macrocluster VIII treats social organization in isolated areas. Though small, it is unique enough to constitute a separate macrocluster. The class strata of Cluster 49 are reported by the Caddo and Natchez as based upon land resources. This is the third such base to appear in the sample. A hereditary base was discussed in Macrocluster

I, which distributes across the Northwest, whereas the singular Quiche report class strata based upon ethnic differences. Despite these social advances beyond lineage considerations, it is somewhat surprising that the farming Caddo do not plant maize.

A deteriorated form of kinship terms for cousins tends to follow a decay of kinship as a structuring agent. The mixed or deviant terms reported by the Natchez are rather expected. That the Caddo do not report them or the domestication of cereal grains suggests that this ethnic unit may be a relatively recent arrival to the area. Alternately, the mixed or deviant kinship terms of the Caribou Eskimo and Takelma might be ascribed in part to their isolation.

Factor Analysis

As a first step to factoring, the matrix was examined for perfect correlations ($\phi = 1.00$). Beside the needless redundancy that results from identical columns and rows, proportionality of this sort would restrict the determinant of the coefficient matrix to $| \Phi | = 0$, thus rendering it inappropriate for factoring. Matrices exhibiting zero determinants are termed non-Gramian and so do not yield factor structures that the investigator may use to reconstruct them. One attribute from each of five perfectly correlated pairs was removed before factoring and later replaced in the factor structure with values identical to its sister variates.

The estimation of communalities reflects the purpose of the factor analysis: to produce results comparable to those of Sawyer and LeVine (1966) and Driver and Schuessler (1968). In such a pursuit, this study is further committed to the goals of these writers. By assigning a value of 1.00 to each communality, we ignore the identity and error components of each of the variates and so instruct the program to transform all of the variance contained in the correlation matrix to factor variance. Like earlier investigators, I follow Thurstone's (1947) suggestion that the resulting factors are not seriously biased when the number of variables is large.

Like Sawyer and LeVine (1966), I wish to identify common dimensions among variables and, like Driver and Schuessler (1968), I wish to see whether the intercorrelations obtained could be due to a few factors that might be given a plausible socio-anthropological interpretation. In addition, I wish to compare my results to those obtained by these writers.

I used the factor analysis program contained in the popular BioMed series, along with a supplementary program that assigned 1's to the diagonal cells. Thus, the factor analysis program was altered to produce factors by the method of principal components. With unities in the diagonals, the computer program will continue to extract as many factors as variates (Kendall, 1957). Since many of these will be of little statistical value, there are procedures available to separate meaningful from trivial factors. Authors of the two studies cited above employed Kaiser's (1958) criterion, which retains those factors whose eigenvalues or characteristic roots exceed 1.0 or, equivalently, whose variance equals $1/n$ or more of the total variance, where n equals the number of variables.

When this criterion was employed in the present sample, it identified 66 factors that accounted for 88.3 percent of the aggregate variance. This compares with reductions of 60 percent by Driver and Schuessler, 66 percent by Sawyer and LeVine, and 71 percent by Smith and Crano. Although names could be attached to each of these factors and their number supported on algebraic grounds (Kaiser, 1958), a review of the factors shows that most of them either load a small number of attributes or treat topics associated with more localized areas. For these reasons we turn to more expedient methods.

Cattell (1966b) suggests that the characteristic roots will drop dramatically in size to a point where further reductions would add little to the information already extracted. He calls this procedure a scree test; the term refers to rubble at the foot of the cliff. In an alternate approach, one would draw an asymptotic line along the "scree" and note the number of factors that leave this limiting position. Cattell and Jaspers (1967) originally suggested taking the first factor on the line but later specified the number immediately before the line. Because I would prefer to run the risk of interpreting too many factors rather than too few, I adopt Cattell's earlier suggestion here and use the first nine factors, explaining 34 percent of the aggregate variance, for interpretation. The Sawyer-LeVine and Driver-Schuessler data were rotated to the varimax criterion, and for similar reasons I adopt that analytic criterion here. This procedure has the advantage for exploratory factor analysis of simplifying the factors rather than the variables, since it maximizes the variances of squared loadings across factors rather than the variances of squared loadings for variables.

The interpretation of factors rests upon loadings that are sufficiently high to indicate a relationship between the variable and the factor. Unfortunately, there is no exact procedure for determining these salient loadings, and the investigator is left to choose among alternatives. He may examine significance levels for lower boundaries (Guilford, 1965; Nunnally, 1967) and face some difficulties (Horn, 1967; Humphreys and others, 1969), he may examine standard errors of correlations in factor structures or he may individualize his criteria for a cutoff point. By tradition these cutoff points have ranged between $\mid \alpha_{ij} \mid \geqslant .30$ and $\mid \alpha_{ij} \mid \geqslant .50$.

Sawyer and LeVine recorded loadings greater than $\mid \alpha_{ij} \mid \geqslant .50$ and observed that their variables did not overlap among factors. Driver and Schuessler interpreted factors having three or more loadings of $\mid \alpha_{ij} \mid \geqslant .40$, "since an ambiguity produced by two variables migh be resolved by a third" (1968, p. 350). With these pioneering studies in mind, I adopt the procedure of Driver and Schuessler. The nine factors are characterized below. (For the loadings and the number of units reporting each trait, see Hudson, 1979.)

Factor I, Subsistence Extremes. This combination of attributes centers upon subsistence practices that have been reported for the most part north of the Rio Grande. Grain agriculture is described at the positive pole and, as the magnitudes of the loadings decrease, incipient agriculture by females and later by males is specified. Females practiced incipient agriculture in a variety of units in the woodland areas over the eastern half of the United States from the Great Lakes to the Gulf of Mexico, whereas male involvement was confined to the Southwest and the Aztecs. Attributes negatively loaded include an absence of agriculture, of pottery manufacture, and of inheritance rules for real property. These absences, often associated historically, are jointly reported over most of the remainder of North America, with the possible exception of the Great Basin. The high loadings of these "absence" attributes offer little of interpretive value except to stress the simplicity of the polar opposite of grain agriculture. This factor is the most important and areally widespread.

With an eigenvalue or characteristic root of 18.75, it accounts for 8.15 percent of the total variance.

Factor II, Settlement Permanence. All of the attributes heavily loaded by this factor refer to architectural style, to construction materials used in dwellings, or to characteristics that correlate with construction procedures.

Circular dwellings were employed over most of the western half of North America, and of these the tipi in its varied forms was the most widespread. Built of skins or occasionally vegetation, this relatively impermanent dwelling appeared on the Plains, the Prairies, and the Basin, where it was usually constructed of skins by females, and in California, where it was built of bark or thatch. An earthen cone-shaped roof over circular pits also appeared in the Subarctic and Plateau regions.

Circular dwellings with dome- or hemisphere-shaped roofs were built in several areas where the conical tipi was also employed. To this extent, the negatively loaded attributes of this factor do not reflect separate geographic areas as do those of Factor I. Dome-roofed dwellings were built of grass and thatch in California, in the Basin, and on the Prairies, and of earth over circular pits by the Eskimo. In addition, a dome-shaped earth lodge without subterranean floors and the wigwam appeared on the Prairies, while the igloo was confined to the Arctic. Such roofs have not been reported on the Plains, on the Plateau, or in the Subarctic. The absence of clans and local exogamy and the relative impermanence of settlements call attention to the temporary nature of many circular dwellings, whether they were built with cone- or dome-shaped roofs.

In contrast, positively loaded attributes characterize permanent and more complex settlements. While the Northwest Coast is the only area for which all of them have been reported, most have been reported in Mexico and California, and at least two more have been reported in each of the remaining areas of the sample. The more permanent dwellings were constructed by males in all areas of the sample.

This is the second most important and areally widespread factor. With an eigenvalue or characteristic root of 13.13, it accounts for 5.75 percent of the total variance.

Factor III, Matricentered Organization. Attributes loaded by this factor treat matrilineally oriented practices or observances. In North America, matrilineal descent is observed in five geographic areas: the Northeast and some adjacent units, the Southwest, the Central Plains, the Northeast, and the Southeast. Since each of these areas includes at least two thirds of the matri-oriented attributes weighted by this factor, no one stands out as a major source of them. With an eigenvalue or characteristic root of 9.75, Factor III accounts for 4.24 percent of the total variance.

Factor IV, Patricentered Organization. With an eigenvalue or characteristic root of 7.91, Factor IV accounts for 3.44 percent of the total variance.

Factor V, Subsistence Hunters. The attributes that constitute this varied assortment do not easily yield to localization. Jointly they reflect a somewhat homogenous set of events which are observed over the central and northern Plains. It is widely reported that Plainsmen raised horses, hunted edible animals from horseback, and strove to obtain multiple wives who used the skins from the hunt to construct clothing and the typical Plains tipi.

Not all subsistence hunters lived on the Plains, however. Men of the Subarctic hunted without horses, and their wives also worked the skins for clothing and dwellings. Eskimo wives of the Arctic worked skins of animals that were taken from the sea, while women of the southern Plains and the Pueblo area raised horses for use as plow animals. All of these areal variations are reflected in Factor V. Factor V has a characteristic root of 6.86 and accounts for 2.98 percent of the total variance.

Factor VI, Southwestern Farmers. Attributes loaded by this factor are largely confined to the intensive agriculturalists of the Pueblo Southwest and Mexico. They jointly describe an egalitarian pattern of inheritance among matrilineages, neolocal residence in compact communities of adobe-walled structures, and the use of plow animals by males in the practice of agriculture. Local endogamy without segmentation to clan-barrios is the most commonly reported form of community organization. Only the Zuni community was segmented by local clans.

With a factor sum of squares of 6.15, Factor VI accounts for 2.67 percent of the total aggregate variance.

Factor VII, Localized Effects—Tlaxcalans. This factor loads attributes that derive largely from Mesoamerica. As in the case of Factor VI, the Mesoamerican coverage of this sample is too limited to support reliable interpretations. Together the attributes of Factor VII uniquely describe economic and political characteristics of the Tlaxcalans, the one unit of the sample that reports all of them. No other social unit occurs frequently. Factor VII has a characteristic root of 5.73 and accounts for 2.49 percent of the total variance.

Factor VIII, Boat Construction. Attributes loaded by this factor identify differences between social units that lie along waterways and those that do not. The construction of boats by males is associated with the patrilineal rule for the inheritance of movable property and specialization by females in the dressing of skins. This unique combination of characteristics is broadly reported for the Arctic, the Subarctic, the Northwest Coast, the Plateau, California, and the East.

In units more removed from drainage areas, males were occupied in the dressing of skins, rules or patterns of inheritance for movable property were absent, and gathering was a chief mode of subsistence. These small and relatively simple groups were most frequently found in the California and Basin areas. With a characteristic root of $\lambda = 5.20$, Factor VIII accounts for 2.26 percent of the aggregate variance.

Factor IX, Localized Effects—Aztecs. Loading another odd assortment of metalworking by males, ambilineal kinship, and all three types of games, Factor IX reflects parts of the cultural inventory of Mesoamerica. Social characteristics such as ambilineality, primogeniture distribution of movable property, and large settlements were also observed on the Northwest Coast. Only the Aztecs exhibited all of the attributes positively loaded by this factor. With a latent root of $\lambda = 4.68$, Factor IX accounts for 2.03 percent of the total variance.

Clusters and Factors Compared

The comparisons that follow are organized around six topics that appear throughout the studies discussed.

Agriculture. Three clusters center upon three separate forms of agriculture in North America. An incipient form (Cluster 14) is variously reported over the eastern half of North America, an intensive form (Cluster 25) in the Southwest, and an extensive form (Cluster 28) below the Rio Grande. While all of the factor analyses produce an agriculture factor that loads both the domestication of cereal grains and permanent, compact, or nonmigratory settlements, the Smith-Crano and Hudson factors are more inclusive. The former groups agriculture by males, rules for the inheritance of real property, and the intensive form of agriculture. Cluster 25, the largest cluster to treat agriculture, is built upon this intensive form. It further specifies dwelling characteristics, the election of the headman, and other attributes common among Pueblo and other Southwestern peoples.

The Hudson factor groups incipient agriculture by females in lieu of the intensive form. Incipient agriculture provides the base of Cluster 14, a set that also groups agriculture and pottery manufacture by females, clan-segmented communities and, less frequently, two levels of jurisdictional hierarchy beyond the community. These traits are most frequently found in the eastern half of North America.

The remaining form, extensive or shifting cultivation, is grouped by Cluster 28 with equal participation in bovine husbandry and a relative absence of games. Units exhibiting these attributes lie in Mexico and Mesoamerica, areas that are not fully represented in the sample.

Matrilineage. Again, all factor analyses produced a similar matri-oriented factor. Matrilineal descent is loaded by all of them, but is not elaborated by the loadings as widely as is agriculture. Besides matrilineal descent the Hudson factor loads matrilocal residence, a practice which relates closely to the matrilineal exogamy loaded by the remaining three. Unlike agriculture, matri-oriented attributes are numerous and are grouped by seven of the clusters.

Cluster 18 treats matrilineal descent on the Northwest Coast, in the Southwest, on the Plains, and in both the Northeast and Southeast. The cluster also includes matrilocal residence, Crow kinship terms for cousins, and moieties as the largest matrilineal group. All of these attributes are loaded by the Hudson factor. The grouping of attributes from four distinct clusters by one factor underscores the relatively broad coverage of this factor. As when both the incipient and intensive forms of agriculture were loaded by factors, the Hudson matrilineage factor groups matrilineal descent, inheritance, and residence with inheritance by other matrilineal heirs.

Patrilineage. Almost all the attributes loaded by factors of the four studies are grouped by Cluster 38. Beginning with patrilineal descent, the most heavily loaded by the factors, and with patrilocal residence, the cluster includes clan-organized communities, an absence of cognatic kin groups, moieties as the largest patrilineal unit, and Omaha kinship terms for cousins. This relatively close correspondence between factors and clusters suggests an underlying simplicity to the distribution of patri-oriented attributes.

Other Subsistence Activities. Other subsistence activities consist of fishing, hunting and gathering, and animal husbandry. Only the fishing factor occurs in all of the four studies. The combined or scaled categories of Driver-Schuessler, Sawyer-LeVine, and Smith-Crano produce factors that show male involvement in fishing, whereas the Hudson factor cites fishing as a dominant mode of subsistence. Both attributes are grouped by Cluster 6. The cluster treats small and relatively underdeveloped social units that do not cultivate grains and are more prone to fish than to hunt.

Varying combinations of hunting, gathering, and animal husbandry identify the factors of Sawyer-LeVine, Smith-Crano, and Hudson. These combinations reflect joint occurrences over North America, as in the hunting and animal domestication factor of Hudson, and the scaling procedures of Sawyer-LeVine, which combine hunting and gathering. Sawyer and LeVine obtain an "Animal Husbandry" factor that correlates highly with male involvement. It should be noted that this factor rests upon the domestication of horses and not of other animals.

Sociopolitical Complexity. This designation of Naroll (1970) proves to be the most complex and varied of all. Much of this variation, already discussed in the section on factor analysis, appears to follow from the several ways in which the Murdock columns are combined, scaled, or divided into attributes.

Stated in terms of the Murdock columns of the *Ethnographic Atlas*, the combined categories of Driver and Schuessler provide one factor that loads family organization, social stratification, and slavery. The scaled data of Sawyer and LeVine support a factor that combines the two components of family organization and household size, a category that was not used in the present study. A second Sawyer and LeVine factor combines class stratification and slavery but loads succession of the headman and jurisdictional hierarchy so weakly as to rule them out for interpretation.

Smith and Crano obtain three factors that variously combine the five columns. The first groups family organization with the local jurisdictional component of jurisdictional hierarchy. The second loads the remaining component, suprajurisdiction, along with succession to the office of headman, and a third dwells upon slavery.

With the Murdock columns decomposed to attribute form, the present study produces 22 clusters that classify components of the five Murdock columns with one or more of the remaining attributes. Only seven of these group two or more sociopolitical components within one cluster. A slavery characteristic accompanies a class stratification attribute in Clusters 3 (Northwest Coast), 5 (Northwest Coast adjacency), and 20 (strata-free societies), while some form of polygynous marriage (family organization) accompanies a form of jurisdictional hierarchy in Clusters 6 (nonagriculturalists), 41 (small extended families), and 44 (migratory peoples) and accompanies succession of the local headman in Cluster 36 (an artifact). It appears that the statistical attractions between Murdock columns, which variously describe the sociopolitical factors over North America, are grounded largely in the associations illustrated in these clusters. Additional exploratory studies will perhaps add to these combinations of variables as new methods of combining or arranging component attributes of the columns are used.

Only the Sawyer-LeVine and Smith-Crano analyses contain factors that treat the marriageability of first cousins. The Smith-Crano factor loads two similar variables: types of permitted cousin marriages and cousin kinship terms. These designations follow from the listings of Murdock's Columns 25 (cousin marriage) and 27 (kinship terminology for cousins).

In Retrospect

Though not anticipated, the relative independence of so many attributes of the sample is perhaps the most significant finding of the study. This independence persists into the upper levels of the tree diagram and contrasts sharply with the Q-mode pattern of Driver (1972). At a correlation of $\phi = .48$, where Driver obtained 10 classes to compare with Murdock's (1967) 10 cultural areas, 98.2 percent of the original Q-mode classifications are contained in clusters with an average of 26.8 attributes each. Only 45.2 percent of the R-mode classifications have clustered, with an average of 2.8 attributes per cluster. When singletons are included, the total set of Q-mode classifications is now reduced by 94.5 percent, while the R-mode classifications are reduced by only 29 percent. This overall reluctance of attributes to group in clusters corroborates a strong and similar tendency in the factor analysis. Both underscore the point that large geographic areas are likely to introduce so much variability in social and cultural inventories that reduction procedures cannot adequately handle them without prior reductions afforded by scaling or the combining of categories.

In biology, numerical classification is largely used to group floral and faunal specimens with a view toward identifying taxa. When social scientists produce similar groupings, they are often called exploratory, and few of them are incorporated into subsequent forms of analysis. It would seem that there is now enough information about social and cultural dimensions to enable the investigator to look to more elaborate research designs in which classifications become topical components of hypotheses and are constructed subject to the constraints of these hypotheses.

5

Maximum Likelihood Clustering of Binomial Data Sets

Pascale Rousseau
David Sankoff

Most clustering procedures begin with estimates of resemblance among entities. These estimates, assembled in matrix form, are then transformed so as to identify a structure within the original data. This paper is concerned with an alternate method of classifying binomial data, one that proceeds directly from data to classification and thus relieves the investigator of the need to choose and calculate a measure of resemblance.

Iterative partitioning methods have been extensively used to group I points, in N-dimensional space, into K clusters. The principle is to identify, at each iteration, the kernel (centroid, mean, most central point, and so on) of each cluster and then reassign each point to the cluster whose kernel is the closest. This approach has recently been generalized in several ways (Diday and Simon, 1976), including a broadening of the kind of entity to be classified, the development of more diverse and complicated kernels, and the use of various definitions of closeness of a point to a kernel.

Here we investigate one such generalization. The entities to be classified are sets of binomial experiments, each set associated with a given object or individual under a variety of conditions. The kernel of each cluster is a linear model in several parameters that describes the effects of the experimental conditions on the binomial parameter. The model has the same form from cluster to cluster, but the estimates for a given parameter may differ. The criterion for clustering an object with a kernel is maximum likelihood—the same criterion that is maximized to estimate the parameters within each cluster.

The Model

Let $A_{ij} = b\,(T_{ij},\,p_{ij})$ be a binomial variable; A_{ij} is the number of successes in T_{ij} independent trials, where the probability of success in a trial is p_{ij}. Suppose $i = 1, \ldots, I$ indexes a set of individuals or objects to be classified into K disjoint clusters, and $j = 1, \ldots, n_i$ indexes a vector $\vec{Y}_{ij}$ of R explanatory factors, binary, discrete, or continuous, affecting p_{ij}. (Note that these vectors are numbered separately for each i. There is no connection between $\vec{Y}_{i_1 j}$ and $\vec{Y}_{i_2 j}$. In particular, many or most of the possible configurations of the R factors may not occur with some or all individuals, so n_i may vary widely, depending on i.)

The usual model (Cox, 1976) for evaluating the effects of the explanatory factors is to postulate a logistic-linear model of form

$$\log \left\{ \frac{p_{ij}}{1 - p_{ij}} \right\} = \vec{Y}_{ij}\,\vec{\beta} \tag{1}$$

which ensures that $\hat{p}_{ij} \epsilon [0,1]$ under maximum likelihood, while the parameters in $\vec{\beta}$ are free to take on values in $[-\infty, \infty]$. (See Haberman, 1977; Rousseau, 1978; Rousseau and Sankoff, 1978a for the problem of singularities in the estimates.)

In classifying the individuals into K clusters, we postulate the existence of K parameter vectors $\vec{\beta}^{(1)}, \ldots, \vec{\beta}^{(K)}$ such that

$$\log \left\{ \frac{p_{ij}}{1 - p_{ij}} \right\} = \vec{Y}_{ij}\,\vec{\beta}^{(k)} \tag{2}$$

if the individual i is in the kth cluster.

The iterative partitioning scheme employed here is related to those summarized by Blashfield (1977) but is particularly in the spirit of Diday's "typological analysis" (Diday and Simon, 1976). At each cycle of the algorithm, using the K clusters calculated in the previous cycle, $\vec{\beta}^{(k)}$ is estimated by maximum likelihood within the kth cluster, for $k = 1, \ldots, K$, and each individual is then reassigned to the cluster that maximizes its likelihood. It can be shown (Rousseau, 1978) that starting from any initial partition, this algorithm converges to a local maximum in a finite number of steps.

Within a subset S of individuals, the log-likelihood of a parameter vector $\vec{\beta}$ is

$$\sum_{i \in S} \sum_{j=1}^{n_i} A_{ij} \log p_{ij} + (T_{ij} - A_{ij}) \log (1 - p_{ij}) \tag{3}$$

where the p_{ij} depend on $\vec{\beta}$ through (1). In order for (3) to have a unique maximum, it is necessary to take into consideration linear or other functional dependence among the explanatory factors. In the linguistic variation data that motivate our work, each binary explanatory factor is associated with one or more other factors to form a *nominal* factor F. In each $\vec{Y}_{ij}$, exactly one of the binary factors making up F is equal to 1; the rest are zero. This relationship can be taken into account by constraining the estimation through

$$\sum_F \beta = 0 \tag{4}$$

for each nominal factor F. (This resembles the setting of row and column means to zero in ANOVA. Analogous to μ in ANOVA, it requires the introduction of an "overall" effect β_0 where the zero-th component in each $\vec{Y}_{ij}$ is 1.) In practice, one of the β in each F is eliminated from (3) using (4), so that estimation may proceed unconstrained. Details of the Newton-Raphson procedure employed, as well as a documented program, are given by Rousseau (1978).

Reassignment of Individuals. There are two ways of going about reassignment each time new estimates $\hat{\vec{\beta}}^{(k)}$ are found. If each object or individual is simply characterized by various explanatory factor values that are either shared or in contrast (for example, sex, residential area, ethnic group) or are numerically comparable (for example, age, education, social rank) with other individuals, the reassignment of individual i proceeds by seeing which k maximizes

$$\sum_{j=1}^{n_i} A_{ij} \log p_{ij}^{(k)} + (T_{ij} - A_{ij}) \log (1 - p_{ij}^{(k)}) \qquad (5)$$

Another way of characterizing or identifying individuals involves defining a nominal factor to contain the first I binary explanatory factors (after the zero-th or "overall" factor). The binary factor corresponding to individual i has value 1 in $\vec{Y}_{ij}$, $j = 1, \ldots,$ n_i and value 0 in $\vec{Y}_{hj}$, $j = 1, \ldots, n_h$ where $h \neq i$. In this case reassignment is most meaningfully accomplished through the trial maximization of (5) with respect to $\beta_i^{(k)}$, $k = 1, \ldots, K$ prior to choosing the k that gives the highest value of (5).

Equation (1) allows $\hat{p}_{ij} = 1$ or $\hat{p}_{ij} = 0$, but this requires $\hat{\vec{\beta}}$ to contain infinite components. Once this occurs in a cluster at any iteration, it can lead the algorithm into a very unlikely local maximum, especially at early iterations (right after the initial partition). This follows from the fact that the reassignment step of the algorithm cannot assign any individual i to a cluster having infinite parameters unless $A_{ij}/T_{ij} = 1$ or $A_{ij}/T_{ij} = 0$ wherever the value of p_{ij} predicted by (5) is 1 or 0 respectively. (Any contrary assignment would lead to zero likelihood.) Thus, once such a singular cluster has been obtained, it remains through all further iterations, since any individuals whose data might remove a singularity cannot be reassigned to this cluster.

One way of avoiding this would be to change the reassignment method by carrying out a trial maximization of (5) for each $k = 1, \ldots, K$, not only with respect to $\beta_i^{(k)}$ but also with respect to all the $\beta_h^{(k)}$, $h = 1, \ldots, R$. Unfortunately, this approach is not computationally feasible.

Instead, we arbitrarily reset any infinite estimate to vC (or $-vC$ where appropriate), where C is a positive constant, and v is the number of iterations already performed by the algorithm. C is large enough so that, while it gets the algorithm out of undesirable early singularities, it does not perceptibly perturb the results (even if singular) of later iterations.

An Example

The particulars of our computer implementation were motivated by the nature of linguistic variation data and were tested on Laberge's (1977) *on—tu/vous* data, among others.

The indefinite subject pronoun in Montreal French can be either *on*, as is normatively prescribed, or one of the second-person forms, *tu* (singular and familiar) or *vous* (plural or formal). The choice of *on* (which we arbitrarily call a "success" of the binomial trial) or *tu/vous* is affected by two aspects of the discourse in which the pronoun is to be used. One is the syntax: whether the pronoun is found in an implicative type of structure, in a sentence embedded in a presentative matrix, or concurrently with a lexical marker of indefiniteness. This can be represented by one nominal explanatory factor, consisting of three binary factors, exactly one of which takes on the value 1 in any particular case. Another nominal factor is the "pragmatic" factor, distinguishing between two discourse effects, one that may be called situational insertion and the other, formulation of a moral.

In Laberge's study, data from 120 speakers were collected, but 26 of these individuals used only *on* or only *tu/vous* and were not subjected to statistical analysis, so that $I = 94$. The extent of the data is represented by

$$\sum_{i=1}^{94} \sum_{j=1}^{n_i} T_{ij} = 3861 \tag{6}$$

We will discuss two approaches to the analysis of these data, both of which use maximum likelihood clustering. The first associates a binary explanatory factor with each individual and has been worked out in some detail. The second uses sociological variables to characterize speakers, and only preliminary results will be presented.

How Many Clusters? Linguistic arguments can be made to the effect that if the three syntactic factors differ in their effects, the implicatives should have the smallest and the presentatives the largest, and that the formulation of a moral should have a greater effect than situational insertion. These arguments are supported by the results of fitting model (1) to the entire data set, as depicted in Table 1. We omit the 94 individual parameters and use the transformation

$$p = e^{\beta}/(1 + e^{\beta}) \tag{7}$$

so that all effects are in the interval [0, 1].

Table 1. Single-Cluster Analysis of *On—Tu/Vous* Data

Number of Individuals	Syntactical I L P	Discourse S M	Overall Effect	Log Likelihood
94	.31 .50 .70	.35 .65	.70	−1550

I = implicative   *L* = lexical marker   *P* = presentative
S = situational insertion   *M* = formulation of a moral

Source: Based on data compiled by Laberge.

Proceeding to an analysis where K = 2, we encounter the problem of local optima. The two solutions that occurred most frequently are presented in Table 2.

Table 2. Two-Cluster Analysis of *On—Tu/Vous* Data

Solution Cluster	Number of Individuals	Syntactical I L P	Discourse S M	Overall Effect	Log Likelihood
A 1	57	.18 .59 .76	.38 .61	.72	−1485
2	37	.52 .48 .50	.33 .67	.71	
B 1	54	.20 .71 .63	.35 .65	.71	−1482
2	40	.43 .39 .67	.37 .63	.71	

Source: Based on data compiled by Laberge.

Both of these solutions conserve the difference, first detected in the single-cluster analysis, between situational insertion and formulation of a moral, in both clusters. Solution *A* divides the individuals into one cluster that exaggerates the difference between the syntactic effects and a second cluster in which this difference disappears. Solution *B* shows parallel differences between implicatives and presentatives in both clusters but classifies individuals according to whether the lexical marker effect is high or low. Despite the slightly higher likelihood of this latter solution, it occurs less frequently as a local optimum than solution *A* and has no linguistically meaningful interpretation, while *A* does.

Table 3. Three-Cluster Analysis of *On—Tu/Vous* Data

Cluster	Number of Individuals	Syntactical I L P	Discourse S M	Overall Effect	Log Likelihood
1	43	.17 .72 .65	.38 .62	.68	−1448
2	35	.30 .40 .78	.38 .62	.74	
3	16	.70 .50 .30	.24 .76	.77	

Source: Based on data compiled by Laberge.

Considerations external to the purely statistical results also shed doubt on the three-cluster analysis in Table 3. While not the only local optimum, it is the only one that recurred many times with only minor modifications, and it has a distinctly higher likelihood. The main feature that distinguishes it from a mixture of solutions A and B in the two-cluster analysis is a group of 16 speakers who use relatively more of the *on* variant (overall effect = .77), who exaggerate the distinction between discourse effects, and who completely reverse the syntactic effect. An examination of the data further reveals that these speakers tend to have relatively few data and tend to have $A = T$ when the component of $\bar{Y}_{ij}$ corresponding to M is 1. This explains why the discursive effect, which is quite stable across all clusters in the other analyses, is exaggerated here, and this poor distribution of the data can be shown to be at least partially responsible for the reversed syntactic effect, as follows. By modifying our program to include the condition that the discursive effect must be identical in all three clusters, we still obtain a cluster with syntactic effects reversed, but only to the extent of a 0.6 : 0.4 comparison between implicatives and presentatives, rather than 0.7 : 0.3.

Thus, the introduction of external arguments favors solution A, a two-cluster analysis. Are there statistical criteria to back this up? As a first approach to this question, we carried out the following simulation study: Given the parameters of the single-cluster analysis in Table 1, we generated five random data sets with the same characteristics as the real data. That is, we generated a random binomial variable A_{ij} corresponding to each T_{ij}. Each complete data set so generated constitutes a typical sample under the single-cluster hypothesis.

We then carried out, on each artificial data set, a single-cluster analysis and a two-cluster analysis. We reasoned that if a single-cluster analysis were all that was warranted for the real data, then the increase in likelihood with a two-cluster analysis should be about the same as the increase for the random data sets. The random increases, however, ranged from 22 to 38, while the real data showed a jump of 65, strongly supporting a two-cluster analysis.

To test whether a three-cluster analysis is better than a two-cluster configuration, we carried out the same procedure, except that the artificial data were generated using two formulas of type (1) and by using the parameters of solution A. The real data showed an increase in likelihood of 37 for the three-cluster analysis, compared to a range of 13 to 28 for random data. This tends to support the three-cluster analysis over the two-cluster analysis, but not as unequivocally as solution A was preferred over a single-cluster analysis. Finally, a four-cluster analysis increased the likelihood of the data no more than that of random data.

The simulation experiment, then, confirms the presence of at least two but no more than three clusters, but does not help us further in deciding between these possibilities.

Partially Constrained Analyses. In the previous section, we referred to a modification of the program that permits some parameters to have identical values in all clusters while the algorithm searches for clusters and simultaneously estimates both these and cluster-dependent parameters. We illustrate further with an application to the *on—tu/vous* data. As will be seen, this is only partially successful, but it demonstrates well the potential of the method.

Laberge (1977) discovered that, whereas young women tended to use more of the *on* variant than did older individuals, young men strongly preferred the *tu* form. That these tendencies were statistically significant for each sex is evident from 2 × 2 contingency tables, which divide younger from older individuals at age 40.

Accordingly, we set up the maximum likelihood cluster program to search for two clusters, requiring the linguistic parameters, discussed in the previous section, to take on the same values in both clusters. Individuals were characterized not by individual binary explanatory factors but by their ages, and the parameters expressing the age effect and the "overall" effect were estimated separately for each cluster. The individual's sex was not included as an explanatory factor. All 120 individuals, not just those who varied in *on—tu/vous* usage, were included in the analysis.

The results of this were disappointing. The speakers clustered about two "regression" lines whose slopes (the age effects) vere very small. The lines intersected at age 111 rather than 40 or 50 as suggested by Laberge's results, and the two clusters did not show segregation by sex. Attempts to find a local optimum with lines intersecting at an earlier age failed.

An examination of the data showed that the attempt, in essence, to fit the *on—tu/vous* data with two intersecting curves of form

$$\hat{p} = \frac{e^{\text{age} \times \hat{\beta} + \hat{\beta}_0}}{1 + e^{\text{age} \times \hat{\beta} + \hat{\beta}_0}} \tag{8}$$

was thwarted by the presence of a few middle-aged individuals with either 100 percent *on* or 100 percent *tu*. In order to overcome this, to see whether the method would work with appropriate data, we tried weighting, by a factor of three, the data of three or four individuals toward the middle of the age range who had variable usage of *on* versus *tu/vous*. Forcing the regression curves to intersect in this way produced two clusters that accorded well with Laberge's results.

One cluster contained about two-thirds men and indicated a decrease in *on* usage with decreasing age. The other contained about two-thirds women and showed increasing *on* usage with decreasing age. The two curves intersected at age 58. Despite the fact that the desired type of intersecting was obtainable only by tampering with data, it is of interest that, once obtained, these clusters bear out the sex difference observed by Laberge. (Further application of maximum likelihood clustering to linguistic variation data has been discussed by Rousseau and Sankoff (1978b).)

6

Classifying Social
and Cultural Data
by Factor Analysis

Karl F. Schuessler
Robert Nash Parker

This chapter is an extension of earlier papers by Driver and Schuessler (1957, 1968). In the first, territorial populations were classified by their trait distributions, the centroid method was used, and practically all calculations were carried out by hand; in the second, cultural traits were classified by their population distributions, the principal factor method was used, and practically no calculations were done by hand. In both studies, we had to select a correlation coefficient, to fix the number of classes, and to choose a class for each variable. In all of these decisions, there was an element of discretion; none was based on a purely analytical criterion.

Here we ask whether these matters are substantially less discretionary today because of innovations in factor analysis (Jöreskog, 1969). Our answer, with minor reservations, is that recent work,

Note: We are indebted to Harold Driver, John Fox, and Howard Wainer for commenting critically on a preliminary draft of this chapter.

which is more concerned with fitting models than finding patterns, has only a marginal bearing on these issues and that their resolution is as much a matter of judgment today as it was a decade or so ago. The investigator must still decide on the best correlation coefficient, the best number of classes, and the best class for each variable.

Our clustering of cultural traits then raised two major questions: (1) Why did we choose the method of principal factors (PF) over the maximum likelihood (ML) method? and (2) Would we have obtained different results if we had used the ML method? To begin with, the ML method was hardly mentioned in the writings on which we relied for guidance at the time (Harman, 1960), and computer programs for ML factor analysis were not readily available, although some had been written. Our work reflected the state of the art of factor analysis during the early 1960s.

With regard to the second question, we would have obtained practically the same results with the ML method if all other operations had stayed the same. The reason is the necessarily close correspondence between loadings on the first k principal factors and the ML loadings for a model of k uncorrelated factors with no other constraints (Lawley and Maxwell, 1963). On the other hand, we might have come up with different clusterings if we had used the tetrachoric coefficient $r(t)$ instead of the product-moment coefficient $r(\phi)$, or if we had lifted the restriction of no correlation between factors. The choice of coefficients and the imposition of restrictions contribute as much to differences in classification as do factoring methods.

In emphasizing this point, we address decisions that must be made before variables are ever classified—selecting a correlation coefficient, settling on criteria for class membership—and show that PF and ML loadings produce very similar patterns once those decisions have been made. We do not argue that factor analysis is superior to alternative methods (for example, Goodman, 1975), merely that one's method of calculating loadings, or weights, is immaterial when the sole purpose is to classify a set of n binary variables.

To illustrate this process of decision making and to compare arrangements based on PF and ML loadings, we draw on 27 binary (dichotomous) measures of social life attitudes (cynicism, fatalism, and so forth) based on a national probability sample of 1,522 United

States (excluding Hawaiian and Alaskan) adults. These measures are similar to the 31 cultural traits analyzed by Driver and Schuessler (1968) in form and in the distribution of their correlations. These similarities and the convenient availability of these data on tape are our justification for using them in this demonstration.

Choosing a Correlation Coefficient

Factor analysis applies to the product-moment correlation coefficient, or the covariance. When that coefficient is based on binary (0, 1) variables, or 2 × 2 correlation tables, as in this study, it may be subject to adjustment before it is analyzed. Such adjustments rest on assumptions about underlying bivariate distributions. (See MacRae, 1970, for a more relaxed point of view. In his work on legislative roll calls, he factors Yule's Q, and the plausibility of his findings seems to justify his pragmatic approach.)

Although investigators may entertain any assumption about the distribution underlying a 2 × 2 table, in practice they are limited to assuming that it is either normal or rectangular (as specified below). The assumption of bivariate normality justifies replacing the product-moment coefficient for a 2 × 2 table r (ϕ) with the tetrachoric coefficient r (t). The assumption that the joint frequencies n_{ii} and n_{ij} are uniform among themselves but unequal to one another justifies replacing the product-moment coefficient r (ϕ) by the ratio of that coefficient to its maximum possible value (Carroll, 1961). Since few if any empirical distributions are known to conform to this pattern, assuming that they do in order to justify the use of r (ϕ) /max r (ϕ) would appear to be quite risky. For that reason, we exclude this adjusted coefficient from our discussion.

Table 1 gives the frequency distributions and a few of the statistical characteristics of our r (ϕ) and our r (t). Comparing means, we see that $\bar{r}(t)$ is larger than $\bar{r}$ (ϕ). This result inheres in the correction procedure: Pearson's approximation formula $r(t) = 2\sin\theta$ $(ad - bc)/N^2$ cannot be smaller than r (ϕ) and is generally larger. Since the smaller mean correlation $\bar{r}$ (ϕ) = .16 is fairly large, there would appear to be no point in testing the hypothesis that all intercorrelations in the population are zero. However, that test would probably be run as a matter of course in an actual problem.

Table 1. Frequency Distributions of $r(\phi)$ and $r(t)$

Class Interval	$r(\phi)$ F	$r(\phi)$ %	$r(t)$ F	$r(t)$ %
.00–.05	19	5.4	7	2.0
.05–.10	91	25.9	18	5.1
.10–.15	77	21.9	63	17.9
.15–.20	57	16.2	58	16.5
.20–.25	40	11.4	43	12.3
.25–.30	28	8.0	44	12.5
.30–.35	24	6.8	25	7.1
.35–.40	11	3.1	26	7.4
.40–.45	1	.3	13	3.7
.45–.50	1	.3	23	6.6
.50–.55	2	.6	17	4.8
.55–.60	0	0	9	2.6
.60 +	0	0	5	1.5
	351	100.0	351	100.0
Mean	.163		.266	
Standard Deviation	.094		.146	
Skew	.883		.728	

Note: Correlations Between 27 binary variables in a sample of 1,522 cases.

Although the $r(\phi)$ and the $r(t)$ differ in both dispersion and skew, they have a product-moment correlation of 0.99+, and we expect them to be very similar in their classifications of variables. This expectation is borne out, except that the percentage of common factor variance within classes is necessarily smaller for the $r(\phi)$.

Criteria for Classes

A classification by factor analysis involves arranging and rearranging variables until classes satisfy or approximate their formulated criteria. This implies that criteria are formulated before variables are ever sorted into classes. (It would be possible to fit alternative schemes by trial and error and accept the best-fitting one. In this case, rules for classes are formulated after variables have been grouped.)

For an exercise, we held that correlations among variables within classes are reducible to one factor, no correlation exists between classes, and no class includes fewer than four variables (since intercorrelations of three variables are always reducible to one factor). The rule of no class with fewer than four variables, or no more than $n/4$ classes, where n is the number of variables, implies that some variables may go unclassified. For a set of 27 variables, as in this demonstration, the maximum of six may leave as many as three variables with no class. By adding another variable for a total of 28, we might get a seventh class and so leave no variable unclassified. On the other hand, we could produce just one more unclassified variable. Empirical classifications based on factor analysis will generally be incomplete in the sense that some variables will be unclassified. We could get a complete classification by setting up classes with no minimum number of variables.

The double requirement of uncorrelated classes whose internal correlations are rank 1 implies no classes within classes, or no hierarchy. We could produce hierarchy by relaxing that requirement in some way. For example, we might allow for a general class of rank 2 and two or more subclasses of rank 1, after adjusting for the effect of the general class or factor. That model would fit variables composed of A or B, but not both, and C, as in the following diagram:

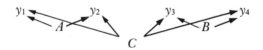

Classifying these variables gives a hierarchical arrangement with C at one level and A and B at another. Such an arrangement would be impossible to obtain under the rank 1 rule, since that rule makes no provision for classes of rank 2.

We might, on the other hand, get a hierarchy by permitting a correlation between classes. If that correlation were attributable to a common factor, it would warrant a combination of classes. After combining classes with a common element, we would have a composite class and two or more component classes, or a two-level hierarchy.

Uncorrelated classes may be represented by separate clumps

and correlated classes by clumps attached to a trunk

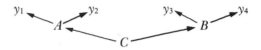

In this latter diagram, the clusters have internal correlations of rank 1. We may thus retain the rank 1 rule and still get hierarchy if we allow for correlation between classes and if we combine classes on the basis of that correlation.

Classifying Variables

Approximating class criteria—no more than $n/4$ classes of rank 1—would appear to be a simple matter: (1) Set up as many classes as there are significant factors, with every variable in every class at the start; (2) Drop variables from classes making only a negligible contribution to their variances; and (3) Drop classes with fewer than four variables.

One difficulty is that *negligible* is a relative term—it has no constant value and therefore must be defined before variables can be assigned to classes or dropped from them. Here, so as not to leave every variable in every class, we define a negligible contribution as less than 9 percent. A contribution of at least 9 percent, in other words, is a prerequisite for class membership. (As utilized here, this definition excludes joint contributions. With uncorrelated factors, there are no joint contributions; with correlated factors, there are both direct and joint contributions.) A significantly smaller value would leave every variable in every class; a significantly larger would leave most variables unassigned to a class.

Setting this screening value might seem to clear the way for assigning variables to classes, but there is still another snag: Contributions of factors to variables have no constant values. Their magnitudes depend on the positions of the factor vectors, and since these positions are arbitrary, they must be fixed before screening values are calculated.

Since, for a given variable, a quartimax rotation tends to increase the contribution of one factor at the expense of the others and, for all variables, tends to simplify structure, that rotation (or positioning of vectors) seems a priori best suited to our task. For comparative purposes, we also run a varimax rotation and, to determine whether our classification would change if we relaxed the rule of no correlation between classes, we carry out an oblique rotation, subject to the restriction of no interfactor correlations larger than 0.70 (interfactor correlations range from .30 to .55).

After performing these rotations and copying down loadings, we assign every variable to every class contributing at least 9 percent to its variance. We make these assignments for two methods (ML and PF) by two correlation coefficients $[r(\phi)$ and $r(t)]$ and by three rotations (quartimax, varimax, and oblimax).

Table 2, Columns 1–4, gives significant eigenvalues (calculated with communalities on the diagonal) for correlation coefficients according to method. In the first tier, Columns 5–10, we give the number of PF loadings larger than .30 (.09) for both correlation coefficients and for all three rotations; in the second tier, we give the same information for the ML method. With this setup, we may compare methods within coefficients by rotation, and vice versa; with a little more trouble, we may compare rotations under comparable controls.

From Table 2, we see that method makes very little difference. Both methods have the same eigenvalues (correlation constant) and the same class frequencies (correlation and rotation constant). Both call for dropping Classes 4 and 5, since neither class has the minimum number of four variables.

Rotation makes a difference in Class 3 for the $r(t)$ but not for the $r(\phi)$; Class 3 frequencies corresponding to quartimax, varimax, and oblimax rotations are, respectively, 13, 11, and 9. No such differences occur for the $r(\phi)$.

Comparing coefficients, we see that the $r(t)$ have an appreciably larger common factor variance than the $r(\phi)$—49.4 to 31.5—this by reason of the conversion formula. For the same reason, the $r(t)$ have more large loadings—193 to 178—over all comparisons. Frequencies in Classes 4 and 5 are uniformly less than the minimum of four for both correlation coefficients.

Table 2. Significant Eigenvalues and Number of Large Loadings ($a_y > .30$) by Factoring Method, Correlation Coefficient, and Rotational Criterion

Method	Factor	Eigenvalues $r(\phi)$ λ_i	λ_i/n	$r(t)$ λ_i	λ_i/n	Loadings Quartimax $r(\phi)$	$r(t)$	Varimax $r(\phi)$	$r(t)$	Oblimax $r(\phi)$	$r(t)$
Principal Factor	1	4.712	.175	7.633	.283	10	10	10	10	10	10
	2	2.035	.075	3.164	.117	8	8	8	8	8	8
	3	.987	.037	1.500	.056	9	13	9	11	8	9
	4	.444	.016	.533	.020	2	1	2	3	2	1
	5	.326	.012	.481	.018	1	1	1	1	1	1
			.315		.494	30	33	30	33	29	29
Maximum Likelihood	1	4.683	.173	7.435	.275	10	10	10	10	10	10
	2	2.037	.075	3.228	.120	8	8	8	8	8	8
	3	1.006	.037	1.547	.057	9	13	9	11	8	9
	4	.467	.017	.644	.024	2	2	2	2	2	2
	5	.311	.012	.444	.016	2	1	2	2	1	2
			.314		.492	31	34	31	33	29	31

The conclusions we draw from Table 2 are that method has no effect on the frequency pattern of variables, that rotation makes a difference only in Class 3 for the $r(t)$, and that the correlation coefficient makes a difference in the number of large loadings and hence in class frequencies. But we would produce three classes regardless of which combination of method, correlation, and rotation we applied to the data set.

Class assignments may differ even though class frequencies are closely similar. Therefore, our next question is whether different factoring methods will produce different class assignments (after controlling for correlation coefficient and rotation) and whether coefficients and rotations will differ under comparable controls.

Tables 3a through 3c show first that different methods do not produce different specific class assignments, after we control for coefficient and rotation. They show, second, that in every comparison the assignments based on the $r(\phi)$ are included among those based on the $r(t)$, but not vice versa. Thus, given a quartimax rotation and PF loadings, the assignments based on the $r(t)$ include all assignments based on the $r(\phi)$, plus additional assignments for Variables 15, 16, 17, and 27. Third, when the correspondence between assignments is less than perfect, those based on the quartimax include those based on the varimax, and those based on the varimax include those based on the oblimax. This nesting pattern occurs for the $r(t)$ but not for the $r(\phi)$.

In summary, neither method nor rotation makes a difference in class composition, given $r(\phi)$; given $r(t)$, rotation makes a difference but method does not. It would thus appear that $r(\phi)$ is more robust (loosely speaking) than is $r(t)$ in the face of changes in method and rotation and might therefore be preferred for classifying binary variables, other things being equal. It bears repeating that, with correlation coefficient and rotation fixed, it makes no difference whether loadings are calculated by the ML method or the PF method.

Testing Class Homogeneity

We specified in advance that correlations within classes have rank 1, or that variables within classes have only one common factor. Since empirical correlations can never attain that standard, it

Table 3a. Principal Factor and Maximum Likelihood Solutions After Quartimax Rotation

Variable Number	Principal Factor $r(\phi)$ F_1	F_2	F_3	$r(t)$ F_1	F_2	F_3	Maximum Likelihood $r(\phi)$ F_1	F_2	F_3	$r(t)$ F_1	F_2	F_3
1	57			71			57			71		
2	54			68			54			69		
3	53			67			54			68		
4	49			65			49			65		
5	50			66			51			67		
6	61			78			61			78		
7	59			73			59			73		
8	47			60			47			60		
9	37			47			36			46		
10	47			60			46			59		
11		63			78			63			81	
12		40			53			40			54	
13		50			62			50			61	
14		53			69			54			71	
15		57			68	31		57			68	32
16		57			71	30		56			69	33
17		55			66	33		63			65	33
18		46	35		57	42		45	36		55	45
19			46			57			45			56
20			58			75			58			75
21			47			58			48			58
22			46			58			46			58
23			46			58			46			59
24			38			48			37			47
25			42			52			42			52
26			48			60			47			60
27						40						39

Table with grouped headers: **Principal Factor** and **Maximum Likelihood**, each containing $r(\phi)$ and $r(t)$ sub-groups with columns F_1, F_2, F_3.

Variable Number	PF $r(\phi)$ F_1	PF $r(\phi)$ F_2	PF $r(\phi)$ F_3	PF $r(t)$ F_1	PF $r(t)$ F_2	PF $r(t)$ F_3	ML $r(\phi)$ F_1	ML $r(\phi)$ F_2	ML $r(\phi)$ F_3	ML $r(t)$ F_1	ML $r(t)$ F_2	ML $r(t)$ F_3
1	57			71			57			70		
2	54			68			54			69		
3	53			67			53			68		
4	49			65			49			65		
5	50			66			51			66		
6	61			77			61			78		
7	59			73			59			73		
8	47			60			47			60		
9	36			47			36			46		
10	47			60			46			59		
11		64			79			64			80	
12		41			54			41			55	
13		51			63			51			63	
14		54			71			55			73	
15		58			70			58			70	
16		58			73			58			71	
17		56			68	30		64			65	33
18		48	33		60	40		48	34		58	42
19			45			56			45			55
20			58			74			58			74
21			47			57			47			57
22			45			57			46			57
23			45			57			46			58
24			37			47			37			47
25			41			51			41			51
26			47			60			47			59
27						39						37

Table 3c. Principal Factor and Maximum Likelihood Solutions After Oblique Rotation

Variable Number	Principal Factor r(φ)			r(t)			Maximum Likelihood r(φ)			r(t)		
	F_1	F_2	F_3	F_1	F_2	F_3	F_1	F_2	F_3	F_1	F_2	F_3
1	58			72			58			72		
2	56			70			55			71		
3	53			66			53			67		
4	51			67			51			67		
5	51			67			51			67		
6	63			79			63			80		
7	60			75			60			75		
8	48			61			47			61		
9	37			47			36			46		
10	47			61			47			60		
11		70			86			70			88	
12		43			57			42			57	
13		55			67			54			66	
14		58			75			58			77	
15		60			72			60			72	
16		60			75			58			72	
17		56			67			54			63	
18		44			55			42			51	
19			46			57			47			57
20			62			80			63			81
21			46			56			48			58
22			49			62			50			64
23			46			57			47			60
24			40			52			41			51
25			42			53			43			54
26			48			62			49			62
27						37						36
$r_{F_1F_2}$	.308			.322			.309			.327		
$r_{F_1F_3}$	.303			.318			.334			.352		

becomes necessary to test the degree to which they approximate it. That approximation may be good in one class and poor in another or uniform over all classes. These approximations serve to verify our starting premise that variables may be grouped into $n/4$ or fewer classes, with no class showing more than one common factor.

In our case, the degree of approximation to rank 1 is an open question: Our 9 percent rule does not guarantee that variables within classes will have only one factor in common; it merely specifies that every variable in every class should be at least 9 percent dependent (in a statistical sense) on that class. On the other hand, that rule does not eliminate the possibility that variables within classes will have only one common factor—9 percent dependency and rank 1 can coexist.

To gauge homogeneity of variables within classes, we rely on the Tucker and Lewis (1973) Reliability Coefficient—abbreviated hereafter to TLRC. This coefficient rests on a comparison between the observed correlations and the correlations implied by k factors and gives the percentage improvement in the implied correlations attributable to k factors. When $k = 0$, TLRC = 0; when $k = n$ (the number of variables), TLRC = 1.00; for intermediate k, TLRC falls between 0 and 1. For $k = 1$, the model tested here, TLRC gives the percentage improvement in the implied correlations (or the percentage reduction of error) due to one factor. For large samples, it is the difference between χ_0^2/df_0 and χ_1^2/df_1 divided by χ_0^2/df_0. It is the complement of this ratio that is tested for significance.

In Table 4, we give the TLRC and χ^2 for every combination of variables for every class. No comparison between ML and PF methods is required, since these methods yield identical TLRCs (for $k = 1$), other things being equal. Nor are comparisons between rotations called for, since at issue is the homogeneity of a given set, not the rotation producing it. For these reasons, the only required comparison is between the $r(\phi)$ and the $r(t)$, as set up in Table 4.

In this table, we see that for a given combination of variables, the $r(\phi)$ always has the larger TLRC and the smaller χ^2. This contrast shows that, for classes that are common across coefficients, the combination with the largest number of variables, Class 1, has the largest TLRC and that the smallest, Class 2, has the smallest TLRC for both $r(\phi)$ and $r(t)$. However, we should not extrapolate this

Table 4. Tucker-Lewis Reliability Coefficients and χ^2s for Classes 1, 2, and 3

Class No.	Combination	Class Size	$r(\phi)$ TLRC	χ^2	df	$r(t)$ TLRC	χ^2	df
1		10	.960	118	35	.933	360	35
2		8	.865	296	20	.812	925	20
3	(a)	8	.956	65	20			
	(b)	9	.954	86	27	.914	259	27
	(c)	11				.733	1028	44
	(d)	13				.717	1804	65

finding: Class 3(d), which is largest with 13 variables, has the smallest TLRC—0.717.

The statistical results in Table 4 argue against grouping all 27 variables into three homogeneous classes. Class 1 and Class 3(b) are homogeneous by the criterion of a TLRC above 0.90, but in neither of these two combinations is the residual correlation lacking in significance. For Class 2, not only is χ^2 significant, but the TLRC is below 0.90. If we shuffle class assignments to reduce the significance of the residual correlation, we run the risk of leaving many variables unclassified. On the other hand, if we let matters stand, we in effect give up our requirement that variables within classes share only one common factor.

At this juncture, purpose and possibly time and energy come into play. A pragmatic social scientist would probably let the classification stand and make the most of it in substantive research; a methodological purist might continue to shift class assignments until the rank 1 rule is met. As this instance exemplifies, it is difficult if not impossible to make a decision on the basis of significance level alone. Our own inclination would be to accept at least tentatively the classification based on the $r(\phi)$ and make the most of it in our research.

Discussion

We have emphasized that factor analysis is no machine for classifying social and cultural traits. In using it for the first time, the investigator will shortly discover that it leaves many matters up in the air and that these uncertainties will have to be resolved judgmentally before the task can be completed.

Nevertheless, in classifying social and cultural traits by factor analysis, different analysts will be unlikely to come up with radically different results. With some sets of data, there will be few uncertainties to resolve. When traits are strongly correlated within subsets and weakly correlated across them, that is, when correlations are highly structured, both the number and composition of classes will be clear and unmistakable. In this case, different analysts will necessarily come up with very nearly identical classifications. Even when ambiguities are present in the data, specialists familiar with both the theoretical problem and the empirical facts are likely to consider the same points: plausibility of alternatives, time and place of data, sampling and measurement error. Our opinion is that the subject-matter experts will assess these factors similarly and will therefore arrive at nearly identical classifications.

Classifying social data by factor analysis involves the frequent exercise of judgment, but this holds equally for all so-called objective methods. If social classifications based on factor analysis have seemed arbitrary and jumbled, this is probably due not to factor analysis but rather to the imprecision of social data and the idiosyncratic nature of social life.

7

Progressively Complex Linear Transformations for Finding Geometric Similarities Among Data Structures

James C. Lingoes

An investigator who confronts more than one result or solution to a problem must ask: "What are the similarities and differences among these events?" Although this is a common problem for scientists in general, I wish to address it in a fairly specific context, that of individual differences in multidimensional configurations, regardless of the manner in which they were obtained. We shall suppose that such configurations are mere n-tuples of numeric assignments and that the array or matrix of such n-tuples can be given a geometric representation in a Euclidean space of greater than one dimensionality. I wish to invoke a dictum attributed to Newton, "Natura est simplex," as a basis for choosing a subset of transformations among the infinite variety available. This subset must help me to discern similarities among configurations, to quantify existing communalities, to diagnose the complexity of analysis needed for sufficient explanation, and to give precise form to the nature of the transformation. I therefore confine myself to linear transformations (because of their simplicity) and vary these according to their mathematical and psychological, or perceptual, complexity.

I shall give concrete form to my stated goals with an actual computer program and model (PINDIS, an acronym for **P**rocrustean **IN**dividual **DI**fferences **S**caling). This employs data whose immediacy is not, for the most part, apparent in more discipline-bound examples. The data are taken from geometric forms that are specifically biological in nature (fish, leaves, skulls, and genetic maps) and are embedded in a two-dimensional space. I shall place a minimum emphasis upon the mathematical foundation for the PINDIS model, since these details are adequately covered elsewhere (Lingoes, 1975; Lingoes and Borg, 1976a, 1976b, 1978; Borg and Lingoes, 1977, 1978; Borg, 1979). I shall, however, give mathematical expression to intuitively obvious geometric changes made in the configurations and shall quantify the similarity in terms of predictable variance, r^2 (Lingoes and Schönemann, 1974).

The first example involves two related species of fish, the common *Diodon* or porcupine fish and the allied, but quite different in appearance, sunfish (or suckling pig fish), *Orthagoriscus mola*. This example is abstracted from Thompson's (1948) fascinating chapter, "On the Theory of Transformations or the Comparison of Related Forms."

Some simple changes in Figure 1 may make the planar representation of these fish more amenable to comparison. First, I shall orient the two fish so that they are facing in the same direction. This change will involve an orthogonal rotation of A (*Diodon*) (a 45° turning in the plane of the page about some fixed, arbitrary point in A) and a reflection of B (*Orthagoriscus*) parallel to the bottom of the page (as depicted in Figure 2). Together these movements constitute what is known as an improper rotation when carried out on the same configuration. The rotation of A is known as a clockwise rotation, while the reflection of B is equivalent to lifting B off the page and turning it over or to looking at the figure from the reverse side of the page.

Figure 1. *Diodon* and *Orthagoriscus* Arbitrarily Oriented and Translated

Source: Adapted from Thompson, 1948.

**Figure 2. *Diodon* Orthogonally Rotated and *Orthagoriscus*
Horizontally Reflected**

Source: Adapted from Thompson, 1948.

My next elementary transformation will be a translation or displacement of A such that the head-to-tail axes of the two fish (appropriately centered) are in alignment. Then A is moved to the right until the right-to-left areal bisectors of the fish are coincident. By superimposing A on B in this manner, I can gain an immediate perception of size and structural relationships between the fish. In effect, I am lessening the distance between all corresponding points of A and B. Figure 3 demonstrates this type of movement in the plane.

To further decrease the distances between homologous points, since size may not be the most relevant feature, I can uniformly dilate or enlarge A. By selecting a set of 29 points for *Diodon* and a corre-

Figure 3. *Diodon* Translated

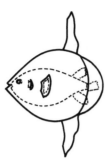

Source: Adapted from Thompson, 1948.

sponding set for *Orthagoriscus* (depicted in schematic form in Figures 4 and 5), I am able to illustrate the superimposition and dilation in Figure 6. Each figure shows the above four elementary, linear transformations which preserve the figure as figure; all relative distances within each fish are maintained; and the angles between any two points, using a third as a point of reference, are unchanged in magnitude. The mapping, in other words, is conformal. For a detailed elementary discussion of these transformations and others, the reader is referred to Green and Carroll (1976). For a sketchier development, see Lingoes (1975).

By imposing a coordinate system (rectangular, in this case) on Figures 4, 5, and 6 and by introducing a scale for both axes, I can express the position of any point for either fish, can measure the distances between points, and can give symbolic or mathematical expression to the transformations. For any given configuration of points, let **X** denote the coordinates of an $n \times m$ matrix of n points (rows) and m dimensions (columns) with elements x_{ia}. The four transformations can now be expressed in terms of these elements, that is, the projections of the points on the axes. The coordinate resulting from these transformations will be designated as x^*_{ia}, being an element of **X***, the transformed matrix or coordinate system. Thus, for a translation, we have the equation

$$x^*_{ia} = x_{ia} + t_a \qquad (1)$$

Figure 4. *Diodon* with 29 Selected Points

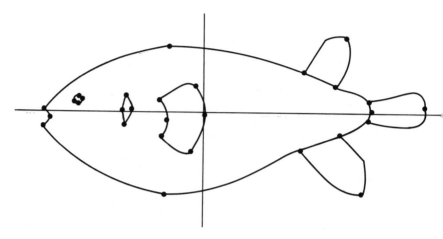

Source: Adapted from Thompson, 1948.

For a reflection,

$$x^*_{ia} = -x_{ia} \tag{2}$$

This involves an odd number of dimensions only; otherwise, we would have a rotation through 180°. For a dilation or contraction, we obtain

$$x^*_{ia} = cx_{ia} \ (c \neq 0) \tag{3}$$

Finally, for an orthogonal rotation (the only kind I will discuss in this paper and the only kind used in PINDIS), we have

$$x^*_{ia} = x_{ia} \cos\theta - x_{ib} \sin\theta \tag{4}$$

and

$$x^*_{ib} = x_{ia} \sin\theta + x_{ib} \cos\theta \tag{5}$$

for a pair of dimensions, a and b, representing a clockwise rotation. The preceding can be compactly expressed as

$$\mathbf{X}^* = c\mathbf{X}\mathbf{R} + \mathbf{j}\mathbf{t} \tag{6}$$

where $\mathbf{R}$ is an $m \times m$ orthogonal matrix, $\mathbf{j}$ is an n-element column

Figure 5. *Orthagoriscus* **with 29 Selected Points**

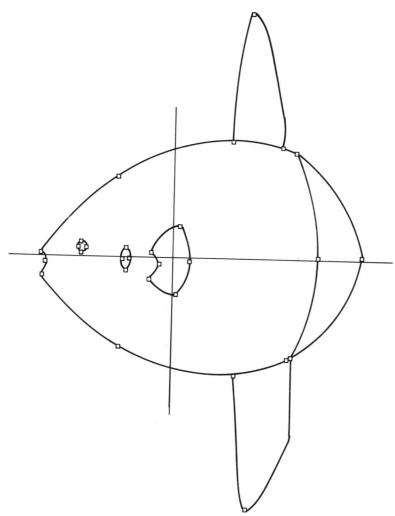

Source: Adapted from Thompson, 1948.

vector of 1's, **t** is an *m*-element row vector of positive or negative numbers indicating the magnitude and direction of translation, and *c* is a scalar. Since our measure of common or predictable variance, r^2, for pairs of configurations is invariant under uniform stretching (central dilation), we can conveniently norm **X** and **Y** to unit length and

Figure 6. *Orthagoriscus's* Procrustean Fit to *Diodon*

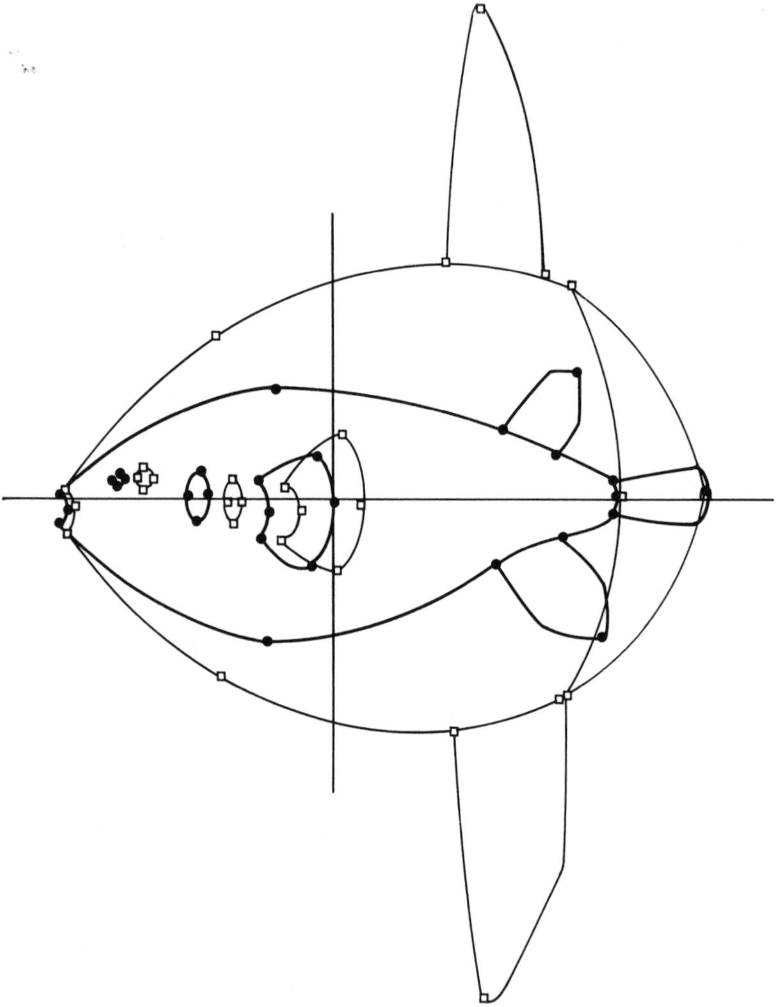

Source: Adapted from Thompson, 1948.

eliminate the c in (6). **X** will designate the matrix to be fitted and **Y** the target configuration. If **R** has a positive determinant, then no reflections are involved.

   The solution for the orthogonal rotation (Schönemann and Carroll, 1970) constitutes the first step of a PINDIS analysis. The communality between the two fish under this isotonic (angle preserving) transformation is r^2 ($\mathbf{X}^*$, $\mathbf{Y}^*$) = .72, which could be considered fair (see Figure 6 for the visual counterpart to this measure of fit). It should be noted that, at this stage of the analysis, an orthogonal (proper or improper) rotation leaves relative distances within $\mathbf{X}$ invariant. $\mathbf{R}$ is chosen such that the distances between corresponding points in $\mathbf{X}$ and $\mathbf{Y}$ will be minimized.

At the next level of complexity, I introduce an m-square matrix of weights, $\mathbf{W}$, whose off-diagonal elements are null. $\mathbf{W}$, in other words, is diagonal, and its effect is to differentially stretch or shrink each dimension so as to minimize the distance between $\mathbf{X}$ and $\mathbf{Y}$. As one might surmise, these dimensional weights are from the Horan-Bloxom-Carroll-Chang model of subjective metrics. The model, first incompletely solved by Bloxom (1968), was algebraically formulated by Schönemann (1972). Horan (1969) originally proposed its use in the INDSCAL algorithm (Carroll and Chang, 1970). Without comparing the details of the INDSCAL and PINDIS weights at this time (see Borg, 1979), I would like to point out that in PINDIS the weights are a direct function of the two sets of coordinates and are simply related to various communality indices among the configurations. Because optimal dimensional weighting is dependent upon the positions of $\mathbf{X}$ and $\mathbf{Y}$, I seek a unique orientation for both, a simultaneous orthogonal rotation of $\mathbf{X}$ and $\mathbf{Y}$ such that the distance between $\mathbf{X}^*$ and $\mathbf{Y}^*\mathbf{W}$ is minimal. For just two configurations, $\mathbf{X}$ and $\mathbf{Y}$, Carroll and Chang's IDIOSCAL (1972) provides a solution, although, in contrast to that of PINDIS, their solution is not unique.

In Figure 7, the weights are applied to the target configuration. Figure 8 portrays the desired goal. Figure 9 presents a more direct comparison between $\mathbf{X}^*$ and $\mathbf{Y}^*\mathbf{W}$ in terms of the 29 points. The measure of fit under this distance-distorting transformation is r^2 ($\mathbf{X}^*$, $\mathbf{Y}^*\mathbf{W}$) = .87, which represents about a 15 percent improvement over the unweighted, Procrustean fit. Although Figure 9 is closer to our goal, certain parts of *Orthagoriscus*, the back, belly, and tail, are rather poorly fitted by this transformation. To some extent, this lack of fit is a function of the number of points used and their locations. Because there is an inherent conflict in different parts of both fish (the left and right halves), the solution represented in Figure 7 is but a compromise.

Figure 7. PINDIS's Dimensionally Weighted *Diodon*

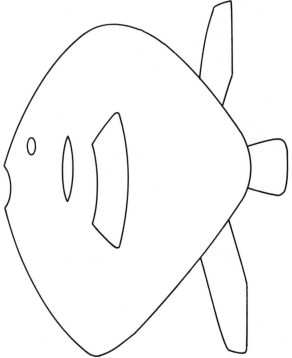

Source: Adapted from Thompson, 1948.

The third stage of PINDIS generalizes the subjective metrics model of dimensional weighting to that of vector weighting. Each point is conceived to be the terminus of a vector; an optimal rotation of **X** and a set of weights for **Y**, **V** (a *n*-square diagonal matrix) are determined, such that the distance between **X*** and **VY** is as small as possible (Lingoes, 1975). Although the centroid is optimal for dimension weighting, it may not be best for vector weighting and thus requires a shift as well as a rotation in the to-be-fitted matrix. The distorted *Diodon* (**VY**) appears in Figure 10. The success of this transformation is more apparent in Figure 11, where the left half matches excellently but the right very poorly indeed. Again we have a conflict that the transformation is inadequate to resolve. Our fit is

Figure 8. *Orthagoriscus*

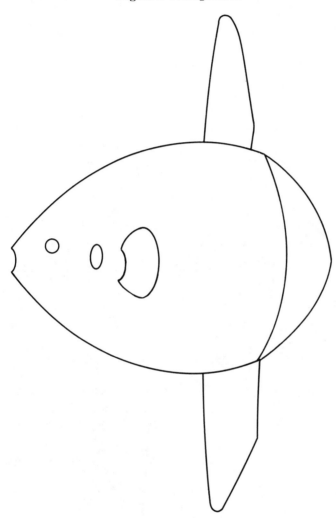

Source: Adapted from Thompson, 1948.

about 6 percent better than the simple Procrustean fit under rigid motions, r^2 ($\mathbf{X}^* + \mathbf{jt}$, $\mathbf{VY}$) = r^2 ($\mathbf{X}^*$, $\mathbf{VY} - \mathbf{jt}$) = .78, and is 9 percent poorer than dimensional weighting. The expense of these improvements is the use of 29 more parameters. Obviously, the needed transformation must still be sought.

Figure 9. Point Representation of Dimensionally Weighted *Diodon*

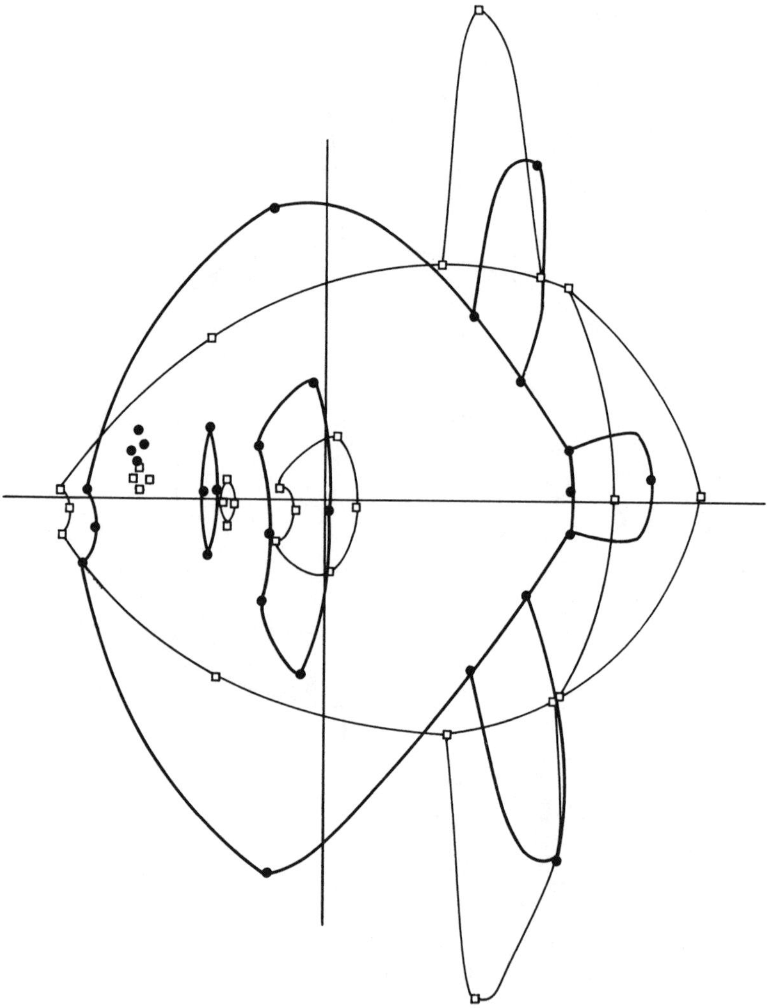

Source: Adapted from Thompson, 1948.

     In the last stage of PINDIS, weighting from both the left and right vectors and dimensions is combined, as suggested by Lingoes (1975). The transformed *Orthagoriscus* appears in Figure 12 and the superimposed figures in Figure 13. Here, r^2 ($\mathbf{X^*}$, $\mathbf{VY^*W}$) = .96, representing about a 9 percent improvement in predictable variance

Figure 10. PINDIS's Vector Weighted *Diodon*

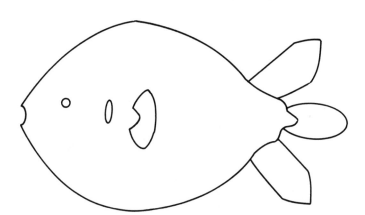

Source: Adapted from Thompson, 1948.

over simple dimension weighting, our best solution to this point. Without addressing the number of parameters needed (equal to that of vector weighting, $m + n$ for the double-weighting solution), the statistical significance of the r^2's (see Neel, Rothhammer, and Lingoes, 1974), or the psychological rationale for such a complex transformation (since the aim here is a purely descriptive one), the use of linear transformations for this particular problem has come a long way.

As an epilogue for this fishy example, Thompson's graphical solution (1948, p. 1064, Figs. 525 and 526) seems to represent a fairly uniform, albeit nonlinear, nonisogonal transformation. For other nonanalytic transformations based on Tissot's Theorem (1881), the reader is referred to Tobler (1961, 1963).

Akin to the fish example is the following PINDIS analysis of the common tobacco leaf taken at two stages of growth, initial sprouting and maturity. The relevant parameters and measures of fit will be presented in lieu of the numerous figures involved in this analysis. In this example, 56 measurement points are scattered symmetrically and uniformly within the leaves. The Procrustean fit with **Y** rotated at

Figure 11. Point Representation of Vector Weighted *Diodon*
Superimposed on *Orthagoriscus*

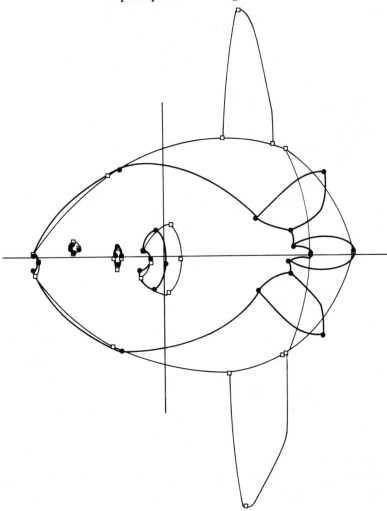

Source: Adapted from Thompson, 1948.

about a 45° angle from the larger, horizontal axis yields an $r^2 = .96$. This indicates that growth was fairly uniform throughout the leaf, considering the prior norming where both **X** and **Y** are of unit length. An optimal dimension weighting yields unit weights for both dimen-

Figure 12. PINDIS's Doubly Weighted *Diodon*

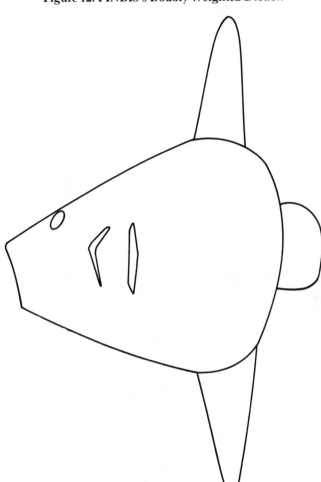

Source: Adapted from Thompson, 1948.

sions ($r^2 = .96$ or no improvement), essentially confirming the surmise about uniform growth.

If vector weights with an appropriate origin are applied, the
communality is increased by roughly 4 percent ($r^2 = .9974$), but the
points on one half of the leaf are approximately unity, while the

**Figure 13. Point Representation of Doubly Weighted *Diodon*
Superimposed on *Orthagoriscus***

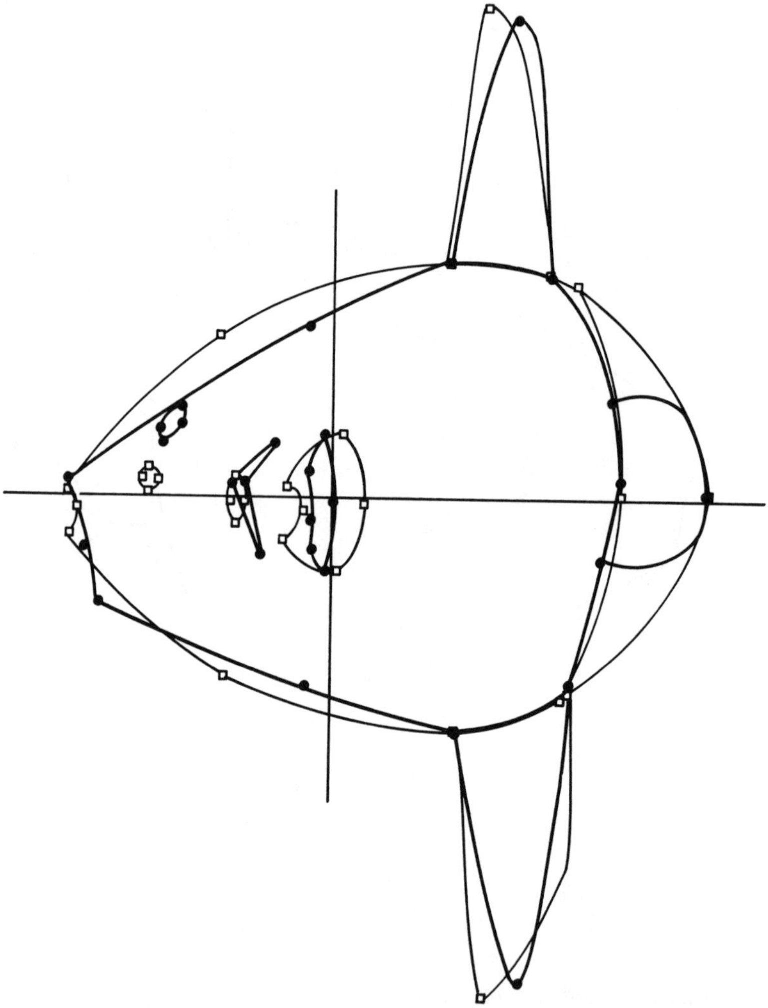

Source: Adapted from Thompson, 1948.

remaining points are less than unity. (The range of weights is from
.56 to 1.38 with one exception: a large negative weight of −2.51 near
the origin.) While the increment in fit may not be statistically significant, the systematic change in weights suggests that growth is differ-

Figure 14. Thompson's Graphic Transformational Solution

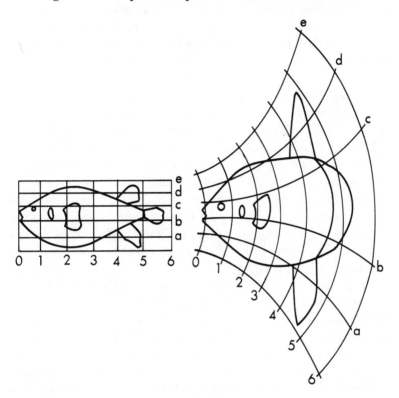

Source: Thompson, D'A. W. *On Growth and Form.* (2nd ed.) New York: Macmillan, 1948, p. 1064, Figs. 525 and 526.

ential in this example, which for a botanist may be informative. The final, combined transformation produces no improvement over vector weighting.

A third example of growth (evolutionary) is based upon 20 homologous skull loci of early (*Australopithecus*) and modern man (*Homo sapiens*). Here, as in the previous example, the Procrustean fit is quite good ($r^2 = .93$), and dimensional weighting brings about a slight improvement only ($r^2 = .95$). Introducing vector weights increases the fit by about 4 percent ($r^2 = .99$), and double weighting does not improve upon this. The dimension weights are in the ratio of 4:3, while the vector weights are all positive in the range of .35 to 1.60.

Once again, differential changes in various parts of the skull better account for the differences than does change along the dimensions. Although these data were previously analyzed (Lingoes, 1975), the rotation problem had not at the time been solved in an optimal way. Much progress has been made in the PINDIS algorithm since its inception.

As a cautionary note, it should be mentioned that the two-configuration case ($N = 2$) is an anomaly for most applications of PINDIS. As a consequence, fitting **X** to **Y** is not equivalent to fitting **Y** to **X** for any of these transformations, except simple Procrustean fits in terms of r^2. One should, therefore, obtain a solution both ways in such instances and choose the solution that makes more sense or has the better fit. That this asymmetry exists for the fit measure should be evident when one considers that r^2 is a composite of weighted covariances and that the weights will, in general, be different for the two solutions. The above examples, basically didactic and descriptive, have ignored this caveat.

A final example involves a reanalysis of some genetic maps of the Yanomama Indians (Neel, Rothhammer, and Lingoes, 1974), which were analyzed pairwise originally. The principal aim of the study was to compare distance matrices based on three different sets of biological data (9 dermatoglyphic characteristics, 12 anthropometric measurements, and gene frequencies at 9 loci) among seven Yanomama villages in Venezuela and Brazil. The three genetic maps yield 7×7 matrices of Mahalanobis D^2, and a geographic map of the approximate locations of the villages serves as a basis of comparison to determine the extent of fissioning and centrifugal expansion of the tribe. Using a number of metric and nonmetric techniques, I conclude that the correspondences among these four maps are statistically significant, with some pairs (six in all) yielding higher similarities than others. My aim here will be to see if transformations other than the isotonic (Schönemann and Carroll, 1970) will reveal additional points of similarity. To this end, I have chosen the geographic map as the target to which the three genetic maps are to be fitted.

The D^2 matrices were preprocessed by MINISSA-I (Guttman, 1968; Lingoes, 1965, 1973; Lingoes and Roskam, 1973; Roskam and Lingoes, 1970), and very good fits were obtained in two dimensions for all. A simple rotation of all three matrices simultaneously to best fit the target (a modification of the Gower, 1975, process) resulted in $r^2 = .63$, which is fair and, most likely, statistically significant. Dimension weighting improved the fit by 7 percent; idiosyncratic (Carroll and Chang, 1972) rotations of the hypothesis (target) configuration (geographic map) improved the fit by an additional 4 percent. Vector weighting, on the other hand, improved upon dimension weighting by yielding a communality of .90. The double (duo-affine) weighting, however, added only about a 1 percent improvement over the rotations.

In terms of individual differences, marker genes, then anthropometrics, and then dermatoglyphics constituted the best order for dimensional weighting, yielding communalities of .80, .72, and .70, respectively. In the case of vector weighting, a very different order emerged: anthropometrics ($r^2 = .98$), dermatoglyphics ($r^2 = .88$), and marker genes ($r^2 = .85$). This seems to suggest that the distribution of villages among Yanomama Indians might be explained by more obvious genetic differences (discrimination?) and that village dispersion can primarily be explained by angular separations from an optimally computed origin, which I find interesting indeed!

Other features and applications of the PINDIS model may be pointed out in summary form. First of all, although I have used only two-dimensional examples, the PINDIS program will handle mixed dimensionalities up to a ten-dimensional solution with up to 1,000 configurations for as many as 100 points. The procedure will allow for the use of a hypothesis or target configuration; if one is not available, the program will generate a common space that best explains all configurations. Because it is a direct procedure (using configurations rather than some derivative, such as distances, squared distances, or scalar products), a wider range of data structures is amenable to analysis (rectangular, nonsymmetrical, with missing cells, metric, nonmetric, and so on) without invoking questionable assumptions about the relationship of input to output.

Because the PINDIS procedure is sequential and progressive, it provides a better idea of just what is needed and where and for whom. For example, in a reanalysis of some consumer behavior (Green and Rao, 1972), Borg and Lingoes (1978) not only found some unsuspected communalities but also discovered that, while the "subject space" may show a nice distribution of dimensional weights, a simple Procrustean (nondistorting) fit may explain as much variance as does dimensional weighting. This fact is obscured by other forms of analysis. Using Feger's (1974) data on political attitudes, Borg and Lingoes (1976) found that the "group space" may not represent anyone in particular; some are unpredictable. One is cautioned to take neither space for granted. Using them as a basis for clustering S's or inferring the "underlying" dimensions may have a number of pitfalls. A PINDIS analysis does, however, provide a foundation for obtaining more homogeneous groups within the limited repertoire of transformations presently available. Other, more technical issues, such as norming, partitionability of variance, uniqueness, negative weights, and nonorthogonality of the group space-dimensions, will not be specifically addressed here, but all of these details are properly handled by PINDIS.

Recently, an important modification has been made in the vector weighting portion of the PINDIS algorithm, that of a simultaneous translation of both **X** and **Y** in order to maximize predictability. This change, for example, results in an almost perfect prediction of *Diodon* from *Orthagoriscus* ($r^2 = .9964$). Note that this involves a reversal of what is to be fitted to what and that the origin has been shifted from the centroid to a point near the front central point of *Orthagoriscus's* tail fin. This vector weighting (linear) transformation has accomplished the same fit as Thompson gives (see Figure 14), without sacrificing conformality (angles from the new origin are preserved).

All other reported findings are essentially the same, except for the genetic example, where vector weighting improves the $r^2 = .96$ under optimal translations. The new origin for the target configuration thus has important substantive implications, but space precludes a discussion here.

Although PINDIS may not be able to "make a silk purse out of a sow's ear," it has proved to be adequate and instructive for analyzing many different kinds of data. It is hoped that the foregoing examples will suggest what can be done with linear transformations as a first approximation to some other complex structures.

8

Selective Aspects of Measuring Resemblance for Taxonomy

John Fox

The last two decades have witnessed the proliferation of automatic classification methods in a variety of disciplines. For examples of the diverse applications of numerical taxonomy, see Hartigan (1975a) and Sneath and Sokal (1973). Although terminology is far from standard, it is important to distinguish techniques for the construction of classification schemes from methods of assigning objects to previously defined classes. A number of authors (see Cormack, 1971, for example) have drawn this distinction. The former sort of method has been variously termed cluster analysis, classification, and numerical taxonomy, as well as a plethora of other names. Placing objects in predefined classes is often called identification or assignment, but the term *classification* is also common. In the present paper, we are concerned with the development of classification schemes and shall

Note: The author would like to thank William Carroll, York University. and the participants in the workshop for helpful comments on an earlier draft of this paper.

employ the terms cluster analysis, classification, and numerical taxonomy synonymously to describe this process.

Most numerical classification procedures do not proceed directly from data to a clustering of these data. Rather, a derivative structure, comprising measures of resemblance among the entities to be classified, mediates between the data and their classification. This two-stage approach to classification is characteristic of what are probably the two most important works on numerical taxonomy: Sokal and Sneath (1963, and the more recent Sneath and Sokal, 1973) and Jardine and Sibson (1971). There are, however, a number of clustering techniques that are not based on the intermediate calculation of measures of resemblance. Hartigan (1975a) presents several interesting examples.

The subject of the present chapter is the measurement of resemblance for cluster analysis. This topic has been discussed and debated repeatedly in the literature on numerical taxonomy, and it is unlikely that I shall have much that is new to add to the discussion and debate. Nor do I propose to survey the literally dozens of measures of taxonomic resemblance that have been proposed; such a survey would be tedious and of dubious value. Nor shall I organize this discussion around the formal properties of measures of resemblance, though, of course, these properties will be of some concern (see Jardine and Sibson, 1971; Williams and Dale, 1965; and Gower, 1966). Rather, I shall begin with a consideration of the different sorts of data on which classification may be based and shall proceed to describe the methods of analysis appropriate to each.

This chapter, then, has more the character of a text than of a formal literature review or definitive synthesis. It is primarily directed toward an audience interested in the measurement of taxonomic resemblance but largely unfamiliar with the issues in this area. In the spirit of such an undertaking, I shall avoid detailed references and attributions but shall, at appropriate points, direct the reader to sources that supplement this account. The most comprehensive bibliography on methods of numerical taxonomy is found in Sneath and Sokal (1973). Less exhaustive and somewhat easier to use are the bibliographies in Cormack (1971) and Everitt (1974). Hartigan (1975a) includes a nicely annotated set of references.

In data analysis generally and in numerical taxonomy in particular, there exists a largely healthy tension between the formal development and analytical investigation of methods on the one hand and the ad hoc construction and practical application of techniques on the other. The two approaches are by no means mutually exclusive: To a great extent, one supplements the other. Jardine and Sibson (1971) argue convincingly for formal study, and their contribution is exemplary in this realm. It is probably fair to say that most other work in numerical classification has been in the "practical" tradition. If the present paper has a bias, it is toward the formal approach. The reader who wishes to pursue this issue will find the exchange between Cormack and Gower, following Cormack's 1971 review essay, stimulating and informative.

Data

The fundamental data on which cluster analysis is generally based are scores on a set of variables for a set of individuals. (There are other sorts of data structures that are potentially useful for taxonomy. For example, a matrix of similarities or dissimilarities may be given directly rather than computed from a rectangular "case by variable" data matrix. See Hartigan [1967] for further discussion.) These scores may conveniently be placed in a matrix

$$
\underset{(n \times p)}{X} = \begin{bmatrix} x_{11} & x_{12} & \ldots & x_{1p} \\ x_{21} & x_{22} & & x_{2p} \\ \cdot & & & \\ \cdot & & & \\ \cdot & & & \\ x_{n1} & x_{n2} & & x_{np} \end{bmatrix}
$$

where n rows represent n individuals and p columns represent p variables or attributes (descriptive of persons). The set of possible scores for an attribute is termed its set of attribute states and may be discrete or continuous. The process of data analysis in general and of cluster analysis in particular may be viewed abstractly as a transformation of the data matrix. Before I can intelligently approach the transformation of data into measures of resemblance, however, I shall have to discuss some of the characteristics of data.

Modes of Analysis. Most of the data analysis applications familiar to social scientists examine relationships among the columns of the data matrix, that is, among attributes. Regression analysis, analysis of contingency tables, and factor analysis as it is commonly employed are examples of techniques that are used to explore relationships among variables. This familiar type of analysis, termed R-mode by Cattell (1952), is distinguished from Q-mode analysis, which focuses on relationships among the rows of the data matrix.

Generally, methods of cluster analysis that take as input a set of resemblance coefficients are equally suited for clustering individuals or variables. The measurement of association among variables, familiar to social scientists and simpler than the measurement of resemblance among objects, will not concern us here, however. Nor will I examine certain techniques that construct clusterings of both individuals and attributes (see Tryon and Bailey, 1970; Hartigan, 1975a). The focus here will be the measurement of resemblance among objects, that is, Q-mode relationships.

Individuals and Aggregates. It is common for cluster analysis to study aggregates of individuals rather than individuals themselves. In biological taxonomy, a researcher may wish to classify species of organisms rather than individual organisms. To the extent that attribute states are invariant within aggregates, the distinction between classification of aggregates and classification of individuals becomes unimportant. If there is substantial variation within aggregates, however, this distinction, which is frequently overlooked or ignored, becomes critical.

Jardine and Sibson (1971) have introduced the term *character state* (used by most other authors as synonymous with attribute state) to refer to the probability distribution (or probability density distribution for a continuous attribute) over the states of an attribute for members of an aggregate. The abstract set of character states (the set of possible distributions) is termed a *character*. In the present paper, I shall modify Jardine and Sibson's terminology somewhat, employing the term *character state distribution* for character state and *character distribution set* for character. I hope this usage will avoid terminological confusion and, at the same time, stress the distributional nature of characteristics of aggregates.

Social aggregates are rarely aggregates in the strict sense, since they have properties of a different nature from those of their members.

All but the most intransigent methodological individualist would assent to this statement. For example, in one respect, a nation is a collection of individuals, and its income distribution is a character state distribution in the sense of Jardine and Sibson. Its area and type of government are indivisible attributes, however. The fact that social aggregates are not aggregates in the strict sense need not cause formal difficulties. Attributes of aggregates may be treated as if they were attributes that are invariant within aggregates, that is, character state distributions that "concentrate" all of their probability on single attribute states.

Types of Attributes. At least since Stevens (1946), social scientists have been aware that different varieties of measurement scales exist. (See Torgerson, 1958, for a more complete discussion of measurement scales.) From the point of view of their use in taxonomy, it is probably sufficient to distinguish four varieties of attributes: (1) numerical attributes, (2) ordinal attributes, (3) binary nominal attributes, and (4) multistate nominal attributes.

Numerical attributes include what are generally termed absolute, ratio, and interval scales. What distinguishes these three from other scale types is that they possess a unit of measurement. An absolute scale or count (number of children in a family) has both a natural origin (no children) and a natural unit (the child). Ratio scales (money income) possess a natural zero point (no income) but employ a conventional unit (the dollar). An interval scale attribute (historical time) has both an arbitrary origin (the year zero) and a conventional unit (the year). Sometimes numerical attributes are termed *continuous.* This identification is erroneous, however, since certain numerical attributes (number of children) are clearly discrete. It is often convenient to treat discrete numerical attributes with a large number of states (income, for example) as if they were continuous.

Like numerical attributes, ordinal attributes indicate differences in quantity or amount. Ordinal attributes include rankings (in terms of dominance, for example) and, perhaps more commonly in social science, assignment to ranked categories (occupations ranked according to status, for example). Ordinal scales may have a natural origin (as in the case of Likert-type attitude items with a neutral response category), or they may not (as in the examples given above).

Ranked categories are frequently treated as rankings in which individuals in the same category are "tied."

Nominal attributes code qualitative, not quantitative, differences. Binary or dichotomous nominal attributes possess two states, as their name implies. Often these states denote presence and absence of some characteristic. For example, North American Indian societies may be coded on the basis of presence or absence of waterworks for irrigation. Since certain measures of taxonomic resemblance require binary attributes, it is useful to distinguish these from multistate nominal attributes. Religion, coded in several categories, is an example of the latter.

Commensurability and Conditional Definition of Attributes. The data matrix that serves as input to a classification procedure is likely to contain attributes of different types. A data matrix of this sort is termed *mixed* by Hartigan (1975a). Combining information from different attributes to produce overall measures of taxonomic resemblance among individuals or aggregates is a difficult problem, one that is compounded when the data are mixed.

Even when all attributes are of the same type, they may be incommensurable. Since commensurability depends upon the possession of a common unit of measurement, only numerical attributes may be strictly commensurable. Data matrices that include attributes that are all of the same type but are not all measured on a common scale are termed *heterogeneous.* If all attributes are commensurable, the data are homogeneous.

As Jardine and Sibson (1971) point out, true commensurability of two attributes is rare, even if both are formally measured on the same scale. Although different parts of an organism are measured in centimeters, direct comparisons of the lengths of different parts may be inappropriate. To take an example with more relevance to social research, even though the percentage of murderers and the percentage of married people in a county share a common unit, it is unlikely that the percentages would be treated as comparable. On the other hand, percentile scores from a battery of psychological tests may well be considered commensurable.

The central problem in the construction of measures of taxonomic resemblance is to find a nonarbitrary procedure for dealing with the combined information in a mixed or heterogeneous data matrix. As we shall see below, Jardine and Sibson (1971) have developed such a procedure for measuring the resemblance among a set of aggregates. I am unaware of a wholly satisfactory procedure that can be applied to individuals, although a number of reasonable alternatives have been proposed.

Some attributes are defined only in terms of other attributes. Attributes of this type are said to be conditionally defined (Jardine and Sibson). For example, in a study of Indian tribes, the "use of waterworks in agriculture" would be applicable only for tribes practicing agriculture. The presence of conditionally defined attributes in the data matrix complicates the construction of measures of resemblance. As in the case of incommensurable attributes, the problems raised by conditional definition are most satisfactorily solved for measuring resemblance among aggregates.

In biological taxonomy, it is not always simple to identify corresponding or homologous structures in different organisms prior to measuring attributes based on these structures (Sneath and Sokal, 1973; Jardine and Sibson, 1971). It is unclear whether such problems are likely to arise in the construction of social classifications, though one could imagine, for example, that for societies with radically different social structures it would be difficult to identify corresponding characteristics.

Selection of Individuals and of Attributes. In the R-mode sort of analysis most familiar to social scientists, the individuals in the data matrix are sampled from a population of interest to the researcher. At times, one can think in terms of sampling even when the populations are hypothetical, as are the possible repetitions of an experiment or the potential realizations of a stochastic process. In contrast, the entities to be investigated in a Q-mode analysis (generally termed *operational taxonomic units*, or OTUs, in taxonomy) are likely to comprise a population that is of interest to the researcher. Hence, though they are selected according to more or less explicit criteria, they are not sampled. If the OTUs are aggregates of individuals, however, the individuals chosen for study are likely to be sampled from relevant populations. In this event, the character state distributions of the aggregates or the parameters of these distributions are estimated.

In Q-mode studies, as well as in R-mode research, attributes are chosen, not sampled, since the concept of the population or universe of attributes is not well defined. In the present chapter, the data matrix will be given. The selection of OTUs and attributes will reflect the interests of the researcher. Issues surrounding the process of selection are discussed in a number of sources, including Sneath and Sokal (1973), Jardine and Sibson (1971), and Everitt (1974).

Measuring Resemblance Among Individuals

This section is devoted to a discussion of measures of resemblance among individuals and, by implication, among aggregates whose members are invariant with respect to the attributes under study. Prior to considering the measurement of resemblance for mixed data, I shall separately investigate measures proposed for different types of data.

Measures of resemblance are of two basic types: measures of similarity and measures of dissimilarity. Let $A = \{a_i : 1 \leq i \leq n\}$ represent the set of individuals to be classified, and let x_i' represent the i-th row of the data matrix, that is, the vector of attribute scores for individual i. Then a dissimilarity measure between individuals may formally be defined as a function d from pairs of individuals a_i, a_j (that is, $A \times A$) to real numbers that satisfies the following conditions (Jardine and Sibson, 1971; Williams and Dale, 1965):

(1) $d(a_i, a_j) \geq 0$
(2) $d(a_i, a_j) = d(a_j, a_i)$
(3) $d(a_i, a_j) = 0$ if and only if $x_i = x_j$

Note that (3) implies that $d(a_i, a_i) = 0$. Some of the following measures satisfy the third property for transformations of the data vectors rather than for these vectors themselves.

A dissimilarity measure is said to be metric if it satisfies the triangle inequality:

$$d(a_i, a_j) \leq d(a_i, a_k) + d(a_k, a_j)$$

Dissimilarity measures that can be modeled as distances among points (representing individuals) in Euclidean space are examples of metric coefficients. The ultrametric inequality is even more restrictive:

$$d(a_i, a_j) \leq \max \left(d(a_i, a_k), d(a_k, a_j) \right)$$

Ultrametric distances are more likely to be encountered as the output of clustering than as input (see Hartigan, 1967, 1975a; Jardine and Sibson, 1971).

Clearly, a dissimilarity measure may be transformed into a similarity coefficient by inversion, for example, by subtraction from its maximum realized or theoretical value. Likewise, a similarity coefficient may be transformed into a measure of dissimilarity by inversion; however, it is not always possible to transform a similarity coefficient into a metric dissimilarity measure.

Quàntitative Data. Measures of resemblance that have been proposed for quantitative data are of two general sorts: distance coefficients, which are based upon attribute differences and angular coefficients, which are based upon attribute products (see Boyce, 1969, or Cormack, 1971, for a quick overview of a number of these measures). As we shall see, the two kinds of coefficients are related.

The simplest distance coefficient is Euclidean distance, which is defined in the following manner:

$$d(i, j) = \left(\sum_{k=1}^{p} (x_{ik} - x_{jk})^2 \right)^{1/2}$$

Since the unit of the distance coefficient is the square root of the sum of squared units of measurement of the p attributes, distance is uninterpretable unless the attributes are commensurable, in which case the unit of distance is the common unit of the attributes. For heterogeneous data, therefore, the arbitrary unit of measurement chosen for an attribute will affect its contribution to the distance coefficient. Clearly, if distance is to be a useful measure of dissimilarity for heterogeneous data, some way must be found to make the contributions of different attributes commensurable. Unfortunately, there appears to be no completely adequate procedure for achieving this purpose.

One approach to the problem is to introduce the concept of a weighted distance, together with a reasonable procedure for arriving at weights:

$$d'(i, j) = \left(\sum_{k=1}^{p} w_k (x_{ik} - x_{jk})^2 \right)^{1/2}$$

If weights are chosen as the reciprocals of the variances of the attributes, then we are in effect standardizing the attributes and converting them to unitless, and hence commensurable, quantities. Alternative standardizations are possible: Weights, for example, may be taken to be the inverse of the squared range of each attribute.

Various weighting procedures have been suggested, most of them employing weights that are functions of the data. However, subjective weighting is also possible. For further discussion, see Jardine and Sibson (1971), Sneath and Sokal (1973), Hartigan (1975a), and Morrison (1967). Kendall and Stuart (1976) suggest that numerical data be converted to ranks prior to the calculation of variance-weighted distances. Since the transformed variables are each scored from one to n, their variances are identical so long as all scores on a variable are distinct. If ties are present, the variance of the ranks will vary accordingly, and variable weights, in general, will differ. Kendall and Stuart's measure is also applicable to ordinal data.

It is distressing that standardization (in terms of a measure of dispersion calculated over the whole set of OTUs to be classified) works to the detriment of attributes that are relatively good discriminators among OTUs in different clusters. Once OTUs have been classified into clusters, the variance of an attribute can be partitioned into within- and between-cluster components. Good discriminators among clusters have large between-cluster as compared to within-cluster variance. To maximally differentiate clusters, variables should be standardized in relation to their within-cluster variance, not to their overall variance. Although these observations serve to criticize standardization as a weighting procedure, they do not suggest a practical alternative method of determining weights. As a number of authors (see Fleiss and Zubin, 1969; Hartigan, 1975a) have noted, the optimal calculation of weights requires the division of OTUs into clusters, the very task that motivates the calculation of measures of resemblance in the first place.

In addition to Euclidean distance, quite a number of other measures of taxonomic distance have been proposed (see, for example, Sneath and Sokal, 1973). Among these is the family of Minkowski metrics, defined by the following formula:

$$d_\alpha(i, j) = \left(\sum_{k=1}^{p} |x_{ik} - x_{jk}|^\alpha \right)^{1/\alpha}$$

Within this family of metrics, the familiar Euclidean distance measure is d_2, while d_1 is the absolute or "city-block" metric. Since Minkowski metrics are built upon sums of powers of differences, they all share the commensurability problems (and the partial solution of standardization) associated with Euclidean distances.

Variance-weighted distance attempts to correct for the dependence of the distance coefficient on the measurement scales of the attributes and, indeed, such distances are invariant under changes of unit and origin (linear transformations). Another difficulty associated with the calculation of distances is the correlation of scores of different attributes. In a sense, sets of highly correlated attributes are implicitly given more weight in the calculation of distances than are attributes that are not strongly related to others. Several problems raised by this phenomenon can be clarified by an examination of generalized or Mahalanobis distances, a technique that adjusts for correlation among attributes. The squared generalized distance between a pair of OTUs is defined as

$$D^2(i, j) = (x_i - x_j)' \, \Sigma^{-1}(x_i - x_j)$$

where x_i and x_j are (as before) vectors of scores on a set of p attributes, and Σ is a $p \times p$ variance-covariance matrix for the attributes. We can see that generalized distance is the direct multivariate analog of variance-weighted distance. As such, it is invariant with respect to all nonsingular linear transformations of the attribute scores.

The natural use of generalized distance is in the measurement of distances between aggregates; it will function in this role in the next section of this chapter. In that context, the differences measured are differences in mean vectors between multivariate, normally distributed populations with a common covariance matrix. In the present context, Σ will be the covariance matrix within clusters or, more properly, a pooled estimate of an assumed common covariance matrix. Since the clusters are unknown prior to calculation of a distance function, we are faced with the same problem of circularity that complicated the univariate variance weighting of distances.

If Σ is taken as the variance-covariance matrix for the attributes calculated over the whole set of OTUs, this is likely to create more problems than it solves. The eigenvectors of the variance-covariance matrix provide an orthogonal basis for the space spanned by the original set of (correlated) attributes. If these eigenvectors are scaled in proportion to the square roots of the corresponding eigenvalues, as they are in principal component analysis, distances calculated on the new basis will be equal to those calculated from the original set of variables. The generalized distance measure described above, however, implicitly equates the lengths of all of the eigenvectors; that is, in calculating distances, equal weight is assigned to each of the orthogonal components of the original set of attributes. To the extent that attributes are correlated in the entire set of OTUs because they similarly discriminate among (unknown) clusters, their correlation should not be discounted. On the other hand, one may wish to discount correlation within clusters. Calculation of generalized distances based upon an overall covariance matrix does not solve these problems. For critical discussion of generalized distances, see Cronbach and Gleser (1953), Friedman and Rubin (1967), Hartigan (1975a), and Gower (1966).

The angular separation between two OTUs is defined in the following manner:

$$AS(i, j) = \frac{x_i \cdot x_j}{\| x_i \| \quad \| x_j \|}$$

Here, $x_i \cdot x_j$ is the inner product of the vectors of attribute scores for individuals i and j, and $\| x_i \|$ is the length of vector x_i. This coefficient measures the cosine of the angle between the two OTU vectors; Figure 1 shows how AS is related to Euclidean distance:

$$d^2 = \| x_i \|^2 \sin^2\theta + (\| x_j \| - \| x_i \| \cos\theta)^2$$
$$= \| x_i \|^2 + \| x_j \|^2 - 2 \| x_i \| \|x_j \| \cos\theta$$

Clearly, like unweighted Euclidean distance, angular separation is meaningless if the attributes are incommensurable. Even for commensurable attributes, angular separation removes differences in

Figure 1. The Relationship Between Angular Separation and Euclidean Distance

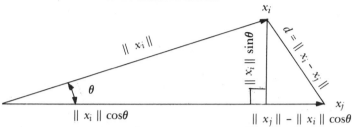

vector length. Converting AS to a distance by the transformation $d^2 = 2(1 - AS)$ is equivalent to projecting the OTU vectors onto the surface of a hypersphere of unit radius prior to measuring the distance between their tips (see Cronbach and Gleser, 1953).

If the OTU vectors are measured as deviations from their means, $\cos\theta$ becomes the Q-mode product-moment correlation coefficient:

$$r(i, j) = \frac{\displaystyle\sum_{k=1}^{p} (x_{ik} - \bar{x}_i)(x_{jk} - \bar{x}_j)}{(\sum (x_{ik} - \bar{x}_i)^2 \ \sum (x_{jk} - \bar{x}_j)^2)^{1/2}}$$

where

$$\bar{x}_i = \sum_{k=1}^{p} x_{ik}/p$$

The mean attribute score for an OTU is not interpretable unless the attributes are commensurable. One undesirable consequence of subtracting OTU means is that the Q-mode correlation is affected by the direction of scaling of individual attributes: In general, if an attribute is reflected, correlations among OTUs will be altered. For commensurable attributes, the correlation eliminates distinctions between OTUs that are attributable to differences in level and dispersion. Therefore, if the attribute scores for one OTU are a linear function of those of another, the two OTUs will be perfectly correlated. In general, this property does not appear to be sensible and disqualifies the Q-mode correlation as a useful measure of similarity for taxonomy, even for homogeneous data.

A critical analysis of Q-mode correlations is provided by Fleiss and Zubin (1969). Cronbach and Gleser (1953) show how distance can be decomposed into components representing differences in "elevation," "scatter," and "shape." Q-mode correlation is an angular version of the shape component (compare Penrose, 1954). Despite the formal difficulties outlined above and developed in greater detail in the references cited, Q-mode correlations have yielded apparently meaningful results in a wide variety of taxonomic studies and, in practice, frequently perform well in comparison with other measures of resemblance (see Rohlf and Sokal, 1965; Mezzich, this volume).

The foregoing analysis of angular coefficients is interesting not only because it casts doubt upon the application of these coefficients in taxonomy but also because it suggests a means of transforming some similarity measures to distances (Gower, 1966). Any positive semidefinite matrix can be interpreted as a matrix of sums of squares and cross-products, that is, of vector inner products; therefore, any similarity measure that yields a positive semidefinite matrix of coefficients can be transformed into a Euclidean distance measure:

$$d^2(i, j) = s(i, i) + s(j, j) - 2s(i, j)$$

If, as is commonly the case, $s(i, i) = 1$ for all OTUs, this formula simplifies to:

$$d^2(i, j) = 2 (1 - s (i, j))$$

Binary Nominal Data. If all attributes have two states, the relationship between a pair of OTUs can be displayed in a four-fold Q-mode contingency table such as the one shown below:

		OTU j		
		1	0	
OTU i	1	a	b	$a + b$
	0	c	d	$c + d$
		$a + c$	$b + d$	$p = a + b + c + d$

Each entry in the table represents the number of attributes for a particular pair of codes; for example, a is the number of attributes for which both OTUs are coded 1. It is somewhat ironic that a simple four-fold table could have given rise to a large number of measures of taxonomic resemblance (see Sokal and Sneath, 1963; Everitt, 1974). If all such similarity measures ranked pairs of individuals in the same order, that is, if these measures were jointly monotonic, the problem of choosing among them would be less acute. It would, in fact, be nonexistent for clustering algorithms that attend only to order. Many of the proposed coefficients, however, are not jointly monotonic, as is simply demonstrated (see Everitt, 1974).

Perhaps the simplest similarity measure that can be constructed for binary attribute data (apart from the number of matches $= a + d$) is the proportion of matches, or the simple matching coefficient:

$$SMC(i, j) = (a + d)/p$$

This coefficient has been widely employed in numerical taxonomy and has a number of attractive features apart from its obvious simplicity. For example, as we shall see in the next section, SMC is simply related to a specialization of the measure developed by Jardine and Sibson (1971) for measuring dissimilarity among aggregates. Further, the complement of SMC is squared Euclidean distance (divided by p) for binary data (Gower, 1969).

The states of binary attributes may be labeled arbitrarily. In certain circumstances, however, all such attributes may code the presence (1) or absence (0) of characteristics of OTUs. Under these circumstances, it is sensible, though not necessary, to exclude negative matches (cell d) from a measure of taxonomic resemblance. The simplest such measure is the coefficient of Jaccard:

$$J(i, j) = a/(a + b + c)$$

Gower (1971) has shown that this coefficient may also be transformed to a dissimilarity measure with Euclidean properties according to the method described above.

Multistate Nominal Data. The methods for binary attributes may be extended to nominal multistate attributes in several straightforward ways. The simple matching coefficient can be calculated for multistate data as the number of matches divided by the number of attributes. Alternatively, each state of a multistate attribute can serve to define a binary attribute of the presence-absence variety. If sets of binary attributes defined in this manner are used with a coefficient such as SMC, however, negative matches will proliferate. These techniques all yield coefficients that can be transformed to Euclidean distances.

A large number of measures of association have been employed in the R-mode analysis of contingency tables (see, for example, Bishop, Fienberg, and Holland, 1975). Measures of association conceivably could be calculated for multistate nominal data where all attributes have the same set of categories. If the categories for different attributes were not identical, the Q-mode contingency table would not be well defined. However, even for homogeneous data, since these coefficients generally measure association rather than agreement, their use in the Q-mode for taxonomic purposes should be discouraged. The difficulties entailed in the use of these measures are similar to those of the Q-mode correlation coefficient discussed earlier.

Ordinal Data. In R-mode analysis, ordinal data often prove embarrassing, since statistical models for these data are relatively underdeveloped. Researchers often treat ordinal variables as nominal (which, of course, discards information) or as interval (adopting an arbitrary metric, which is not strictly justified). Similar problems and similarly unsatisfactory "solutions" arise in the calculation of Q-mode measures of resemblance from ordinal attributes.

One expedient is to treat an ordinal variable as if it were a nominal multistate attribute. Obviously, this strategy penalizes near-matches. Alternatively, mismatches may be weighted by some monotone function of the number of intervening categories. However, such weighting is equivalent to adoption of an interval scale.

Mixed Data. The foregoing discussion of measures of taxonomic resemblance for various types of heterogeneous data reveals the essential arbitrariness of these measures. This arbitrariness is compounded when we examine coefficients suitable for use with mixed data.

It is possible to convert all attributes to binary or multistate nominal form. This process has already been described for ordinal data. If they are relatively few in number, the states of a discrete numerical attribute may serve to define a set of binary attributes (as described above for multistate data) or may directly define the states of a nominal attribute. Similarly, a continuous attribute may be categorized by dissection of its range. Of course, these procedures require one to discard ordinal differences, not to mention differences in magnitude. In addition, when the range of a continuous attribute is dissected into categories, information about within-category differences is lost, although this is a less serious problem when the number of categories retained is relatively large. Of course, as the number of categories is increased, near-matches are increasingly treated as nonmatches.

There are several suggested measures of resemblance for mixed data that do less violence to the measurement scales of the attributes (Cormack, 1971). Gower (1971), for example, has suggested a coefficient that treats binary presence-absence, multistate nominal, and numerical attributes in somewhat different manners. This coefficient is defined by the following formula:

$$G\,(i,\,j) = \frac{\displaystyle\sum_{k=1}^{p} d_{ijk}\,s_{ijk}}{\displaystyle\sum_{k=1}^{p} d_{ijk}}$$

where

(1) for a binary attribute k, $s_{ijk}=1$ for a positive match and 0 otherwise; $d_{ijk} = 0$ for a negative match and 1 otherwise;
(2) for a nominal multistate attribute k (or for a binary attribute for which negative matches are not to be excluded), $s_{ijk} = 1$ for a match and 0 otherwise; $d_{ijk} = 1$;
(3) for a numerical attribute k,

$$s_{ijk} = 1 - \frac{\mid x_{ik} - x_{jk}\mid}{R_k}$$

where R_k is the range of attribute k; $d_{ijk} = 1$.

Gower's coefficient is, therefore, an amalgam of Jaccard's coefficient (for binary data), the simple matching coefficient (for nominal multistate data), and range-standardized absolute distance (for numerical data). Because of its construction, the coefficient can be transformed to a dissimilarity measure with Euclidean properties.

Missing Data and Conditionally Defined Attributes. Conditionally defined attributes, of course, will be undefined for certain individuals. However, undefined attributes may be explicitly excluded from the calculation of measures of resemblance. For measures such as Jaccard's coefficient and the *SMC*, this procedure is straightforward, since undefined attributes can be eliminated from both the numerators and denominators of these coefficients. For measures such as distance, since different distances will be based on different numbers of attribute comparisons, it becomes necessary to correct each coefficient for the number of valid comparisons; for example:

$$\bar{d}' \ (i, j) = (\ \frac{1}{p_{ij}} \ \sum_{k \ = \ 1}^{p} \ w_k \ (x_{ik} - x_{jk})^2 \ )^{1/2}$$

where p_{ij} is the number of attributes simultaneously defined in both OTUs, and $x_{ik} - x_{jk}$ is equal to 0 for undefined comparisons. This measure of average distance is, of course, proportional to weighted distance, as defined earlier, when all attributes are present in all OTUs.

Gower (1971) describes another approach to the treatment of conditionally defined attributes that employs weights. Jardine and Sibson's (1971) technique for treating conditionally defined attributes in measuring dissimilarity among aggregates is described below.

Missing data, though logically distinct from undefined attributes, may be handled in a similar manner (see Sneath and Sokal, 1973). It should also be mentioned that some of the same difficulties associated with the use of pairwise present correlations or covariances in *R*-mode analysis are likely to arise when *Q*-mode measures of resemblance are calculated over different subsets of attributes for different pairs of OTUs. For example, a distance measure may lose its Euclidean properties, and a measure of similarity that ordinarily yields a positive-definite matrix of coefficients may no longer do so (Gower, 1971).

Measuring Resemblance Among Aggregates

Coefficients of resemblance to be used for classifying aggregates are of three general sorts: (1) measures of resemblance for individuals, which are applied to aggregates; (2) measures of the extent to which aggregates can be distinguished on the basis of their character state distributions; and (3) measures of the extent to which distinguishing between a pair of aggregates conveys information about their character state distributions. Jardine and Sibson (1971) term these types of measures *A-similarity*, *I-distinguishability*, and *D-dissimilarity*, respectively. These authors argue convincingly that measures of *D*-dissimilarity are most suitable for taxonomic purposes and proceed to develop an information-theoretical model of *D*-dissimilarity which they call *K*-dissimilarity. In the following pages I shall endeavor to clarify the distinctions among the different sorts of measures of resemblance for aggregates and shall explain, in a simplified manner, the construction of *K*-dissimilarity.

Measures of Resemblance for Individuals Applied to Aggregates. All of the measures of resemblance discussed earlier can be applied to aggregates of individuals. If attributes are invariant within aggregates, that is, if all character state distributions concentrate their probability in single-attribute states, the distinctions between individuals and aggregates and between attributes and character distribution sets become unimportant. Under these circumstances, applying measures of resemblance for individuals to aggregates is straightforward.

On the other hand, at least some attributes are likely to vary among the members of aggregates. In this event, a "typical" attribute state may be taken to be representative of the character state distribution of the aggregate. This is the procedure advocated by Sneath and Sokal (1973). For a nominal attribute, the modal category might be chosen; for a numerical attribute, the mean attribute score could be employed. This approach, in effect, summarizes a distribution by a single parameter and discards information about variation within aggregates. Clearly, it would be desirable to consider within-aggregate variation when one assesses resemblance.

Distinguishability Measures. Unlike the measures of resemblance discussed above, measures of distinguishability take within-aggregate variation into account. These measures indicate the degree to which members of one population can be separated from members of another on the basis of their joint character state distributions. Suppose that an individual is chosen from one of two aggregates:

Given the character state distributions of the two aggregates and the attribute states of the individual, we may assess the probability of correctly reassigning the individual to the aggregate of which he or she is a member. Distinguishability between aggregates increases with the probability of making a correct assignment.

At first blush, distinguishability appears to be an ideal measure for assessing the resemblance of aggregates. It has the following disturbing property, however: Two aggregates may be perfectly distinguished if any one, or any combination, of their character state distributions is nonoverlapping. For instance, two aggregates identical in all but one completely disjoint character distribution set are just as distinguishable as two aggregates that are disjoint in all of their character distribution sets.

The most common measure of distinguishability is the Mahalanobis generalized distance:

$$D^2(i, j) = (\beta_i - \beta_j)' \Sigma^{-1} (\beta_i - \beta_j)$$

where β_i is the population mean vector for aggregate i and Σ is the within-aggregate population variance-covariance matrix, common to the two aggregates. In practice, β_i, β_j, and Σ would be estimated from sample data, the estimate of Σ pooling information from the two samples (or many samples if generalized distances were calculated for many aggregates). D^2 assumes multivariate normal populations with a common covariance matrix. Jardine and Sibson (1971) discuss a related, information-theoretic measure of distinguishability called normal information radius, which is applicable to multivariate normal populations with different covariance matrices:

$$N(i, j) = 1/2 \log_2 \frac{\left| 1/2 (\Sigma_i + \Sigma_j) + 1/4 (\beta_i - \beta_j)(\beta_i - \beta_j)' \right|}{|\Sigma_i|^{1/2} |\Sigma_j|^{1/2}}$$

Here, β_i and β_j are mean vectors, as before, and Σ_i and Σ_j are the covariance matrices for aggregates i and j, respectively. In the case $\Sigma_i = \Sigma_j = \Sigma$, this formula reduces to a simple function of D^2:

$$N(i, j) = 1/2 \log_2 (1 + 1/4 D^2)$$

K-Dissimilarity. The difference between *I*-distinguishability and *D*-dissimilarity (for which *K*-dissimilarity is a model) is, as Jardine and Sibson (1971) have put it, "subtle." As we have seen, the concept of distinguishability involves the probability of correctly classifying an individual into one of two aggregates. In contrast, dissimilarity involves the expected information gain in such an assignment. If I learn that an individual belongs to one or the other of two aggregates, I gain information about that individual's attributes. I shall always expect to gain information unless the aggregates are identical in all of their character state distributions. Further, I can acquire differing amounts of information for pairs of aggregates that are perfectly distinguishable.

K-dissimilarity assesses expected information gain separately for each character distribution set and then combines these separate terms to arrive at an overall measure of dissimilarity between two aggregates. For a particular discrete attribute, the expected information gain, or *information radius*, measures the overlap of the character state distributions for two aggregates:

$$K \begin{bmatrix} \mu_1 & \mu_2 \\ w_1 & w_2 \end{bmatrix}$$

$$= \sum_{k=1}^{m} \sum_{i=1}^{2} \left[\frac{w_i p_i (x_k)}{\sum\limits_{j=1}^{2} w_j} \log_2 \frac{p_i (x_k) \sum\limits_{j=1}^{2} w_j}{\sum\limits_{j=1}^{2} w_j p_j (x_k)} \right]$$

This formidable expression requires some explanation. First, for simplicity, we have labeled the two aggregates 1 and 2. The attribute under consideration has m states: $x_1, x_2, \ldots, x_m$. μ_i represents the probability distribution for aggregate i (1 or 2) over the states of the attribute: $p_i (x_1)$, $p_i (x_2)$, $\ldots$, $p_i (x_m)$. w_1 and w_2 are weights that are proportional to the prior probabilities of assignment to aggregates 1 and 2, respectively. These weights are generally considered to be equal except in the case of conditionally defined attributes. For equal weights, information radius simplifies to:

$$K (\mu_1, \mu_2) = \frac{1}{2} \sum_{k=1}^{m} \sum_{i=1}^{2} \left[p_i (x_k) \log_2 \frac{2 \, p_i (x_k)}{\sum\limits_{j=1}^{2} p_j (x_k)} \right]$$

We can see that when $\mu_1 = \mu_2$ (that is, when $p_1(x_k) = p_2(x_k)$ for all k), $2 p_i(x_k) = \sum_{i=1}^{2} p_i(x_k)$. The ratio of these quantities is 1, the log of which is 0, and $K^j(\mu_1, \mu_2) = 0$. When the distributions μ_1 and μ_2 are dissimilar, $K(\mu_1, \mu_2)$ is large.

If we specialize $m = 2$ (a binary attribute), then

$$K(\mu_1, \mu_2) = 1/2(p_{11}\log_2(2p_{11}/p_{11} + p_{21})$$
$$+ p_{21}\log_2(2p_{21}/p_{11} + p_{21}) + p_{12}\log_2(2p_{12}/p_{12} + p_{22})$$
$$+ p_{22}\log_2(2p_{22}/p_{12} + p_{22}))$$

where $p_{ik} = p_i(x_k)$. Now, suppose that each character state distribution concentrates all of its probability in a single attribute state: If these attribute states are the same (if there is a match) then, for example, for $p_{11} = p_{21} = 1$, $p_{12} = p_{22} = 0$: $K(\mu_1, \mu_2) = 0$. If these attribute states are different (do not match), then, for example, for $p_{11} = p_{22} = 1$, $p_{12} = p_{21} = 0$: $K(\mu_1, \mu_2) = (1/2)(1 + 0 + 0 + 1) = 1$.

The K-terms for different character distribution sets are measured in a common unit, bits of information. Therefore, an overall measure of dissimilarity can be constructed by summing information radius over all p character distribution sets:

$$KD(i, j) = \sum_{k=1}^{p} K(\mu_{ik}, \mu_{jk})$$

where μ_{ik} is the probability distribution for aggregate i over the states of attribute k. For example, if all attributes are binary and invariant within aggregates, KD simply counts the number of mismatches between the aggregates for, as we noted above, each mismatch contributes a K of 1 and each match, 0. Hence, in this case

$$KD(i, j) = p(1 - SMC(i, j))$$

By dealing with character distribution sets singly, that is, by examining marginal distributions (character state distributions) rather than joint distributions, K-dissimilarity avoids the problems associated with measures of distinguishability.

K-dissimilarity can be extended to handle conditionally defined attributes. Suppose that attribute 2 is conditional upon attribute 1 and that, as before, we consider aggregates 1 and 2. For certain states of attribute 1, attribute 2 will be defined; let this set of states be designated S. For states of attribute 1 not in S, therefore, attribute 2 is undefined. The probability distribution over states of attribute 1 is μ_{11}, μ_{21} for aggregates 1 and 2, respectively. μ_{12} and μ_{22} are the conditional probability distributions over the states of attribute 2, given that attribute 2 is defined (that is, given that attribute 1 is in S). Jardine and Sibson show that the K-term (component of K-dissimilarity) for the conditionally defined attribute is:

$$\frac{1}{2}(\mu_{11}\ (S) + \mu_{21}\ (S)\ )\ K\left[\frac{\mu_{12}}{\mu_{11}\ (S)}, \frac{\mu_{22}}{\mu_{21}(S)}\right]$$

In this formula, $\mu_{i1}(S)$ is the probability that attribute 2 is defined in aggregate i or, equivalently, that attribute 1 is in S in aggregate i. The K-term for a conditionally defined attribute, therefore, consists of two factors: the average probability of occurrence of attribute 2 in the two aggregates (called the *occurrence factor* by Jardine and Sibson) and an *information factor*, in which the probabilities of occurrence in the two populations function as weights. If one of $\mu_{11}(S)$ and $\mu_{21}(S)$ is zero, that is, if the conditionally defined attribute never occurs in one of the aggregates, then the information factor and the whole K-term become 0; absent conditionally defined attributes do not contribute to K-dissimilarity, as is sensible. If, for a pair of aggregates, $\mu_{11}(S)$ and $\mu_{21}(S)$ are both 1, the weights in the information factor are 1, the occurrence factor is 1 and, for this pair of aggregates, the second attribute loses its conditional status. Finally, Jardine and Sibson show how the occurrence factor and information factor can be defined for more complicated sorts of conditional definition, where an attribute is jointly conditional on the states of several other attributes.

Thus far, we have considered discrete character state distributions, or probability distributions over the states of discrete attributes. Continuous attributes can be accommodated by replacing the sum over the attribute states in the formula for information radius with an integral. The evaluation of this integral, of course, depends upon the density functions μ_1 and μ_2. Tables of values of K for normally distributed attributes can be found in Jardine and Sibson (1971, Appendix 2). If distributional assumptions are not warranted, the range of a continuous attribute can be dissected into class intervals. Since information radius compares probability distributions (character state distributions) and not attribute values (attribute states), dissection of the range does not treat a quantitative attribute as qualitative but treats a continuous attribute as discrete. Jardine and Sibson note that information radius for the categorized distributions will be no greater than that for the original continuous distributions. The former will approach the latter as the number of categories grows larger.

Information radius is defined in terms of character state distributions, or population distributions of attributes. Since these distributions are generally unavailable, they or their parameters must be estimated from sample data. In the case of discrete distributions, for example, it is natural to estimate attribute state probabilities from corresponding observed proportions. Jardine and Sibson report a numerical investigation of an estimator of K for binary attributes that employs sample proportions. Their experiment reveals that: (1) The estimator is positively biased; (2) the bias is small relative to sampling error and hence contributes only a minor amount to mean square error; (3) the estimator appears to be consistent; and (4) mean square error is quite small, even for relatively small samples.

Conclusion

In this chapter I have examined measures of taxonomic resemblance for various sorts of data and have found that a truly satisfactory measure, K-dissimilarity, can be defined to assess resemblance among aggregates. This coefficient deals with mixed data in a nonarbitrary fashion, takes into account variation within aggregates, and handles conditionally defined attributes in an intuitively meaningful manner.

For measuring resemblance among individuals, the alternatives are somewhat less satisfactory. There are a large number of measures (most not discussed in the present chapter) for various sorts of data; all of these measures have deficiencies, some more serious than others. This is not to say that measures of resemblance among individuals should not be employed for taxonomic purposes. Rather, when these coefficients are used, their deficiencies should be kept in mind. In many cases, it may prove worthwhile to compare results obtained with different coefficients. Improved means for measuring similarity among individuals may be developed in the future. Certain problems, however, like that of commensurability of attributes, may not be solvable in a nonarbitrary way. More satisfactory solutions may well lie in algorithms that do not employ measures of resemblance but instead act directly upon the data matrix (see Hartigan, 1975a; Cormack, 1971; Friedman and Rubin, 1967).

Whether the OTUs are individuals or aggregates, my supposition throughout has been that once resemblances have been calculated, they will be input to a clustering algorithm. In fact, I should note that there are other techniques for the analysis of resemblance data which can replace or supplement cluster analysis (see Cormack, 1971; Sneath and Sokal, 1973).

If a measure of resemblance is Euclidean (or if it is transformable into a Euclidean coefficient), OTUs can be represented as points in Euclidean space. Jardine and Sibson (1971) point out that the ability to represent a measure of resemblance geometrically provides just that: a representation or interpretation of the measure and not a full justification of its use. For instance, Q-mode correlation has Euclidean properties, but its use is questionable.

As Gower (1966) has shown, principal component analysis of a Euclidean dissimilarity measure provides a set of coordinates for the OTUs. If the first few eigenvalues are large relative to the remaining ones, the first few principal components provide a lower-dimensional configuration that accurately (but imperfectly) reproduces the distances among OTUs. Even when the matrix of coefficients is not positive-semidefinite and, hence, has no exact Euclidean representation, if the negative eigenvalues are small in magnitude, an approximate configuration can be obtained. More generally, resemblance matrices may be analyzed by nonmetric multidimensional scaling (see Kruskal, 1964b), which attends only to the order of the input coefficients in constructing a configuration in Euclidean space. Interpretation of OTUs as points in space and division of OTUs into clusters provide a convenient representation of Q-mode relationships, especially if the number of dimensions required is small. If the OTUs do not divide into relatively disjoint clusters, the geometric point representation may still convey important information, while a cluster analysis could prove misleading.

Comparing Cluster
Analytic Methods

■■■■■■■■■■■■■■■■■■■■■■■

Juan E. Mezzich

During the past several years, in line with increasing interest in quantitative classification among scientists in many fields, there has been a great proliferation of methods designed to group sets of entities into clusters. Typically, these methods were developed for taxonomic work. Some of them were not originally constructed for clustering, but were merely adopted for this use. Relatively little effort has been made to evaluate them in a systematic and comprehensive way. Under these circumstances, the use of quantitative taxonomic methods has

Note: H. Solomon was a major collaborator in this study. J. Erickson, P. Damarin, P. Isaac, H. Kraemer, H. Chernoff, and P. Switzer provided advice on various statistical issues. R. Moos kindly provided the treatment environments data base, and L. Cavalli-Sforza, the ethnic populations data base. S. Agras, P. Berger, F. Estess, A. Freeman, T. Gonda, G. Gulevich, J. Kaplan, B. Kopell, G. Krieger, J. Kuldau, F. Melges, A. Pfefferbaum, S. Price, N. Rogers, P. Rosenbaum, T. Roth, R. Sack, E. Solomon, A. Stunkard, W. Wittner, K. Woodrow, and R. Worthington participated in the development of archetypal psychiatric patients. Dwayne Ball provided inestimable assistance in data processing.
   This research was supported in part by Grant MCCPC 1-HVA-051 from the Stanford University School of Medicine, and by National VA Grant MRIS-5692.

been governed much more by what is available at the nearest computer center than by the validity, reliability, and appropriateness of specific methods.

Few empirical assessments of various cluster methods have been reported in the literature. The first study, quite typical in many respects, was carried out by Sneath (1966), who evaluated single-linkage, complete-linkage, and average-linkage hierarchical methods by applying them to a group of randomly spaced points. He used the appropriateness of clustering output to the structure of the input data as his evaluative criterion and measured it with the cophenetic correlation coefficient (Sokal and Rohlf, 1962). Most other studies reported in the literature also evaluated one or more agglomerative hierarchical methods. Half of them evaluated one or two other clustering approaches as well.

The evaluative criterion used by Sneath (appropriateness of clustering output to the structure of the input data) has also been used by Boyce (1969), Cunningham and Ogilvie (1972), Hubert (1974), and Baker (1974). Four of these five studies used taxonomic methods on artificial data sets; Boyce used them on skull measurements for a group of hominoids. A less frequently used evaluative criterion is the ability to recover artificially created data structures (Blashfield, 1976; Everitt, 1974). Another criterion (concordance between clustering output and a classification established by experts in the field) was used by Bartko, Strauss, and Carpenter (1971) in their study of the psychopathological variables of archetypal psychiatric patients. Rogers and Linden (1973) evaluated taxonomic methods by measuring college students on dimensions of self-concept, using replicability of clustering output as the criterion. Finally, Delabre, Bianchi, and Veron (1973) used an index of intercluster to intracluster heterogeneity as the evaluative criterion when they measured the phenotypic characters of a set of bacteria.

As can be noted, each of these pioneering studies evaluated only a few clustering approaches, usually applied them to only one type of data, and employed only one evaluative criterion. This chapter presents an empirical comparison, according to several evaluative criteria, of several major quantitative taxonomic approaches applied to data sets from various fields or disciplines.

Method

Cluster Analytic Methods. As a starting framework for evaluating the great variety of cluster analytic methods developed to date, I classify them by organizing concepts and schemes reported in the literature. All quantitative taxonomic methods are divided into two major groups: (a) representation of multivariate data units (this can be called *unfinished clustering* because it requires additional work, usually from a human being, in order to obtain a finished set of clusters with specified membership) and (b) *finished cluster analysis*.

To represent multivariate data units, some methods, like Q-factor analysis (Harman, 1967), ordinal multidimensional scaling (Kruskal, 1964a, 1964b), and seriation (Guttman, 1966), use a relationship matrix. Others require subjective clustering directly from a graphical representation of multidimensional data, like Chernoff's (1973) faces.

Finished cluster analysis can be either hierarchical or nonhierarchical. Hierarchical procedures include agglomerative methods, which construct a tree from branches to a single trunk, and divisive methods, which begin at the trunk and work toward the branches. Agglomerative approaches are among the most frequently used, and primarily include single-linkage, complete-linkage, and average-linkage methods (Johnson, 1967; King, 1967). The rarely used divisive approach includes monothetic and polythetic methods according to the number of variables used for each splitting of the data set. The nonhierarchical group includes: (1) total enumeration of partitions, and related methods (Solomon, 1970) that are now of only historical interest; (2) the nearest centroid sorting methods, which may involve a fixed number of clusters (as in MacQueen's k-means method, 1967) or a variable number of clusters (as in the sophisticated ISODATA method of Ball and Hall, 1965, 1967); (3) reallocation methods using variance-covariance criteria (as in Rubin and Friedman's optimization technique, 1967); and (4) density search methods (like the elegant and distribution-based NORMAP/NORMIX method, which performs pattern clustering by multivariate normal mixture analysis; see Wolfe, 1971b).

Three measures of relationship between patients, computed across variables, have been used whenever possible with the representative cluster analytic approaches. They are: (a) the Pearson product-moment correlation coefficient, (b) Euclidean distance (where the distance from one point to another is the square root of the sum of their square differences on each variable), and (c) city-block distance (where the distance between points is the sum of their absolute differences on each variable).

Eighteen quantitative taxonomic methods have been assembled and evaluated in the present study (Table 1). Each consists of one of 10 clustering algorithms representing major taxonomic approaches, and one (if any) of the relationship measures mentioned above.

Data Bases. Data bases were obtained from four fields: psychosocial, psychopathological, botanical, and genetic. Each data base has been randomly halved in order to produce two equivalent data sets for studying the replicability and stability of clustering outputs.

The first data base, the psychosocial one, comprises 72 psychiatric treatment environments, each measured on 10 social climate scales and grouped by Professor Rudolf Moos of the Stanford University Social Ecology Laboratory into four clusters: therapeutic, relationship-oriented, insight-oriented, and control-oriented.

The psychopathological data base is composed of 88 archetypal psychiatric patients fabricated by 22 psychiatrists to represent four diagnostic categories (manic-depressive depressed, manic-depressive manic, simple schizophrenic, and paranoid schizophrenic) and scored on 17 psychopathological symptoms and signs.

The botanical data base, published by R. A. Fisher in 1936, is composed of 150 iris specimens belonging to three species (*setosa*, *versicolor*, and *virginica*) and measured on sepal length and width and petal length and width.

The genetic data base is composed of 10 ethnic populations measured on 58 biochemical-genetic variables and grouped by Professor Luigi Cavalli-Sforza from the Stanford University Department of Genetics into five pairs: American, European, African, Oriental, and Oceanic. In this data base, the 58 variables rather than the 10 entities have been randomly halved to produce two data sets for stability studies.

Evaluative Criteria. The performance of the quantitative taxonomic methods has been evaluated according to the following criteria:

Table 1. Quantitative Taxonomic Methods Evaluated in the Present Study

Symbol	Relationship Measure	Clustering Algorithm	Taxonomic Approach	Reference
1A.	Correlation Coefficient	WH-WH Factor Analysis	Q-Factor Analysis	Wherry and Wherry (1971)
2A.	Correlation Coefficient	MDSCAL-5M	Ordinal Multidimensional Scaling	Kruskal (1964a, 1964b)
2B.	Euclidean Distance	MDSCAL-5M	Ordinal Multidimensional Scaling	Kruskal (1964a, 1964b)
2C.	City-Block Distance	MDSCAL-5M	Ordinal Multidimensional Scaling	Kruskal (1964a, 1964b)
3X.		Chernoff's Faces	Data Representation Without Relationship Matrix	Chernoff (1973)
4A.	Correlation Coefficient	Single-Linkage HICLUS	Hierarchical Agglomerative Single-Linkage	Johnson (1967)
4B.	Euclidean Distance	Single-Linkage HICLUS	Hierarchical Agglomerative Single-Linkage	Johnson (1967)
4C.	City-Block Distance	Single-Linkage HICLUS	Hierarchical Agglomerative Single-Linkage	Johnson (1967)
5A.	Correlation Coefficient	Complete-Linkage HICLUS	Hierarchical Agglomerative Complete-Linkage	Johnson (1967)
5B.	Euclidean Distance	Complete-Linkage HICLUS	Hierarchical Agglomerative Complete-Linkage	Johnson (1967)
5C.	City-Block Distance	Complete-Linkage HICLUS	Hierarchical Agglomerative Complete-Linkage	Johnson (1967)
6A.	Correlation Coefficient	King's Centroid Average-Linkage	Hierarchical Agglomerative Average (Centroid) Linkage	King (1967)
7A.	Correlation Coefficient	k-means	Nearest Centroid Sorting with Fixed Number of Clusters	MacQueen (1967)
7B.	Euclidean Distance	k-means	Nearest Centroid Sorting with Fixed Number of Clusters	MacQueen (1967)
7C.	City-Block Distance	k-means	Nearest Centroid Sorting with Fixed Number of Clusters	MacQueen (1967)
8X.	Several	ISODATA	Nearest Centroid Sorting with Variable Number of Clusters	Ball and Hall (1965, 1967)
9X.		Rubin-Friedman Covariance Criterion Optimization	Reallocation Using Variance-Covariance Criteria	Rubin and Friedman (1967)

1. External criterion validity. This was determined by assessing the degree of similarity between the cluster configuration produced by a given quantitative taxonomic method and the cluster configuration previously established by the field expert on the same data set. A contingency table depicts the cross-classification of entities between these two cluster configurations: Concordance between the quantitative taxonomic method and the expert evaluation was based on the ratio of the number of entities on which there is agreement to the total number of entities; values of the derived Cramer's (1946) statistic range from 0 for no association to 1 for maximum association. A correlation coefficient was computed between corresponding entries of two similarity matrices, one derived from the clustering output and the other from the clustering previously established by the expert. The entries of each similarity matrix are equal to 1 if the corresponding entities are in the same cluster, and 0 otherwise.

2. Internal criterion validity. This corresponds to the appropriateness of the cluster configuration to the original structure of the data. It was estimated by computing the so-called cophenetic correlation coefficient (Sokal and Rohlf, 1962) between corresponding entries of a similarity matrix derived from the cluster configuration, and the initial similarity matrix. The entries of the derived similarity matrix are determined to be 1 if the entities involved were in the same cluster, and 0 otherwise.

3. Replicability and stability. This corresponds to the degree of similarity between the two cluster configurations that result when a given quantitative taxonomic method is applied to the two "equivalent" data sets produced by randomly halving the original data base. For each of the first three data bases, the two half data sets include different sets of entities, and the only labeling that is valid across half data sets was determined by the group to which an entity was assigned by the expert. So for all four data bases, similarity between the two resulting cluster configurations was assessed by correlating corresponding entries on the two half data sets.

4. Inter-rater reliability. This was assessed for the three ordinal multidimensional scaling methods and for Chernoff's faces method, by comparing the corresponding configurations produced by two judges who visually inspected the graphical representation of

the same data set. The statistics used here are similar to those used for the assessment of external criterion validity.

Results

First, I have analyzed the performance of the quantitative taxonomic methods according to each of the three major evaluative criteria. In Table 2, the quantitative taxonomic methods are ranked according to external criterion validity values on each of the four data bases and across them. For each data base, the percentages of the concordance with the field expert, the Cramer's statistic values, and the correlation coefficients between derived similarity matrices were averaged between the half data sets, and a ranking of the quantitative taxonomic methods was obtained according to each of these three measures of external criterion validity. Average ranks and overall ranks were then computed for each data base and are shown in Table 2. This table also shows the ranks computed by averaging data base average ranks and overall ranks. There is some variability in rankings across data bases, but there are also some clear patterns. 5A, 5C, and 5B (complete-linkage methods) appear to perform best. Methods 9X (Rubin-Friedman optimization technique) and 6A (centroid-linkage) also perform well. Making the poorest showing are 4A, 4C, and 4B (single-linkage methods). Other low-ranking methods are 10X (NORMAP/NORMIX) and 3X (Chernoff's faces).

Table 3 exhibits the internal criterion validity values (cophenetic correlation coefficients) and rankings of the quantitative taxonomic methods on each of the four data bases and across them. The various data bases show considerable variability but, on the average, 6A (centroid-linkage) performs best, followed by 2A and 2B (ordinal multidimensional scaling methods using correlation coefficients and Euclidean distances), 5B and 5C (complete-linkage methods using Euclidean and city-block distances), and 4A, 4B, and 4C (single-linkage methods). Ranking lowest are 10X (NORMAP/NORMIX), 1A (Q-factor analysis), and 3X (Chernoff's faces).

Table 4 presents the replicability correlation coefficients and rankings of the quantitative taxonomic methods on each of the four data bases and across them. There is noticeable variability across data bases but, overall, 5A and 5C (complete-linkage methods using corre-

… Derived Similarity Matrices) on Each of Four Data Bases
(Treatment Environments, Archetypal Psychiatric Patients, Iris, Ethnic Populations) and Across Them

Quantitative Taxonomic Methods	*Treatment Environments*		*Archetypal Psychiatric Patients*		*Iris*		*Ethnic Populations*		*Across Fields*	
	Overall Rank	*Average Rank*	*Average Rank*	*Overall Rank*	*Average Rank*	*Overall Rank*	*Average Rank*	*Overall Rank*	*Average Rank*	*Overall Rank*
1A. *Q*-Factor Analysis, Correlation Coefficient	8.8	9	10.7	10.5	14	14	10.2	9	10.91	13
2A. Multidimensional Scaling, Correlation Coefficient	10	10	10.7	10.5	10.7	10	11.2	12	10.63	12
2B. Multidimensional Scaling, Euclidean Distance	12.7	13	11.7	12	8	8	5.2	5	9.47	10
2C. Multidimensional Scaling, City-Block Distance	14	14	13	13	9	9	3	4	9.75	11
3X. Chernoff's Faces	12	12	17	17	6.7	7	12.7	13	12.08	14
4A. Single-Linkage, Correlation Coefficient	16	16	15	15	15.8	16.5	10.5	10.5	14.33	18
4B. Single-Linkage, Euclidean Distance	17.5	17.5	14.3	14	15.8	16.5	6.8	6.5	13.62	16
4C. Single-Linkage, City-Block Distance	17.5	17.5	15.7	16	15	15	6.8	6.8	13.75	17
5A. Complete-Linkage, Correlation Coefficient	1	1	5	5	2	2	2.3	2	2.58	1
5B. Complete-Linkage, Euclidean Distance	6.8	7	9	9	3	3	2.3	2	5.28	3
5C. Complete-Linkage, City-Block Distance	6.7	6	5	5	4.2	4	2.3	2	4.55	2
6A. Centroid-Linkage, Correlation Coefficient	4.7	5	2	2	13.5	13	10.5	10.5	7.68	5
7A. *k*-means, Correlation Coefficient	2	2	8	8	18	18	7.8	8	8.96	9
7B. *k*-means, Euclidean Distance	4	4	2	2	11	11	15	15	8.00	7
7C. *k*-means, City-Block Distance	3.3	3	2	2	12.2	12	13.3	14	7.70	6
8X. ISODATA	7.7	8	5	5	4.8	5	16	16	8.38	8
9X. Rubin-Friedman	11.3	11	7	7	1	1			6.43	4
10X. NORMAP/NORMIX	15	15	18	18	6.3	6			13.11	15

Table 3. Internal Criterion Validity Values (Cophenetic Correlation Coefficients) and Rankings for the Quantitative Taxonomic Methods on Each of Four Data Bases (Treatment Environments, Archetypal Psychiatric Patients, Iris, Ethnic Populations) and Across Them

Quantitative Taxonomic Methods	Treatment Environment		Archetypal Psychiatric Patients		Iris		Ethnic Populations		Across Fields	
	Cophenetic Correlation Coefficient	Rank	Cophenetic Correlation Coefficient	Rank	Cophenetic Correlation Coefficient	Rank	Cophenetic Correlation Coefficient	Rank	Cophenetic Correlation Coefficient	Rank
1A. Q-Factor Analysis, Correlation Coefficient	.3730	16	.6230	16	.7750	7	-.1230	16	.4120	17
2A. Multidimensional Scaling, Correlation Coefficient	.5555	6	.7405	3	.8265	4	.6530	9	.6939	2
2B. Multidimensional Scaling, Euclidean Distance	.5678	4	.7025	13	.7655	9	.6822	5	.6795	3
2C. Multidimensional Scaling, City-Block Distance	.4738	11	.6920	14	.7705	8	.6825	3.5	.6547	9
3X. Chernoff's Faces	.3795	14	.6112	17	.5160	18	.2620	14	.4422	16
4A. Single-Linkage, Correlation Coefficient	.2395	18	.8340	1	.8945	1	.6805	6.5	.6621	6
4B. Single-Linkage, Euclidean Distance	.3845	13	.7445	2	.8255	5	.6925	1	.6618	7
4C. Single-Linkage, City-Block Distance	.4170	12	.7285	4	.8150	6	.6860	2	.6616	8
5A. Complete-Linkage, Correlation Coefficient	.6115	2	.7140	8.5	.6185	14	.6345	10	.6446	10
5B. Complete-Linkage, Euclidean Distance	.5490	7	.7155	6.5	.7320	12	.6720	8	.6671	4
5C. Complete-Linkage, City-Block Distance	.5350	8	.7040	12	.7290	13	.6825	3.5	.6626	5
6A. Centroid-Linkage, Correlation Coefficient	.6720	1	.6850	15	.8895	2	.6805	6.5	.7318	1
7A. k-means, Correlation Coefficient	.5845	3	.7155	6.5	.8155	3	.4370	13	.6381	11
7B. k-means, Euclidean Distance	.5050	9	.7270	5	.7420	10	.5710	12	.6392	12
7C. k-means, City-Block Distance	.4990	10	.7055	11	.7360	11	.5880	11	.6321	13
8X. ISODATA	.5565	5	.7140	8.5	.6095	17	.0875	15	.4919	15
9X. Rubin-Friedman	.2900	17	.7115	10	.6110	16			.5375	14

lation coefficients and city-block distances), 8X (ISODATA), and 9X (Rubin-Friedman optimization technique) perform best. The poorest overall ranks were obtained for 4B (single-linkage method using Euclidean distances), although this method ranked first in the Treatment Environments data base, for 10X (NORMAP/ NORMIX), for 2C and 2B (ordinal multidimensional scaling using city-block and Euclidean distances), and for 3X (Chernoff's faces).

Table 5 shows rankings of quantitative taxonomic methods computed by averaging ranks across the three major evaluative criteria (external criterion validity, internal criterion validity, and replicability) on each of the four data bases (Treatment Environments, Archetypal Psychiatric Patients, Iris Specimens, and Ethnic Populations), and an overall ranking computed by averaging ranks across data bases. Again, some ranking variability is noted, but quite consistently the overall best-ranked clustering approaches were complete-linkage (5A, 5C, and 5B) and centroid-linkage (6A); the lowest-ranked were NORMAP/NORMIX (10X) and Chernoff's faces (3X).

Table 6 shows rankings of the ordinal multidimensional scaling and Chernoff's faces methods according to inter-rater reliability within and across data bases. Ordinal multidimensional scaling using correlation coefficients and city-block and Euclidean distances rank higher than the Chernoff's faces method.

A ranking of the relationship measures (correlation coefficient, Euclidean distance, and city-block distance) was computed by averaging ranks across all three general evaluative criteria on each of the four data bases and across them. Each evaluative criterion value was computed by averaging corresponding values of the quantitative taxonomic methods (2, 4, 5, and 7) using all three relationship measures. The overall ranking is not conclusive since, on the various evaluative criteria and data bases, the absolute values for the relationship measures are quite similar to each other and their ranking is variable.

Discussion

Previous evaluative studies reported in the literature overlap in design with some aspects of this study and generally agree with its

Table 4. Replicability Correlation Coefficients and Rankings for the Quantitative Taxonomic Methods on Each of Four Data Bases (Treatment Environments, Archetypal Psychiatric Patients, Iris, Ethnic Populations) and Across Them

Quantitative Taxonomic Methods	Treatment Environment		Archetypal Psychiatric Patients		Iris		Ethnic Population		Across Fields	
	Correlation Coefficient	Rank	Correlation Coefficient	Rank	Correlation Coefficient	Rank	Correlation Coefficient	Rank	Correlation Coefficient	Rank
1A. Q-Factor Analysis, Correlation Coefficient	.908	5	.971	10	.992	5	.423	16	.824	5
2A. Multidimensional Scaling, Correlation Coefficient	.288	16	.782	13	.852	8	.750	8	.668	8
2B. Multidimensional Scaling, Euclidean Distance	.274	17	.891	11	.511	10	.656	10	.583	14
2C. Multidimensional Scaling, City-Block Distance	.155	18	.780	14	.503	11	.772	5.5	.553	16
3X. Chernoff's Faces	.358	15	.438	17	.973	7	.528	13	.574	15
4A. Single-Linkage, Correlation Coefficient	.871	8	.758	15	.000	16.5	.926	2.5	.639	9
4B. Single-Linkage, Euclidean Distance	1.000	1	.068	18	.000	16.5	.540	11.5	.402	18
4C. Single-Linkage, City-Block Distance	.999	2	.786	12	.021	15	.540	11.5	.586	13
5A. Complete-Linkage, Correlation Coefficient	.941	4	1.000	2	.976	6	.772	5.5	.922	1
5B. Complete-Linkage, Euclidean Distance	.540	12	.974	9	.999	2.5	.772	5.5	.821	6
5C. Complete-Linkage, City-Block Distance	.650	11	1.000	2	.999	2.5	.772	5.5	.855	3
6A. Centroid-Linkage, Correlation Coefficient	.968	3	.998	5	.042	14	.926	2.5	.734	7
7A. k-means, Correlation Coefficient	.889	7	.995	8	-.421	18	1.000	1	.616	11
7B. k-means, Euclidean Distance	.818	9	.998	5	.205	12	.500	14	.630	10
7C. k-means, City-Block Distance	.796	10	.998	5	.155	13	.456	15	.601	12
8X. ISODATA	.907	6	1.000	2	.993	4	.730	9	.908	2
9X. R-bis Friedman	.405	13	.997	7	1.000	1			.831	4

(Treatment Environments, Archetypal Psychiatric Patients, Iris, Ethnic Populations) and Across Them)

Quantitative Taxonomic Methods	Treatment Environments		Archetypal Psychiatric Patients		Iris		Ethnic Populations		Across Fields	
	Average Rank	Overall Rank	Average Rank	Overall Rank	Average Rank	Overall Rank	Average Rank	Overall Rank	Average Rank	Overall Rank
1A. Q-Factor Analysis, Correlation Coefficient	10.00	9	12.17	15	8.67	6.5	13.67	15.5	11.13	16
2A. Multidimensional Scaling, Correlation Coefficient	10.67	12	8.83	10	7.00	4	9.67	11	9.04	8
2B. Multidimensional Scaling, Euclidean Distance	11.33	13	12.00	14	9.00	8	6.67	8.5	9.75	10.5
2C. Multidimensional Scaling, City-Block Distance	14.33	17	13.67	16	9.33	9	4.33	2	10.42	14
3X. Chernoff's Faces	13.67	14.5	17.00	17	10.67	13	13.33	13	13.67	17
4A. Single-Linkage, Correlation Coefficient	14.00	16	10.33	11	11.33	14	6.50	6.5	10.54	15
4B. Single-Linkage, Euclidean Distance	10.50	10.5	11.33	13	12.33	17	6.33	5	10.12	13
4C. Single-Linkage, City-Block Distance	10.50	10.5	10.67	12	12.00	15.5	6.67	8.5	9.96	12
5A. Complete-Linkage, Correlation Coefficient	2.33	1	5.17	2.5	7.33	5	5.83	4	5.17	1
5B. Complete-Linkage, Euclidean Distance	8.67	8	8.17	9	5.83	1	5.17	3	6.96	4
5C. Complete-Linkage, City-Block Distance	8.33	7	6.33	5	6.50	3	3.67	1	6.21	2
6A. Centroid-Linkage, Correlation Coefficient	3.00	2	7.33	6	9.67	10	6.50	6.5	6.63	3
7A. k-means, Correlation Coefficient	4.00	3	7.50	7	13.67	18	7.33	10	8.13	5
7B. k-means, Euclidean Distance	7.33	5	4.00	1	11.00	12	13.67	15.5	9.00	7
7C. k-means, City-Block Distance	7.67	6	6.00	4	12.00	15.5	13.33	13	9.75	10.5
8X. ISODATA	6.33	4	5.17	2.5	8.67	6.5	13.33	13	8.38	6
9X. Rubin-Friedman	13.67	14.5	8.00	8	6.00	2			9.22	9
10X. NORMAP/NORMIX	14.67	18	17.33	18	10.00	11			14.00	18

Table 6. Rankings of the Ordinal Multidimensional Scaling and Chernoff's Faces Methods According to Inter-Rater Agreement on Each of Four Data Bases (Treatment Environments, Archetypal Psychiatric Patients, Iris, Ethnic Populations) and Averaged Ranks Across Data Bases

Quantitative Taxonomic Methods	Treatment Environments		Archetypal Psychiatric Patients		Iris		Ethnic Populations		Across Fields	
	Average Rank	Overall Rank	Average Rank	Overall Rank	Average Rank	Overall Rank	Average Rank	Overall Rank	Average Rank	Overall Rank
2A. Multidimensional Scaling, Correlation Coefficient	1.7	2	1	1	1.33	1	1.5	1.5	1.38	1
2B. Multidimensional Scaling, Euclidean Distance	3.0	3	2.33	2	4.0	4	3.0	3	3.08	3
2C. Multidimensional Scaling, City-Block Distance	1.3	1	2.66	3	3.0	3	1.5	1.5	2.12	2
3X. Chernoff's Faces	4.0	4	4	4	1.67	2	4.0	4	3.42	4

findings. Bartko, Strauss, and Carpenter (1971) found that complete-linkage produces clusterings of archetypal psychiatric patients closer to a classification established by experienced psychiatrists than does the Rubin-Friedman optimization technique. The same ordering of these two taxonomic methods according to external criterion validity is found in the present study, both for archetypal psychiatric patients and across data bases. The internal criterion validity ranking of average centroid-linkage, complete-linkage, and single-linkage, reported here in decreasing order of cophenetic correlation coefficients, is in line with the findings of Sneath (1966), Cunningham and Ogilvie (1972), Baker (1974), and Hubert (1974). On the other hand, Boyce (1969) studied a set of hominoids and obtained higher cophenetic correlation coefficients for Q-principal components analysis than for average-linkage. The replicability ranking across data bases found in the present study for Q-factor analysis, average centroid-linkage, and single-linkage methods agrees with the decreasing replicability values obtained by Rogers and Linden (1973) for Lorr and Radhakrishnan's (1967) factor analytic method, Ward's (1963) special agglomerative method (which, according to Everitt's 1974 Monte Carlo studies, behaves similarly to the average centroid-linkage method), and Johnson's (1967) HICLUS program, assuming its single-linkage option.

Proper consideration should be given to the variable rankings of quantitative taxonomic methods across evaluative criteria and data bases described in this study. However, in light of persistent patterns noted here, it is reasonable to recommend in general the complete-linkage as the preferred method and centroid-linkage as a close second. If these procedures are not available, then the k-means method (which is particularly inexpensive), ISODATA, or the Rubin-Friedman optimization technique (which is particularly expensive) may be selected.

Although ordinal multidimensional scaling does not rank high in this study, it may be a valuable approach in two regards. First, it may be used to visualize data and cluster structure, either as the final clustering procedure or preceding the use of another cluster method. Visual inspection may be helpful in clarifying issues such as number of clusters and particular cluster shapes (elongated clusters, for example, would suggest the use of the single-linkage method).

Second, this approach may be used to graphically represent and interpret groups that have been found by other clustering methods.

The use of either multivariate normal mixture analysis (NORMAP/NORMIX) or facial representation of multidimensional points (Chernoff's faces) for clustering purposes, without previous successful testing on data of the type to be analyzed, does not seem to be advisable at this time. No relationship measures can be clearly preferred, but correlation coefficients seem to do at least as well as Euclidean and city-block distances.

It should be noted that the results of a quantitative taxonomic study may be influenced not only by the cluster analytic method used (as shown in this study) but also by the scaling and transformation of the input data (as shown by Bartko, Strauss, and Carpenter, 1971, among others). The present study suggests preferred methods for conducting taxonomic studies in general and in fields that correspond to the data bases considered here. For a narrower or special problem, entities with a known group structure should be analyzed before a specific clustering procedure is selected.

Validating a Cluster Analytic Solution

■■■■■■■■■■■■■■■■■■■■■■■■■

Roger K. Blashfield
Mark S. Aldenderfer
Leslie C. Morey

The validation of a cluster analysis solution remains one of the most difficult problems surrounding the use of clustering methods. Validation includes such problem areas as: empirical evaluation of the properties of clustering methods, determination of the correct number of clusters in the data set, and recognition of an optimal classification. In short, a validation procedure seeks to measure the adequacy of the clustering solution: It may be a mathematical or statistical formula, a way of manipulating data to test the generality of a solution, or a graphical analysis to help the user see if clusters exist in the data. Unfortunately, the various approaches to validation assume markedly different definitions of an "adequate cluster solution."

Note: This research was funded in part by an internal grant from the University of Florida.

Despite the recognition of this problem, little attention has been devoted to the development and testing of reasonable validation procedures. Among the large number of procedures proposed by various authors, few have ever been critically compared. Much of the difficulty of developing validation procedures stems from the extreme diversity of the general literature on cluster analysis (Blashfield and Aldenderfer, 1978a).

At present, cluster analysis is not supported by a widely accepted and well-developed body of statistical theory. Most analysts take a predominantly descriptive and pragmatic approach to the development of clustering methods and differ widely on the issues of how classifications are created and what ends they ought to serve. At least seven families of clustering methods have developed: (1) hierarchical agglomerative (Sneath and Sokal, 1973), (2) hierarchical divisive (Williams, 1976), (3) iterative partitioning (Anderberg, 1973; Friedman and Rubin, 1967), (4) factor analytic (Tryon and Bailey, 1970; Skinner, 1974), (5) mode searching (Jones, 1968), (6) clumping (Peay, 1975), and (7) graph theoretical methods (Day, 1977; Matula, 1977). Each of these families includes numerous methods with different properties. Many can generate different classificatory solutions to the same data set and provoke the following questions: "Which solution is correct?" "Which solution is optimal?" From these questions, the problem of validation has evolved.

This chapter attempts to consolidate information on validation methods that have been proposed in many disciplines (see also Dubes and Jain, 1979). It is not exhaustive, because the task of searching through the voluminous literature on clustering is simply too great. Many validation procedures have been proposed very briefly in articles devoted primarily to the analysis of data. Only a few have been tested on more than one type of data or compared to other validation techniques. It is likely, however, that categories described below cover most of the important families of procedures. It is to be hoped that this chapter will stimulate their comparison and will ultimately lead to the establishment of reliable conditions for their use.

An examination of the literature reveals three major approaches to the validation of clustering solutions: (1) measures, (2) procedures, and (3) graph analysis. The first approach involves the use of statistical *measures* that characterize the quality of the clustering solution. The second approach employs various *procedures* and manipulations to test cluster analysis solutions. Finally, *graphic* methods can visually represent various aspects of the clustering solutions in order to determine if the clusters are separate. These approaches will be further subdivided for ease of discussion.

Measures

Statistical measures address the problem of validation in different ways. *Cophenetic measures* focus on the relationship between the original similarity matrix and the similarity matrix implied by the clustering solution. *Variance measures* examine the homogeneity of entities within clusters. *Interpoint distance measures* assess the "tightness" of the clusters in the multivariate space. *Maximum likelihood measures*, based on a mixture model for cluster analysis, utilize maximum likelihood estimates to determine the parameters of this model.

Cophenetic Measures. Of the two similarity matrices compared in this procedure, one is formed from the raw data, and one is implied by the clustering solution. This latter matrix is usually called the cophenetic matrix.

The most commonly used cophenetic measure is the cophenetic correlation coefficient. This statistic was first proposed by Sokal and Rohlf (1962) and to date has been the most widely used method to test clustering solutions. The measure was designed to be used with hierarchical agglomerative clustering methods. The cophenetic correlation, R_{cs}, is defined as the Pearson product-moment correlation between the elements in the two similarity matrices. Hubert and Baker (1977) discuss some properties of this statistic. Sneath and Sokal (1973) provide a clear discussion of the cophenetic measure and its rationale.

Despite its rather frequent use, the cophenetic correlation has distinct problems. While the computation of the product-moment correlation does not assume normal distributions of variables, some of its interpretations do, and this assumption is generally violated in the distribution of elements from the cophenetic matrix. Secondly, there are $(N*(N-1))/2$ unique elements in the original matrix and only $N-1$ unique values in the cophenetic matrix. Thirdly, the order of the two matrices is different. Other features of the cophenetic correlation are discussed in Cunningham and Ogilvie (1972) and Farris (1969a).

A second category of measures compares the elements in the original and cophenetic matrices but does not utilize the Pearson product-moment correlation to do so. For example, Cunningham and Ogilvie (1972) propose a nonparametric correlational statistic to compare the cophenetic matrix with the original similarity matrix. On this comparison, Baker and Hubert (1975) base a nonparametric statistic for evaluating the results of hierarchical cluster analysis. Hartigan (1967) suggests the following measure:

$$\sum_i \sum_j (s_{ij} - c_{ij})^2 \qquad (1)$$

where s_{ij} is the original similarity value for entities i and j, and c_{ij} is the cophenetic value as implied by the clustering solution. A brief review by Rohlf (1974) provides an excellent introduction to many of the cophenetic measures. Other proposals or discussions of cophenetic measures can be found in Hubert and Levin (1976a, 1976b), Jackson (1969), Jardine and Sibson (1968), Moss (1968), and Williams and Clifford (1971).

Variance Measures. The cophenetic measures were initially proposed for use in testing cluster solutions from hierarchical agglomerative methods of cluster analysis. Variance measures attempt to examine validity by assessing the homogeneity of the entities within each proposed cluster. Thus many of these measures have been suggested in conjuction with iterative partitioning methods of cluster analysis (Anderberg, 1973; Everitt, 1974). Even so, they can be applied to any clustering method that yields a mutually exclusive partition of a data set.

Most measures in this category have been derived from statistics used in analysis of variance. For example, the error sum of squares criterion popularized by Ward (1963; Ward and Hook, 1963) can be used as a variance measure:

$$ESS = \sum_k \sum_i \sum_j (x_{kij} - \bar{x}_{kj})^2 \qquad (2)$$

where k is an index for each cluster, i is an index for the entities being clustered, and j is an index for the variables. Also suggested as variance measures have been Wilk's lambda (Λ) and other statistics used in multivariate analysis of variance (Friedman and Rubin, 1967).

Standard significance testing cannot be appropriately performed using multivariate analysis statistics. Since entities are assigned during the cluster analysis in order to maximize the homogeneity within clusters and to minimize the heterogeneity between clusters, the assignment of entities to clusters can hardly be said to represent the independent sampling process assumed to occur in standard multivariate analysis of variance. Thus these measures can be used to assess the relative adequacy of different cluster solutions, but their absolute values are hard to interpret. Alternatively, it has been suggested that the natural logarithm of the probability value associated with an analysis-of-variance statistic can be used to measure the adequacy of a clustering solution (Gnanadesikan, Kettenring, and Landwehr, 1977). Blashfield and Aldenderfer (1978b), Clifford and Stephenson (1975), Everitt (1974), and Marriot (1971) introduce many of the variance measures.

Interpoint Distance Measures. From a geometric perspective, the entities being clustered are considered as points in a multidimensional space, where each variable in the data set is a dimension. To demonstrate validity, this approach seeks to determine if the clusters comprise relatively tight "swarms" of points. That is, entities in a cluster should be fairly close together, while entities in different clusters should be relatively distant from each other (Rubin, 1966).

Williams and others (1971) point out that three types of distance can be calculated in cluster analysis: (a) the distance between different objects, (b) the distance between objects and clusters, and (c) the distance between clusters. The measures in this category involve these three interpoint distances, and many of the graphic techniques mentioned later in this chapter visually represent them.

As an example of an interpoint distance measure, Williams, Clifford, and Lance (1971) suggest the following:

$$W = \sum_{k} \sum_{l < k} (d_{kl}/D) \tag{3}$$

where d_{kl} is the distance between the centroids of clusters k and l, and D is the median distance between any two entities in the data set being clustered. Good cluster solutions will have relatively large values on this measure; Williams and others (1971) have used it to compare the accuracy of different clustering methods. Other interpoint distance measures can be found in D'Andrade (1978), Hartigan (1977a), Hubert and Schultz (1976), Rubin (1966), and Sneath (1977).

In general, interpoint distance measures are appropriate when a researcher has metric data and is using distance (Euclidean or Minkowski distance, for example) as the similarity measure. When association correlation measures are used as similarity measures in the clustering process, or when nominal data have been gathered, the interpoint distance measures of solution adequacy are not as meaningful.

Maximum Likelihood Measures. Particular to this set of measures is that they stipulate a specific statistical model for clustering, the maximum likelihood method of cluster analysis, and are used to estimate the parameters of this model. Unfortunately, the mixture model, a common statistical model proposed for cluster analysis, has proved to be extremely complex and difficult to solve with maximum likelihood procedures (Hartigan, 1977b). The clustering methods that have evolved from this approach make use of various heuristics that seek to determine the number of clusters as well as the distributional parameters of the data within clusters.

Along with the development of maximum likelihood methods of cluster analysis, attempts have been made to use maximum likelihood measures to test the adequacy of a cluster solution. For instance, Wolfe (1970) proposes the following:

$$- 2q \log \lambda_k \qquad (4)$$

where λ_k is the likelihood ratio associated with k clusters, and q is a constant (see also Scott and Symons, 1971). Wolfe originally suggested that this measure should be distributed as χ^2 and could be incorporated into procedures that test the significance of the cluster solution. However, a later study by the same author (1971a) concludes that this measure cannot be accurately used to test hypotheses.

Procedures

Procedures for testing the adequacy of cluster analysis solutions can focus on the general solution in various ways. First, a good cluster solution will be duplicated if a data set similar to the original is clustered with the identical method; techniques that employ this logic are called *replication procedures. Data alteration procedures* determine how well cluster solutions hold up with the addition of random noise to the data set. *External criterion procedures* examine how well a clustering solution discriminates on variables not used to generate the solution. *Deletion procedures* recluster the data after deleting variables and determine how well this new solution corresponds to the original.

Replication Procedures. It seems obvious that a cluster analysis solution should be replicated if a similar data set were clustered by an identical method. However, this would not occur if the original solution had resulted from a chance pattern in the data set. McIntyre and Blashfield (1980) base a particular procedure upon replication logic. This procedure is similar to one that employs discriminant analysis (Rogers and Linden, 1973). Landwehr (1972) extends the replication logic by proposing the use of jackknife techniques to estimate cluster solutions from multiple samples. Morf, Miller, and Syrotrick (1976) employ a replication procedure that compares cluster analysis methods.

Data Alteration Procedures. It is assumed in this set of procedures that if a solution is good, the same solution should be obtained even when random error is added to the data. Gnanadesikan, Kettenring, and Landwehr (1977) discuss a procedure they describe as *sensitivity analysis,* in which the data are "shaken" by the addition of noise. The shaken data are represented by the model

$$X'_{N \times P} = X_{N \times P} + E_{N \times P} \tag{5}$$

where $X_{N \times P}$ is the original data matrix with N entities and P variables, and $E_{N \times P}$ is a data set of multivariate normal noise. Baker (1974) and Milligan and Issac (1980) use a similar approach to test cluster analysis solutions after noise has been added to the original similarity matrix.

External Criterion Procedure. This procedure differs from all other methods discussed in this chapter in that it addresses the issue of external validity. The usual procedure is to examine how well the proposed classification differentiates between groups on the basis of relevant variables not included in the original analysis.

Examples of this technique may be found in the literature on psychiatric classification. Clustering is performed on data in which the symptoms and behavior of patients constitute the variables, and the patients themselves, the entities being classified. The classification obtained is studied for its ability to differentiate the cluster of patients on other key variables. This approach has been used with some success in the classification of depressive illnesses (Hollister, Overall, and Shelton, 1967; Paykel, 1972; Raskin and Crook, 1976). Sonquist, Baker, and Morgan (1971) and Tryon and Bailey (1970) have also made innovative suggestions concerning the use of external criteria.

Deletion Procedures. This final category includes various techniques designed to assess the generality of a cluster solution across assorted deletions or changes in the original analysis. For example, Jardine and Sibson (1968) suggest that, after a cluster solution is obtained, all entities assigned to a particular cluster be deleted and the data set reclustered. If the solution is stable, the other clusters should remain the same. Similarly, Everitt (1974) suggests that reclustering after deleting a randomly selected variable will reveal the stability of the cluster. Everitt also believes a good solution will remain constant even though different clustering methods are used to obtain it.

Graphics

Generally, graphics display a cluster in some visual manner so that the researcher can get a feel for its meaningful characteristics. Such techniques are susceptible to the subjective impressions of researchers, who may project their conceptualization of the data set onto their interpretations. On the other hand, many researchers consider cluster analysis in general to be little more than heuristics that help a researcher get a better feel for the data at hand. From this perspective, graphics are very useful for analyzing cluster solutions.

The most common graphical displays are the *biplot* and the *discriminant function plot*. To form the biplot, the clusters are plotted in the space defined by the first two principal components, which have been determined by a principal component analysis (Strauss and others, 1976). To aid interpretation, the variables are also plotted as vectors in the principal component space. To form the discriminant function plot, the clusters are plotted in the space defined by the first two discriminant functions, the results of a discriminant analysis (Friedman and Rubin, 1967). Discriminant plots tend to exaggerate the separateness of the clusters because discriminant analysis finds linear combinations of variables that also maximize this separateness. The biplot, on the other hand, tends to blur the distinction between clusters because the principal component analysis assumes that the data come from one homogeneous population.

One problem common to both of these approaches is that the information provided by all but the first two components or functions is lost. Rohlf (1978) proposes a method for representing clusters as solid objects in three-dimensional space. Snygg (1978) suggests a method for representing high-dimensional data as a two-dimensional figure by using a cosine series containing a term for each variable in the data set. If this expression is plotted in terms of polar coordinates, the resulting size and shape of the figure are determined by the distance and direction (respectively) of the entity from the origin in the multidimensional space. Both of these approaches have potential applicability to the graphic analysis of clustering solutions. However, little work has been done to determine how useful these techniques might be in assessing solution adequacy.

Chernoff's faces constitute a unique method of representing a multidimensional solution visually (Chernoff, 1973). In these faces Chernoff incorporates a number of dimensions: One dimension concerns the length of the lips, another the concave or convex angle of the lips, another the length of the nose, and so forth. Turner and Tidmore (1977) have written a program that permits faces to be drawn with a line printer.

Other graphical procedures have been suggested by Gnanadesikan (1977); Hutchinson, Johnstone, and White (1965); and Wishart and Leach (1970) and have been reviewed in more detail by Fowlkes and McRae (1977); Hartigan (1975b); and Gnanadesikan, Kettenring, and Landwehr (1977).

Overview and Comment

As might be expected from the heterogeneous literature on cluster analysis, the literature on the validation of cluster solutions is somewhat confused and difficult to organize comprehensively. This chapter has attempted to represent most of the major themes, although it has by no means been exhaustive. The reader should have a fair number of alternatives from which to choose. Unfortunately, we can offer little guidance about which validation approaches should be used in applied research.

A few additional comments can be made. First, with the exception of the cophenetic correlation, most of these methods have been discussed by one author in one article only. This suggests that a researcher should be careful when incorporating any validation approach. At present, given the lack of established literature on the topic, the reader is urged to use a handful of fairly different validation procedures to test a cluster solution.

Second, most of the articles covered in this chapter are not primarily concerned with the issue of cluster validation. Instead, they may compare the performance of different clustering methods (Milligan and Issac, 1980; Cunningham and Ogilvie, 1972), or propose new methods of forming clusters (Friedman and Rubin, 1967; Snygg, 1978; Wolfe, 1970). The articles that focus especially on testing cluster solutions are few and very recent (Dubes and Jain, 1979; Gnanadesikan, Kettenring, and Landwehr, 1977; Hartigan, 1977a; Rohlf, 1974).

Third, the discussion of cluster validation often involves different perspectives on the goals of cluster analysis. For example, cophenetic measures implicitly assume that the goal of cluster analysis is to represent the structure of a similarity matrix; maximum likelihood measures assume that the data set represents a mixture of different statistical populations.

In light of these general observations, it is impossible at present to recommend any single validation method for applied research. Nonetheless, the issue of validation is crucial for the future of clustering methods and should be an area for important new research.

Blockmodels: Developments and Prospects

■■■■■■■■■■■■■■■■■■■■■■■■■

Phipps Arabie
Scott A. Boorman

The idea of permuting discrete (and typically binary) data into substantively interpretable patterns of blocks was the original impetus behind the development of blockmodels. That is, for one or more types of social ties (where each type gives rise to an $n \times n$ matrix of

Note: This chapter was written at the invitation of Herschel Hudson, who also suggested the topic. The interested reader should note that a more extensive treatment of blockmodeling is given in Arabie, Boorman, and Levitt (1978), from which parts of the present chapter are derived. We are indebted to A. Tellegen, R. L. Breiger, J. D. Carroll, C. H. Coombs, P. Diaconis, S. E. Fienberg, R. L. Graham, P. W. Holland, J. B. Kruskal, P. R. Levitt, and K. Schuessler for helpful discussions of this work. Financial support for this chapter was obtained from NSF Grants SOC 76-24512 and SOC 76-24394 and LEAA Grant 78-NI-AX-0142. Authors' addresses: Phipps Arabie, Department of Psychology, University of Illinois, Champaign, IL 61820; Scott A. Boorman, Department of Sociology, Yale University, New Haven, CT 06520.

sociometric "votes"), a permutation is sought that simultaneously organizes the reported ties into blocks of common membership across the different square matrices. In many applications reported to date, the permuted data have revealed contrasting patterns of high-density ("oneblocks") and low-density ("zeroblocks") areas within the permuted matrix. This chapter focuses on ongoing developments in blockmodeling, with the fortune-teller's goal of pinpointing specific areas of current research and extrapolating to future developments.

Space limitations preclude review of social networks, but it is assumed that readers are familiar with some of the research in this area (for background, see Arabie, Boorman, and Levitt, 1978; Breiger, Boorman, and Arabie, 1975; Breiger, 1976; Boorman and White, 1976; White, Boorman, and Breiger, 1976). The present chapter is divided into sections pertaining to (1) various algorithms and their implementations for obtaining blockmodels, (2) user-oriented considerations, and (3) implications for substantive theory and acquisition of appropriate data bases.

Algorithms and Implementations for Constructing Blockmodels

As an example of a blockmodel, consider the following blocked matrices, respectively coding positive and negative sentiment in a population of seven individuals:

$$
\mathbf{V} = \left|\begin{array}{cccc|ccc}
0 & 0 & 0 & 1 & 0 & 0 & 0 \\
0 & 0 & 1 & 0 & 0 & 0 & 0 \\
0 & 1 & 0 & 0 & 0 & 0 & 0 \\
1 & 1 & 0 & 0 & 0 & 0 & 0 \\
\hline
0 & 0 & 0 & 1 & 0 & 1 & 1 \\
0 & 1 & 0 & 0 & 1 & 0 & 0 \\
1 & 0 & 1 & 0 & 0 & 1 & 0
\end{array}\right|
\qquad
\mathbf{F} = \left|\begin{array}{cccc|ccc}
0 & 0 & 0 & 0 & 1 & 0 & 1 \\
0 & 0 & 0 & 0 & 0 & 0 & 0 \\
0 & 0 & 0 & 0 & 1 & 1 & 0 \\
0 & 0 & 0 & 0 & 0 & 1 & 0 \\
\hline
1 & 0 & 0 & 1 & 0 & 1 & 1 \\
0 & 1 & 1 & 0 & 1 & 0 & 1 \\
1 & 1 & 0 & 0 & 1 & 1 & 0
\end{array}\right|
$$

Positive   Negative
Sentiment   Sentiment

In the permutation shown and with the indicated bipartition, the upper right submatrix of the **V** matrix consists only of zeros, as does the upper left submatrix of the **F** matrix. A compact coding of the aggregate structure is hence furnished by the *image matrices*

$$\mathbf{V} = \begin{bmatrix} 1 & 0 \\ 1 & 1 \end{bmatrix} \qquad \mathbf{F} = \begin{bmatrix} 0 & 1 \\ 1 & 1 \end{bmatrix}$$

where a "0" in the image corresponds to a zeroblock in the data matrix and a "1" corresponds to a block containing at least some 1's. By convention, we will retain the term "block" to refer both to blocked submatrices of the raw data matrices (the 7×7 matrices in this example) *and* to the subsets of the actors defined by the partition. Observe that the ordering of blocks is arbitrary, as is the ordering of actors within blocks.

CONCOR. To date, the most widely used algorithm for obtaining blockmodels and image matrices such as those shown above has been the CONCOR (CONvergence of iterated CORrelations) algorithm. This procedure, published earlier by McQuitty and Clark (1968), accepts continuously varying data (as entries in $\mathbf{M}_0$, the input matrix) and gives as output a dendrogram, characteristic of the discrete output from hierarchical clustering. The formal properties of this algorithm have been presented in Arabie, Boorman, and Levitt (1978) and in Breiger, Boorman, and Arabie (1975). A brief summary follows.

CONCOR is an hierarchical clustering algorithm that exploits the empirically observed fact that when the columns (respectively, rows) of a matrix $\mathbf{M}_i = [m_{jk}\,(i)]_{n \times n}$ are iteratively replaced by the column correlations, obtaining

$$\mathbf{M}_{i+1} = [m_{jk}\,(i+1)\,]_{n \times n}$$

$m_{jk}\,(i+1) =$ correlation between jth and kth columns of $\mathbf{M}_i$

$$= \frac{\sum\limits_{p=1}^{n}(m_{pj}(i) - \bar{m}_j(i))(m_{pk}(i) - \bar{m}_k(i))}{\sqrt{\sum\limits_{p=1}^{n}(m_{pj}(i) - \bar{m}_j(i))^2 \sum\limits_{q=1}^{n}(m_{qk}(i) - \bar{m}_k(i))^2}}$$

where

$$\bar{m}_k(i) = (1/n) \sum_{p=1}^{n} m_{pk}(i)$$

then the limit $\lim_{i \to \infty} \mathbf{M}_i$ exists except in certain anomalous cases (for example, $\mathbf{M}_0$, a cyclic matrix, or a matrix having at least one constant column) and may be permuted into the bipartite blocked form

$$\mathbf{M}_\infty = \begin{bmatrix} +1 & -1 \\ -1 & +1 \end{bmatrix}$$

thus yielding a two-block clustering from the algorithm. To date, all known classes of exceptions to these convergence results are of measure 0 in Lebesgue measure space of all real-valued square matrices of dimension n.

Except as otherwise noted for rectangular matrices where rows and columns are blocked separately, all later analyses will be assumed to converge on *columns*, rather than on rows (thus continuing the emphasis of Breiger, Boorman, and Arabie (1975) on *received* sociometric choices). Given a choice between columns and rows, strong support for the former is given by the following "worst-possible-case" situation. If a respondent gives erroneous votes to all the members of the group (so that the actor's row of the sociomatrix is thus noise), then a blocking based on rows will yield an inaccurate result for the individual, and the block that should have contained that actor. But if blocking is done on columns, then the respondent will have contributed a much smaller error to the column vectors (specifically, one erroneous entry per vector) for the members of the group. Thus the reliance on columns is less vulnerable to the situation just described. Once the initial bipartition is obtained, the same procedure may be applied to split one or both of the two obtained blocks in turn, so that finer partitions may be obtained corresponding to the desired number of blocks. The following empirical fact makes CON-COR highly effective in the search for blockmodels: when a sparse data matrix $\mathbf{M}_0$ is permuted to conform to CONCOR-derived blocks, the permutation will generally reveal zeroblocks or near-zeroblocks in the data. Furthermore, extension of the method to handle multiple network data is straightforward: it is only necessary to "stack" the k given data matrices, each of dimension n, to obtain a single $kn \times n$

matrix, and then to converge columns of the derived matrix using CONCOR (as discussed below).

As a caveat to sociologists and social psychologists employing these methods, it should be noted that "hierarchical clustering" as in a dendrogram refers to the nesting of successive levels of blockmodel refinement, not to any actual or presumed identification of social hierarchy or dominance structure (that is, an ordering of individuals) in the given data (as in the sense of Landau, 1951, 1965). Regarding graph images such as those at the beginning of this paper, observe that each level of the hierarchical clustering, that is, of blockmodel refinement, will produce its own image matrices [such as those illustrated earlier for (**V,F**)]. As the degree of refinement increases, the successive image matrices more and more closely approximate the original network, until in the limit, where n blocks are used, each actor occupies a singleton block and the "images" are simply the original data. The opposite extreme is a single block comprising the entire population; in this case the mapping of data onto the image matrices is trivial. Thus, the problem of blockmodeling is one of choosing which level or levels of refinement generated through CONCOR provide the optimal degree of aggregation for understanding the data. This problem is, of course, a standard one in hierarchical clustering, when the data analyst must decide which level(s) of a dendrogram (where each level is a partition of the set of n actors) correspond most closely to the original data. Impressive first steps in looking at this problem have been taken by Hubert and others (Baker and Hubert, 1976; Hubert, 1973; Ling, 1975), considering the problem of best fit between a single (2-way) matrix and competing partitions of the entities depicted by the matrix. The problem posed by blockmodeling is more complex. Specifically, for a data matrix representing k types of ties between n actors, we have a (3-way) matrix of dimensions $k \times n \times n$ to compare with the chain of partitions having increasingly "finer" cells, as output from CONCOR, or whatever hierarchical algorithm is employed. Although research to date has always assumed that the same partition "best" depicts the blockmodel structure across each of the k matrices, there is no a priori reason why that assumption should be correct. That is, some type of tie might well support a finer level of interpretation (more blocks) than another type of tie. A goodness-of-fit statistic to indicate the best fitting partition(s) for each of the k separate square matrices could be of considerable use. Moreover, if distinct partitions were to yield differential fidelity to the separate matrices "stacked" in M_0, the 3-way flavor of blockmodel analysis would be enhanced.

Arabie, Boorman, and Levitt (1978) have noted the advantages of CONCOR over its discrete predecessor BLOCKER (Heil and White, 1976). The latter program uses an algorithm designed to partition simultaneously each of the k square matrices into blocks of actors. The partitioning is subject to the constraint that the cells (of the partition) must yield image matrices prespecified by the data analyst, and that zero entries in the image matrices must correspond to submatrices that are entirely zeros in M_0. As noted in Arabie, Boorman, and Levitt (1978), BLOCKER thus makes extreme demands (1) on the data analyst's intuition for the data, in having to specify k image matrices in advance, and (2) on the data, which must be binary and susceptible to forming zeroblocks that are all zeros. Since the advent of CONCOR, BLOCKER has been used infrequently. It is, however, still occasionally useful for locating "floaters" (that is, actors that may be ambiguously affiliated with more than one block) once a CONCOR solution has already been found.

Statistical indigestion concerning CONCOR arises on two issues. First, there is no general proof of convergence to the ± 1 form shown above (compare Schwartz, 1976). Second, it is not clear what objective function (if any) is being minimized or maximized by CONCOR. Moreover, recent unpublished work by J. B. Kruskal at Bell Telephone Laboratories and one of the present authors (P. A.) suggests that answers to either of these problems are not close at hand. Thus CONCOR remains an unvalidated algorithm that has been useful empirically in producing interpretable blockmodels. Given this state of affairs, an alternative discrete approach to CONCOR (and free of BLOCKER's drawbacks) would be of considerable use.

Alternative Discrete Clustering Algorithms. Hubert and Baker (1978b) have pointed to recently proposed combinatorial clustering algorithms (Bhat and Haupt, 1976; McCormick, Schweitzer, and White, 1972; Slagle, Chang, and Heller, 1975) as potential rivals to CONCOR for obtaining blockmodels. Summarized briefly, these algorithms permute the rows/columns of a rectangular matrix with nonnegative entries in order to maximize sequentially an objective function. This function differs across the papers cited, but generally takes the form of a sum of the products of neighboring elements in the array. The result, for binary data, tends to be matrices that are permuted to reveal clumps or blocks of zeros, separated from those of ones. Thus, although there is no formal link between the definition of structural equivalence (Lorrain and White, 1971) and the recent combinatorial approaches, these algorithms are intuitively appealing in their attempts to form homogeneous blocks within a 2-way matrix. [It will be recalled that the intuitive appeal of CONCOR lies in the idea of gauging the *consistency* of actors via correlation. The substantive implication of "structural equivalence" (Lorrain and White, 1971, p. 63) was that actors within a block are interchangeable and thus positionally consistent—in contrast to earlier emphasis on connectedness (for example, Ross and Harary, 1959). For more recent approaches to structural equivalence, see Sailer (1978) and Boyd (1979/80).]

Since these combinatorial clustering algorithms could in the future supplant CONCOR, we first note four technical impediments to their present usage. The first is that the initial configurations for these algorithms begin with arbitrarily choosing a specific row/column to relocate within the matrix. Similarly, successive rows/columns are also chosen arbitrarily, although, of course, each is sequentially placed so as to maximize the objective function. Given this situation, a data analyst would certainly want to try a variety of different initial configurations, and costs could mount for moderately large sets of data.

The second drawback is disguised as a theoretically elegant property, namely that as pointed out by Lenstra (1974), these combinatorial methods of clustering are equivalent to minimum spanning path approaches to the classical traveling-salesman problem. Techniques for dealing with the latter problem are highly relevant to data analyses in the behavioral sciences (Hubert and Baker, 1978b; Hubert and Schultz, 1976). Moreover, Gower and Ross (1969) showed that minimum spanning trees[1] are isomorphic to the output produced by single-link cluster analyses. Thus the combinatorial clustering algorithms cited above are, in effect, analogous to implementations of single-link clustering, applied to the rows/columns of the rectangular data matrix, where the various objective functions proposed in

those papers determine which rows/columns are closest at any particular step of forming the minimum spanning tree. So far there is no
difficulty, and the combinatorial algorithms are thus on a more
familiar (formal) ground. However, it is empirically the case that
single-link clustering suffers from "chaining" effects (Lance and
Williams, 1967). That is, over successive levels of the dendrogram,
frequently the only change is the accretion of a single item to an
ever-stretching cluster (of which there are only a few). Thus the
single-link clustering representation tends to yield singletons as clusters for many levels of the dendrogram. In the context of blockmodels,
the predicted "chaining" effects from applying the combinatorial
algorithms might easily approximate many blocks composed only of
individual actors, which is inherently an uninformative pattern.[2]

A third problem in using the combinatorial clustering algorithms (Bhat and Haupt, 1976; McCormick, Schweitzer, and White,
1972; Slagle, Chang, and Heller, 1975) concerns the choice of objective function for quantifying the "lumpiness" of the blocks of homogeneous elements within an array. There is first the problem of extend-
ing the usage of these methods from a 2-way array to which the papers
cited above limited their discussions, to a 3-way matrix consisting of
the $kn \times n$ square matrices (one for each type of tie). The obvious and
straightforward generalization is to sum the 2-way objective function
over each of the k matrices. Each tentative reordering of a row/
column in the 2-way case can simply be done in parallel across the k
matrices in the 3-way case. However, the selection of a loss function
from any of those proposed by the authors cited earlier is problematic,
and there is little evidence currently available to suggest which, if any,
of the various loss functions would give superior results for blockmodels. McCormick, Schweitzer, and White presciently noted the
arbitrariness of their loss function and stated that "different choices
may significantly alter the array ordering" (1972, p. 995).

A fourth problem, somewhat related to the preceding problem,
is that these combinatorial clustering approaches produce homogeneous groups of entries within a nonnegative data matrix, but do
not delineate blocks or cluster the rows/columns—that is, these
methods permute the rows/columns to rearrange the matrix into a
patterned form, but do so without any concomitant partition forth-
coming for the rows/columns. Thus it is left to the data analyst to

partition the matrix into blocks of actors in order to obtain a block-model. Clearly, some measure of goodness-of-fit (refer to the next section) is needed to decide between competing blockings, and the measures presently available are generally inadequate to the task— although it is possible that the work of Phillips and Conviser (1972) might offer a solution to this problem. In particular, the representation of a "floater," which was handled so deftly by BLOCKER (Heil and White, 1976), would seem to be a special problem with which the combinatorial clustering approaches would have to come to grips.

In conclusion, we note that the computational vehicle for blockmodeling can be of a traditional multivariate approach (Hayashi, 1952; Lambert and Williams, 1962; Schwartz, 1976), or CONCOR, or the combinatorial clustering methods considered above. Since CONCOR is currently the most widely used algorithm and will probably continue in that role for several years, we now turn to specific technical considerations raised by CONCOR (as well as by some multivariate techniques).

Practical Considerations

Form of the Input Data. As noted in the Breiger, Boorman, and Arabie (1975) discussion, the input matrix M_0 for CONCOR is required only to be an $m \times n$ matrix of real numbers consistently coding relations within a population of actors. It is not even necessary to delineate a priori whether the relations so coded describe similarity/dissimilarity, liking/disliking, or any of the other traditional bipolar variables; in fact, we will argue below that the best results are obtained by the juxtaposition of many contrasting types of relations in the same stack, when the input data are entered in the prescribed manner. In spite of this generality, most applications to date have entered only integer-valued matrices that are either binary or ordered choices. Moreover, it has become empirically clear that data in binary form (dichotomized, if necessary) usually provide the best candidates for substantive interpretation through the blockmodel formalism. A similar advantage for binary data has been reported by plant ecologists using principal components analysis (Austin and Greig-Smith, 1968; Hill, 1974, p. 350). We would like to suggest a possible basis for this fact, and then suggest various ways of preprocessing nonbinary data in order to obtain binary M_0. It is to be stressed that this part of the research area remains in a largely premathematical state, though by the same token constituting the field where the next major mathematical advance is perhaps most likely to occur.

The principal empirical advantage of binary data once a blockmodel has been obtained from CONCOR is that such data seem to enhance the pattern of contrasting densities between potential zeroblocks and oneblocks. That is, although the presence of continuous data in M_0 poses no difficulty for computing correlations, cases blockmodeled to date indicate that such data are usually less likely to yield a bimodal distribution of block densities (see also Breiger, Boorman, and Arabie, 1975, pp. 353,355).[3] Because, as we have seen, such an obtained distribution facilitates a clear distinction between zeroblocks and oneblocks, the interpretation of blockmodels is much easier in these cases, and efforts to produce a binary M_0 seem justified.

Although this argument is an empirical conjecture, there are certain examples of nonbinary data for which theoretical reasons can also be adduced. Thus consider an M_0 having both positive and negative entries (for example, where the actors report both positive and negative affect toward each other, and both types of ties, presumed to be mutually exclusive, are summarized in the same M_0). Once the permutation of M_0 has been determined through CONCOR, if the densities within blocks are naively computed, then positive and negative entries may tend to cancel out, giving a spurious impression of zeroblocks. Accordingly, it seems desirable to *fractionate* such a matrix into distinct matrices of positive and negative affect, stack the matrices, and execute CONCOR on this stack (as was done in the analyses of the Sampson monastery data (1969) reported by White, Boorman, and Breiger, 1976; see also Boyle, 1969, pp. 108–111). Following determination of a blockmodel partition by the algorithm, a common permutation may then be applied separately to each of the stacked matrices in order to compute the block densities and interpret the pattern.

Another class of frequently encountered nonbinary data is ranked choice data (for example, forced-choice sociometric data where choices are recorded in order, top person first) or, similarly, category scale data. The objection to naive application of CONCOR to such data matrices is a classical one, namely that the "equal-intervals" assumption about category scale or rank-order data is questionable (Luce and Galanter, 1963, pp. 261–264; Stevens, 1971; see also Campbell, 1954). In blockmodel applications involving such data, the data have usually been initially dichotomized on the basis of choice level, as in the analysis of the Newcomb (1961) data given in Breiger, Boorman, and Arabie (where only the top two choices are taken, and each is coded as 1). When possible, category scale data are fractionated into several distinct ties and entered as a stacked binary matrix. In many cases, these preliminary coding procedures should also improve the robustness of the data, in view of the probable unreliability of intermediate choice levels across replications and the tendency of such intermediate-level ties to be unstable in participant-reported social structures.

An example of fractionation is given by Breiger (1976, p. 119) in preprocessing of network data on researchers studying hypotha-lamic regulatory mechanisms. These data were reported by Griffith, Maier, and Miller (1973) in an unpublished study, and consist of questionnaire responses from a random sample of 107 individuals who were asked to rate the extent of interaction with fellow researchers of a seven-point category scale of professional contact. The extreme categories of the scale had verbal labels of "Present association [is] continuing personal contact" and "Unaware of man and his work" (Griffith, Maier, and Miller do not indicate whether all researchers were in fact males). Breiger fractionated the data into several distinct matrices, such as "mutual contact," "asymmetric awareness," and "symmetric unawareness." By selecting which of these fractionated matrices to enter as CONCOR input, he was able to obtain highly interpretable and quite striking results (Breiger, 1976; see also Arabie, 1977 and results reported in White, Boorman, and Breiger, 1976). Although it is not obvious that the procedures used by Breiger are canonical (for example, he suppresses "asymmetric con-tact"), there is a sound and very useful strategy at issue here. Specifi-cally, as stressed at the beginning of this section, the most interesting interpretations are likely to follow when a blockmodel is formed on multiple types of network displaying maximal *relational contrast*, for example, symmetric ties versus asymmetric ties, or positive senti-ment versus antagonism (see also Mullins, Hargens, Hecht, and Kick,

1977). Unfortunately, in all too many sociometric data sets, even the most ingenious fractionation fails to generate sufficient contrast to provide interpretive interest, typically because fractionation produces unacceptably low densities in the raw data (for example, owing to zero columns, causing the correlations that CONCOR requires as intermediate input to be undefined, as well as other interpretive difficulties). By contrast, the best existing data sets, such as the one represented in Sampson's massive empirical study (1969), furnish multiple axes for contrast arising from competing and often contradictory networks.

The experienced data analyst will have noticed that stacking such contrasting matrices to create M_0 will assign implied weights to each component type of tie if the component matrices are differentially sparse. To date, there has been no systematic investigation of weighting effects arising through CONCOR, and each matrix in the column stack has been entered without correction (such as centering on column means or some alternative weighting-normalization method). It seems clear, however, that weighting effects in blockmodels is a substantively important topic that should be investigated in the future. For example, it is by no means clear that *failure* to have heard of a colleague (as in Breiger's symmetric and asymmetric unawareness) should be assigned the same weights as maintenance of a professional contact, which requires effort and time investment. A second example arises in the analysis of the Roethlisberger and Dickson (1939) data, as blockmodeled in Breiger, Boorman, and Arabie (1975). For the tie of "helping" (on the job), inspectors were ineligible to participate with the wiremen and soldermen, and therefore necessarily have columns and rows of zeros in the sociomatrix for the "helping" tie (Breiger, Boorman, and Arabie, 1975, Table V). Weighting would be one device to compensate for the mandatory exclusion of the inspectors from the "helping" network data, when the stacked M_0 is being formed. Theoretical ideas on appropriate weighting procedures may be derived from the job information flow model of Boorman (1975), where the parameter $\lambda > 1$ serves as a natural weighting factor giving strong ties predominance over weak ones when both are entered in the same stack.

Diagonals. As a consideration in constructing blockmodels, we are concerned with diagonals at two conceptually and physically distinct levels: (1) in M_0 and (2) in the reduced image matrix that is the essence of a blockmodel hypothesis. In both instances we are talking only about a data base where the rows and columns index the same items, since an $m \times n$ matrix $(m \neq n)$ in effect has no (principal) diagonal. Turning first to diagonals in the raw data matrix M_0, it is often the case that the diagonals are either undefined or in some other way unavailable. Diagonals are not furnished at all, for example, in the several hundred sociomatrices contained in the Davis-Holland-Leinhardt data bank (Davis, 1970; Davis and Leinhardt, 1972). Schwartz (1976) has presented arguments as to why diagonals should not be included in the computation of correlations in CONCOR, even when diagonal entries are defined in the data. In the applications presented in Breiger, Boorman, and Arabie (1975), the diagonals were included for purposes of correlation (each sociomatrix being assigned a zero diagonal), but not for calculating image matrix densities. In retrospect, it would perhaps have been preferable to exclude the diagonals from both phases of the analysis.

To elaborate on the mechanics of excluding the diagonal entries from correlations, consider first a single $n \times n$ matrix. In correlating columns i and j, the four entries (i,i), (i,j), (j,i), (j,j) are excluded $(i \neq j)$, and the value $(n - 2)$ is used in the Pearson correlation formula rather than n. These same entries will also be omitted in the computations producing M_{j+1} from M_j for $j \geqslant 1$. For a stacked matrix consisting of k types of ties and thus having dimensions $kn \times n$, each of the k diagonals in M_0 is ignored during computation of M_1. Thus, there are $k(n - 2)$ entries for each column being correlated when M_1 is generated. For the subsequent sequence of matrices produced by iterated correlation, M_2 through M_∞, each having dimensions $n \times n$, there is only a single diagonal to ignore in each iteration.

It should be noted that when a constant column arises in a matrix, the CONCOR algorithm (unlike BLOCKER) terminates prematurely, faced with the zero denominator of any correlation coefficient that involves that column (Breiger, Boorman, and Arabie, 1975, p. 335). While it is possible to get around this formal difficulty by defining the correlation between any nonconstant column and a constant column to be 0, this artifice creates further problems with the $(-1, +1)$ blockability by the limit matrix M_∞, as well as chaining problems in any clustering solution inferred. When diagonals are excluded from the columns for computing correlations, the vulnerability of CONCOR to constant columns is enhanced. Specifically, each binary column of a sparse matrix must have at least two off-diagonal unities if the procedure is to be executed without including the diagonals in the correlations. (A single off-diagonal entry in row i of column j will be excluded when columns j and i are correlated, thus leaving j as a constant zero column.) Thus, sociomatrices collected through the use of one-choice procedures (see cases cited by Holland and Leinhardt, 1973) are not amenable to CONCOR analysis, although this limitation is probably inconsequential because such data in any case have doubtful utility for other reasons (Holland, 1977).

At the level of the blockmodel resulting from the image matrix, there is also a principal diagonal, even though the principal diagonal of M_0 may itself be undefined. The investigator who is seeking cliques among the actors would expect to find oneblocks on the diagonal for a tie of positive affect (such as alliance or friendship). Thus, in this case, blockmodel analysis subsumes (nonoverlapping) clique detection as a special case; although CONCOR does not explicitly search for cliques or for a block diagonal pattern, cliques present in the data will normally be identified by the algorithm.

For other types of tie (such as "aspires to resemble someday"), a oneblock on the diagonal of the image matrix seems intuitively implausible. For this reason, the density of diagonal blocks in such a matrix may help to suggest a useful cutoff density for discriminating zeroblocks from oneblocks in the image.

Goodness-of-Fit. As in the testing of any hypothesis, some measure of goodness-of-fit is desirable for a proposed blockmodel. Although several alternatives are available, none has yet seen extensive usage in blockmodel applications. A recent proposal of considerable promise is given by Hubert and Baker (1978a) and is summarized and discussed in Arabie, Boorman, and Levitt (1978). Moreover, Hubert (1979) has recently generalized the earlier work on goodness-of-fit to encompass 3-way data matrices. Other recent work has been done by Carrington, Heil, and Berkowitz (1979/80).

Miscellaneous Considerations. The present discussion of blockmodels began with square binary matrices, where the rows and columns index the same set of actors. As noted elsewhere in this paper, for the alternative case of $m \times n$ matrices, whose rows and columns index disjoint sets, CONCOR can be separately applied to the rows and to the columns. For such data, m usually does not equal n, so that we have used the descriptor "rectangular" for those matrices. The reader who is familiar with the theoretical history of social network analysis during the 1950s and 1960s may be disturbed by the manifest indifference of CONCOR toward the distinction between rectangular and "true network" data, the latter being data that are formally equivalent to a directed graph (Berge, 1962):

In the history referred to, investigators with a structuralist bias frequently tried to distinguish network analyses from conventional contingency table methods associated with attribute cross-classifications (see related discussions in White, 1970, for the case of mobility data). Formally, of course, contingency tables are a case of rectangular data in the sense we have specified, so that any attempt to preserve this distinction in the CONCOR formalism is lost as soon as the algorithm's applicability to the rectangular case is recognized. However, on the basis of better empirical understanding now available (and in part made possible by the development of blockmodels), the uniform handling of the square and rectangular cases actually appears as an asset of the procedure. As has progressively become clearer, what the early theorists actually found objectionable was not the concept of attribute-by-attribute or item-by-attribute classification per se, but rather the almost invariable association of such classifications with predigested aggregations of both columns and rows into a few a priori categories (thus rows might be ethnicities and columns political party affiliations). By contrast, whenever CONCOR is applied to rectangular data, the same principle already made clear for square matrix cases continues to apply without change: the data are allowed to determine their own most appropriate aggregation (namely, the blocks that emerge), and congruence between the obtained blockings and various other categorical groupings is enforced by the data rather than imposed upon them (compare emphases in Coombs, 1964, and Coombs, Coombs, and McClelland, 1975). An example developed in Breiger, Boorman, and Arabie (1975) is based on Levine's study (1972) of directorship interlocks in American industry, where the primary data are recorded in a rectangular matrix with the rows indexing corporations and the columns index-ing banks (see also Breiger, Boorman, and Arabie, 1975, Figs. 4–6).

Note that the idea of a stacked matrix where each of the k stories is an $n \times n$ matrix on the same set can be generalized to rectangular data. Specifically, one could start with k matrices each of dimension $m \times n$, recording relations between a fixed row set of size m and column set of size n. These k matrices could then be stacked in two alternative ways to produce two separate stacked matrices of dimensions $km \times n$ and $m \times kn$, respectively. Applying CONCOR to columns and to rows respectively, one would obtain blockings of both index sets incorporating data from the full three-dimensional input array. Such a generalization of the stacking procedure has not yet been explored empirically, but there will normally be no difficulty with the convergence, since a square matrix will be obtained in each case after just one iteration.

An aspect of data analysis rarely mentioned in discussions of clustering algorithms is the problem of missing entries (but see Hartigan, 1975, p. 267), although it seems probable that capabilities for handling missing data could be developed for several of the more commonly used algorithms. The earlier procedure for excluding diagonal entries could be generalized to handle this problem in the case of CONCOR. The robustness considerations this generalization raises remain to be analyzed (for promising results along related lines, see Devlin, Gnanadesikan, and Kettenring, 1975). An alternative strategy for missing values in CONCOR applications would be to supply zeros for the missing data entries. The rationale is that the resulting analysis will tend to be a conservative one, in the sense that *if* interpretable blockmodel structure exists, this structure will proba-bly be revealed by the default of supplying zeros—whereas supplying ones may mask blockmodel structure that is objectively present by introducing impurities into zeroblocks.

Prospects

Methodology. Because it is all too simple to obtain a prolifera-tion of blockmodels, many problems of evaluation may be expected to arise as the area advances. Far too little is yet understood about the senses in which one blockmodel is valid and another is not. We have already touched briefly on one aspect of evaluation, the statistical assessment of blockmodel fit relative to some statistical null hypothesis. One important further problem, also bearing on evaluation issues, is that of comparing different blockmodels, whether based on the same data or on entirely different populations. Since the ordering of blocks in a blockmodel is arbitrary, comparison questions are not immediately amenable to direct Hamming or other metric comparisons between matrices (Boorman, 1970; Boorman and Arabie, 1972).

One approach to these problems has been proposed by Boorman and White (1976) and has its origins in formal ideas on the generation of compound roles in complex social structures. Any blockmodel may be used to generate a semigroup of Boolean matrices, which may be substantively interpreted as an accounting of all possible compound roles implied by primitive (generator) roles in the data (thus: my friends [**P**]; my friends' friends [$\mathbf{P}^2$]; my enemy's friends [**NP**]; and so forth).

Formally, define:

Definition: Let **B** be an arbitrary $m \times m \times k$ binary array, for example, as determined by a blockmodel. The *Boolean semigroup* SR (**B**) is the set of all Boolean relations that may be obtained by multiplying finite products of the *k generator matrices* constituting **B**, which may be separately designated $\mathbf{G}_1$, $\mathbf{G}_2$, . . . , $\mathbf{G}_k$.

Obviously the classical prototype of this construction is transitive closure. If ordinary arithmetic matrix multiplication is used (as in Luce, 1950), the semigroup obtained will be infinite in almost all cases. The finiteness of SR (**B**) obtained by Boolean multiplication follows from the fact that there are only 2^{m^2} distinct binary relations on a set of size m. In practice, the computability of SR (**B**) depends on the semigroup having a size that is much smaller than 2^{m^2}. In the empirical cases analyzed by Boorman and White (1976), the obtained SR (**B**) seldom had sizes larger than 30, even when m was 5 (5-block models of the Sampson, 1969, data); see also Boorman (1977) for analytic calculations in the case of a regular tree. Recent work by Kim and Roush (1978), adapting methods of Erdös and Rényi (1968), shows promise as a techique for more refined estimates of the upper bound on the size of such semigroups. The comparison of blockmodels may now proceed by means of the purely algebraic analysis of relations between the associated Boolean semigroups. Given two arbitrary binary arrays, B_1 of dimensions $n \times n \times k$ and B_2 of dimensions $p \times p \times k$, assume only enough outside knowledge of the kind of information coded in the generator matrices to establish a fixed 1-1 correspondence between generators across the two arrays. Without loss of generality, use the same symbols $G_1, G_2, \ldots, G_k$ to denote the matched generators in either case (thus G_1 might denote alliance, G_2 antagonism, G_3 information transfer, and so forth). Then both SR (B_1) and SR (B_2) may be interpreted as homomorphic reductions of the same free semigroup FS $(G_1, G_2, \ldots, G_k)$ over the generator symbols G_i (Clifford and Preston, 1961; Crowell and Fox, 1963). Using one of the basic theorems of universal algebra (Cohn, 1965), the quotients of FS $(G_1, G_2, \ldots, G_k))$ will be endowed with a natural lattice structure defined by homomorphic reductions (that is, congruence relations on FS $(G_1, G_2, \ldots, G_k))$. Then the natural *algebraic* measure of similarity between B_1 and B_2 will be the algebra that is the joint homomorphic reduction of SR (B_1) and SR (B_2) in this lattice, and is thus the largest possible semigroup which is a common reduction of SR (B_1) and SR (B_2); see Boorman and Arabie (1980). If numerical similarity measures are desired, as will be the case for most applications, a variety of natural measures are suggested by the same construction, such as those obtained by adding the entropies of the partitions of SR (B_1), SR (B_2) that are induced by the inverses of the homomorphisms, τ, θ

where JNT (B_1, B_2) is the joint reduction (see Boorman and White, 1976, p. 1422 for details).

The power of the joint reduction algebra JNT (B_1, B_2) as a basis for comparisons between the blockmodels B_1, B_2 is evidenced by the fact that the algebraic procedure may be employed regardless of whether B_1 and B_2 describe the same population, or even possess similar numbers of blocks. Thus the technique affords the possibility of a highly general taxonomy of concrete social structures.

Two independent algorithms for calculating the joint homomorphic reduction of two finitely presented semigroups on the same generator symbols have been developed in APL by Harrison White (JNTHOM algorithm) and by François Lorrain (MASTERGLB algorithm).

Substantive Theory. From a substantive standpoint, the essence of a blockmodel consists in its complete accounting of social relations within a system of positions, developed simultaneously for multiple types of tie. Classical theory within either social psychology or sociology has no close substitutes for this level of detail; conventional descriptions of complex social structures normally pay attention only to a highly limited fraction of the total number of relations actually present. Ambiguity is thereby generated, and attempts at summary become controversial. Only too frequently, a complicated theoretical analysis is rendered unworkable solely because "hierarchy" or "servitude" or some similar concept denotes distinct kinds of social structure in two different settings (compare Marc Bloch's assault, 1960, on the comparison of land tenure systems in France and England in the Middle Ages). By furnishing a systematic language for relational description, it is to be hoped that blockmodels may provide a substantial cure for some traditional ills of social structural analysis.

Another aspect of blockmodeling is suggested by typical blockmodel results. Such propositions (thus: Block 1 is the ally of Block 2, but Block 1 is internally a clique, whereas Block 2 is not) have a transparent quality, in the sense that the reader may refer to the data and observe directly whether the proposition finds support (see Tables 1 and 3 of Breiger, Boorman, and Arabie). This essential simplicity of blockmodel hypotheses stands in marked contrast to the results obtained by most data analysis procedures. When applied in sociology and social psychology, such procedures invariably focus attention on relationships among highly derived measures—factor loadings, partial and multiple correlations, structural equation coefficients. Once such a level of aggregation has been achieved, it usually proves impossible to unravel, and the only feasible course is the further manipulation of aggregate quantities.[4] By contrast, blockmodels are always able to recover the reference standpoint of the individual, which may be evaluated against the communal viewpoint assigned by the blockmodel to this actor's block. To relinquish this standpoint is to concede the greater part of the small advantage that mathematical sociology and social psychology now possess over the far more imposing edifice of mathematical economics: namely, the promise of the former fields to proceed with analyses of concrete populations so alien to the models of the latter area (compare observations in Koopmans, 1957).

It is appropriate to conclude with the number of substantive challenges relevant to the future of mathematical analysis in the area. Significantly, each involves issues of data as well as of formal theory.

First, there is the problem of moving beyond affect ties. Subjectively important as these may be in determining the "mood" of a social structure, there is overwhelming evidence, much of it derived from economic analysis, that most social structure persists regardless of how the actors feel about it or about each other. Other types of tie provide the sinews of everyday functioning: contact, alliance, command, legal liability, and debt are just a few of the possible examples. On the other hand, no one has ever reported complete networks for most of these examples, perhaps largely because such networks will tend naturally to outbreed (so that it is hard to restrict data collection to a small population), and also because tie definitions are hard to establish consistently across even moderately far-flung populations.

Second, there is the problem of relational contrast. As we have already seen, the most interesting blockmodel interpretations are those built around contrasting images whose internal patterns differ radically. Balance theory is the classical illustration (**P** versus **N**), but by no means the only case: other examples are found in Breiger's study (1976), already discussed, as well as in Boorman's combinatorial model (1975), which pits strong against weak ties. Nevertheless, the majority of sociometric studies completely fail to generate contrast (for example, forced-choice studies recording only top choices by each individual). Moreover, contrast is not always easy to reveal in a nonexperimental setting. White (1961), a study of management in a small company, encountered major difficulties in extracting negative sentiment choices from managers, most of whom presumably feared the consequences of revealed factional strife to their own positions.

In the future, attention should be directed to such concealment and masking effects, as well as to the general problem of network definition.

Finally, there is the problem of macroscopic social structure. Even the scarce existing work on large-scale networks (disproportionately owing to historians: for example, Badian, 1958) leads to fresh vantages on some of the most promising areas in social science—among others, the structure of elite access and recruitment (White, 1970), small worlds and their manipulation (Fienberg and Lee, 1975; Shotland, 1976), and grey areas between formal and informal organization (Williamson, 1975). Even the form of the proper questions to be asked remains unknown or is only vaguely guessed, perhaps because the global pattern of a large, open network is not directly apparent to any one participant. Instead, the investigator is first thrown back on the supporting culture and to the prevailing wisdom as to the attributes of various positions and their interrelations. Social scientists have generally assigned far more than due credit to such wisdom. Even when common knowledge about the structure and functioning of the system is tolerably correct, unperceived regularities will exist, if only because each participant is consigned to a single highly local vantage point. Blockmodels should furnish a promising means for new discoveries of global pattern and invariance.

Notes

1. For data that can be seriated along a continuum, the minimum spanning path will be a minimum spanning tree.

2. In Breiger, Boorman, and Arabie (1975, pp. 349, 357) single-link clustering was applied to the first correlation matrix, M_1, for the Sampson (1969) data and for the Roethlisberger and Dickson (1939) data. Particularly for the former data set, there was little evidence of chaining. Subsequent unpublished work that also used single-link on other sociomatrices has tended to produce much more chaining.

3. A potentially useful significance test for bimodality has been devised by J. B. Kruskal (see Giacomelli, Wiener, Kruskal, Pomeranz, and Loud, 1971).

4. This facet of blockmodels may help explain why similar approaches appear independently throughout social science literature. For a recent example in styles of French architecture, see Maroy and Peneau (1977), who (p. 511) used hierarchical clustering and a goodness-of-fit measure based on chi square to determine the row/column permutations for their data matrices. Explicit details were not given. Still another example, brought to our attention by Persi Diaconis, is the work of Bertin (1973).

Blockmodels and Spatial Representations of Group Structure: Some Comparisons

■■■■■■■■■■■■■■■■■■■■■■■■

James G. Ennis

Demonstrating the systemic properties of groups has been a persistent concern of sociologists. We have sought social structure in the fundamental relations that underlie observed reality and have sought to display the pattern of these relations in interpretable and economical form.

Two approaches to these tasks will be reviewed below. The first uses underlying dimensions as axes for geometric representation

Note: I am grateful to Robert F. Bales, Daniel Perschonok, and the members of the group studied for providing the data on which this work is based, and to Ronald L. Breiger, Charles M. Judd, and Steven D. Penrod for specific comments and criticisms that led to notable improvements in the paper. This research was supported by a grant from the Department of Psychology and Social Relations, Harvard University, and by NSF grant SOC 76-24394.

of social structure. The second uses algebraic methods to aggregate individuals and to examine the relations among these aggregates across a range of social ties. The complementarity of these approaches will be demonstrated by the analysis of an illustrative small group.

Spatial Representations of Group Structure

The recurrent metaphor of a "social space" (McFarland and Brown, 1973) represents the dissimilarity between two objects by the distance that separates them in a theoretical space (usually Euclidean). Because n objects may require $n - 1$ dimensions to show their relations, we desire some method for selecting a more compact or theoretically interesting set of dimensions.

Factor analysis (Harman, 1967) and multidimensional scaling (Shepard, 1962; Shepard, Romney, and Nerlove, 1972; Kruskal, 1964a; Kruskal and Wish, 1978; Carroll and Arabie, 1980) have been used to generate spatial configurations and to isolate underlying dimensions for analysis (for factor analysis, see Bock and Husain, 1952; MacRae, 1960; Wright and Evitts, 1961; Schwartz, 1976; Breiger, in press; for multidimensional scaling, see Jones and Young, 1972; Young, 1978; Forgas, 1978; Laumann and Pappi, 1976). The details of these procedures are well known and will not be discussed here. Rather, I turn to some applications of these methods to small group structure.

Dimensions derived from factor analysis or multidimensional scaling for a given group may not be optimal for other groups of the same kind. Robert F. Bales and his colleagues have sought to develop and refine a set of dimensions that will be general to a range of groups (Bales, 1970; Bales, Cohen, and Williamson, 1979). Their project is a direct outgrowth of Bales's earlier specification of analytic categories for the study of interaction (Bales, 1950, 1968; see also Strodtbeck, 1973). Bales's SYMLOG system (**SY**stematic **M**ultiple **L**evel **O**bservation of **G**roups) consists of three dimensions used for observation and theorizing. The first, Upward-Downward (U-D), refers to the relative dominance (U) or submissiveness (D) of group members. The second, Positive-Negative (P-N), corresponds to friendly versus hostile orientations. The Forward-Backward dimension (F-B) taps a continuum from task-oriented, instrumental behavior (F) to emotional, expressive behavior (B).

The dimensions were based upon a series of R factor analyses of personality test data, value statements, observations of interpersonal behavior, and ratings of self and interpersonal perceptions (Bales, 1970, p. 381; Couch, 1960). They are closely related to dimensions found by others in different settings (Osgood, Suci, and Tannenbaum, 1957; Mehrabian, 1980). In their study of perceived typical role relations, Wish, Deutsch, and Kaplan (1976) found dimensions that are virtually identical to Bales's, along with a fourth dimension (intensity of relation).

Having derived the dimensions, Bales imposes them as research categories for the observation and analysis of new groups. He and his colleagues (Bales, Cohen, and Williamson, 1979) have also developed and regularly employ a system of scoring interaction, act by act, and an overall rating system of persons. If observers score group behavior or group members rate one another, the results can be used to locate persons in the space defined by the three dimensions. For example, an "authoritarian boss" would be located in the UNF (dominant, hostile, task-oriented) part of the space; a "cooperative worker" would be rated PF; and so on. The method's generality is one of its greatest virtues. The SYMLOG space can be used to depict the structure of a group at a given point in time, or the development of individual and group behavior over time. As a general analytical system, SYMLOG is equally appropriate to persons, value statements, institutions, and other social objects (Bales, Cohen, and Williamson, 1979).

The SYMLOG rating data form three square nonsymmetrical matrices, whose cell values consist of group members' ratings of their own and each other's behavior on each dimension (U-D, P-N, F-B). Because these ratings are descriptive rather than evaluative, they pertain directly to the attributes or behaviors of the person rated, and only indirectly to relations between individuals. Thus, Bales conventionally averages across raters to derive a mean score for each person on each dimension.

This procedure yields a social distance that is somewhat different from the traditional conception in sociology (McFarland and Brown, 1973). In the SYMLOG space, proximity reflects the common behavioral styles of two individuals, rather than any close relations that may exist between them directly. SYMLOG therefore defines a property space (Barton, 1955), rather than a relation space. For example, persons who regularly engage in fistfights might be placed together in the *UNB* part of the space, but there is no implication that these individuals fight with one another or even with the same third parties. Thus grouping on the basis of shared attributes leaves open the question of relational structure. Conversely, scaling on the basis of direct relations does not address the question of shared attributes (Breiger and Ennis, 1979).

Algebraic Representation of Group Structure: Blockmodels

The blockmodel approach to social structure (White, Boorman, and Breiger, 1976; Breiger, Boorman, and Arabie, 1975; Boorman and White, 1976; Arabie, Boorman, and Levitt, 1978; Breiger, 1979; see also the preceding chapter) foregoes the spatial representation of structure. Rather, it partitions individuals into subgroups (blocks) and examines the pattern of relations among these subgroups (blockmodel images) across a number of different social relationships. White, Boorman, and Breiger argue: "First, social structure is regularities in the pattern of relations among concrete entities; it is *not* a harmony among abstract norms and values or a classification of concrete entities by their attributes. Second, to describe social structure we must aggregate these regularities in a fashion consistent with their inherent nature as networks . . . sociological analysis needs explicit models of the structure in observed populations, *not* measures or statistical indices of deviations from convenient ideal structure" (pp. 733–734, 737). The data for blockmodel analysis are measures of the specific social ties (such as like, dislike, business association, communicates with, patron-client, and so on) among members of a population, represented in matrix form. These may be binary, ordered choices, or integer ratings of one's relation to all group members. These ties form the links of networks; rearranging these ties, by permuting the rows and columns of the original matrices, reveals a pattern of relations among blocks. Thus blocks define positions and the relations among blocks define roles (Boorman and White, 1976).

Members are blocked together according to their social ties with the same third parties, across multiple, simultaneous networks. Blockmodel analysis thus uses the principle of consistency, rather than the sociometric idea of connectivity (see Breiger, Boorman, and Arabie, 1975, p. 333). In contrast to sociometric or graph theoretic approaches, individuals are classed together not on the basis of their mutual ties, although these may exist, nor on the basis of their accessibility through paths of varying lengths but rather on the basis of their sending and receiving ties in a homogeneous fashion.

Blockmodel analysts emphasize the significance of multiple relations for the determination of overall structure because this multiplicity is inherent in human interaction. In addition, as Nadel (1957) argues, structural studies must consider how different types of relationships define networks and how these networks interrelate.

Following the aggregation of individuals into blocks, blockmodel images are formed.* These are reduced-form, square, binary matrices that report in stylized fashion the presence or absence of ties between blocks. With n blocks, the blockmodel image for a given type of tie will be of size $n \times n$, the (i, j)-th entry representing the presence or absence of that tie from Block i to Block j. These blockmodel images operationalize the network structure of a given type of tie among blocks.

The most significant difference between blockmodel analysis and spatial representations is the blockmodel analyst's persistent return to the original relational data for interpretation. It is the network structure of the ties themselves, rather than some composite distance measure, that is interpreted. The issue of "role structure," or relations among types of ties, will not be dealt with here, though the question is addressed by Boorman and White (1976). The present chapter will emphasize the direct interpretability of the blockmodel images.

When full ratings are available, cell means are calculated by block. If there are s_i individuals in block i and s_j individuals in block j, sum entries in that submatrix of the original sociomatrix defined by the s_i rows and the s_j columns in question. Calling this sum n_{ij}, entry $[i, j]$ in a matrix (for example, Table 3) is defined by $n_{ij}/s_i \times s_j$. Since the diagonal entries in the original sociomatrix have no substantive meaning, they are excluded from the computation of n_{ij}. When the data represent choices among the members of a block (when $i = j$), means are computed by $n_{ij}/s_i (s_i - 1)$. If the data consist of binary choices ("best friend") or ranked choices ("three closest associates"), one can proceed similarly. These block means are subsequently binarized according to a given criterion to compose a blockmodel image.

Illustrative Analysis: A Small Group

The above methods offer differing analytical strengths; their results can be counterposed to mutually reinforce and illuminate one another. The complementarity of these techniques is demonstrated below with reference to a single empirical case of a type well known in the literature: the self-analytical groups conducted by Bales and his colleagues (Slater, 1966; Bales, 1970). Its aim was to provide, through concrete observation and instruction in the SYMLOG system, insights into individual personalities, group dynamics, and their interrelations (Bales, 1970, p. 512; Bales, Cohen, and Williamson, 1979). The format was an open discussion of topics initiated by the members, alternating with analysis of the interpersonal dynamics of a given session.

The group met over a period of seven weeks, three times a week, for one and one-half hours each session. It consisted of 12 members and a leader, a professor of psychology. During the fourth and seventh weeks, members rated one another on the SYMLOG Adjective Rating Form (Bales, Cohen, and Williamson, 1979, Appendix C). This instrument yields a rating by each person for each participant, including himself or herself, on each of three dimensions, based on the private recollection of behavior across the history of the group. In addition, each member completed sociometric rating scales (0–7) of liking, disliking, and perceived similarity of other to self, for each other member (see Bales, pp. 413, 432; Breiger and Ennis, 1979: note 7). The resulting matrices are of size 13 × 13. Finally, each member except the leader rated the overall similarity of all possible pairs of members, thus producing a symmetrical 13 × 13 matrix for each rater.* These will be referred to as the *pairwise similarity ratings* in order to distinguish them from the *other-self similarity ratings.*

Results

To aggregate group members into blocks, the divisive hierarchical clustering algorithm CONCOR (Breiger, Boorman, and Ara-

---

The wording of the pairwise similarity question was as follows: "Overall, to what extent do you feel that each of the following pairs of group members are similar or dissimilar? Please take into account any aspect of their behavior or personality that you find significant. Rate each pair on a scale of from one to seven, where 1 = very dissimilar, and 7 = very similar." The leader did not complete the pairwise similarity ratings.

bie, 1975; Schwartz, 1976; Arabie, Boorman, and Levitt, 1978; Arabie and Boorman, this volume) was applied to the matrices for like, dislike, similarity, and their transposes, collected during the final week. The transposes of the sociomatrices were included so that the CONCOR results would reflect the pattern of sent as well as received choices. The 13 members, denoted by lower case letters, were divided into blocks of nine and four:

$$(b \ d \ f \ g \ h \ i \ j \ k \ l) \quad (a \ c \ e \ m)$$

Reapplication of CONCOR to the larger block led to the following partition:

$$(d \ h \ i \ j \ k \ l) \quad (b \ f \ g)$$

which leads to the overall partition

$$(d \ h \ i \ j \ k \ l) \quad (b \ f \ g) \quad (a \ c \ e \ m)$$

These blocks are numbered sequentially so that, for example, $(b \ f \ g)$ = Block 2.

The number of blocks derived is arbitrary. At one extreme, a group may be a single block; at the other extreme, each individual may be a block. The challenge is to choose a level of refinement that is substantively interpretable. Small changes in the number of blocks produce small and internally consistent changes in the resulting models of given networks (Breiger, 1976, p. 121; Arabie, Boorman, and Levitt, 1978, p. 37).

In order to compare the blockmodel analysis to multidimensional scaling of the same data, the first correlation matrix M_1 (resulting from the correlation of the vectors of participants' sent and received choices from the like, dislike, and similarity matrices) (Breiger, Boorman, and Arabie, 1975, p. 334) was used as input to the nonmetric multidimensional scaling program KYST (Kruskal, Young, and Seery, 1973; Kruskal and Wish, 1978). The resulting solution in two dimensions appears in Figure 1.

There is good agreement between the multidimensional scaling and the CONCOR blocking of these data, since the clusters are relatively tight in the dimensional space. While scaling illuminates the position and role of individuals, social psychological interpretation of the differences among blocks requires investigation of the typical differences among the blocks with regard to their attributes

Figure 1. KYST Two-Dimensional Solution, Stress = .103, Formula 1

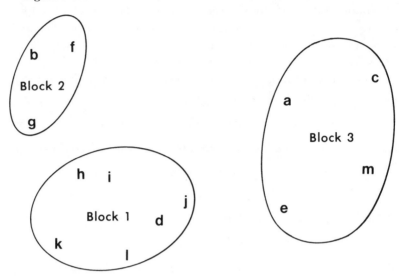

Note: Blocks defined by CONCOR are circled.

Table 1. One-Way ANOVA, Block by Mean SYMLOG Position

	Block Means		
Block	UD	PN	FB
1	1.67	10.0	0.67
2	−0.33	6.0	−1.33
3	1.75	3.25	−1.50
F	0.61	9.64	0.63
P	n.s.	< .01	n.s.

Note: df = (2, 10) for each column.

or patterns of sociometric choice. One-way analysis of variance in the SYMLOG ratings (see Table 1) reveals a statistically significant differentiation along the *P-N* (affective) dimension, with Block 1 rated most positive, Block 2 intermediate, and Block 3 most nearly negative.

It is uncommon for a person to receive an overall negative rating. This positive bias in the SYMLOG ratings means that some sort of recentering on the *P-N* dimension may be appropriate for analytical purposes. That is, the members who are rated closer to *N*, even though they are technically rated positive, may be perceived essentially negatively by other members of the group. For a theory of group roles, relative position may be as important as absolute position.

The characterizations in Table 1 are in close agreement with observations of this group made by the author. The members of Block 1 were most friendly and outgoing, and generally set the topic and tone of the discussion. They may be thought of as *leaders*.

Individuals in the second block tended to be more withdrawn and generally remained silent unless directly questioned. Although they would sometimes express satisfaction with the progress of group discussion, they would seldom take part in it. These persons were primarily *onlookers*.

Person *g* was an exception to this pattern. In the early weeks of the group, she was quite outspoken and directive, and made explicit attempts to channel the group discussion in a work-oriented (*F*) direction. Approximately halfway through the group's life, however, she came under heavy criticism from other members for being too controlling. She subsequently became rather withdrawn and sullen and spoke mostly of her resentment about this rejection. Although she later became an "onlooker," CONCOR places her in the leaders' rather than the onlookers' block at midterm. Finally, *g*'s position is illuminated by the multidimensional scaling plot in Figure 1, where she appears as that member of Block 2 closest to Block 1.

The third block most frequently engaged in disagreements and arguments, especially concerning leadership and power in the group. They attacked the leader for his nondirective style and criticized the members of Block 2 for "not contributing to the group." Person *m* was styled "the anti-leader" in group discussion, and the members of Block 3 were referred to as a "revolutionary coalition" by the other group participants. I will refer to these persons as *rebels*.

These descriptions are suggestive, but insufficient in themselves to reveal an overall pattern of relations among blocks. That is, characterizations of member attributes say little about the pattern of concrete relations among subgroups. A blockmodel based on the specific networks of relations addresses this issue.

Cell means by block for the permuted sociomatrices are presented in Table 2. These means indicate the average relation of members of one block to members of another block on a given scale. To form binary blockmodel images, I code a cell as 1 if its value is greater than its corresponding row mean; otherwise, I code it as a zero. In effect, I am coding the presence of a tie from Block i to Block j if the magnitude of the tie sent by i is greater than its average sent magnitude for that type of tie. This procedure (see Breiger and Ennis, 1979) emphasizes the relative distribution of each block's choices. For ease of visualization, the table also includes graphical representations of the binary blockmodel images, equivalent to the matrix representations.

These images show that the blocks defined above are also cliques, that is, subgroups within which positive relations predominate and between which asymmetrical or mutually negative relations predominate (Davis, 1970, p. 843). Each is marked by a reflexive liking and similarity tie (the diagonal values for similarity are the

Table 2. Three-Block Model of Group: Block Means Resulting from Application of Partition P3 to Like, Dislike, and Similarity Matrices

LIKE			$\overline{X}$	LIKE > ROW MEAN	
5.80	3.94	3.67	4.62	1 0 0	
6.72	6.00	2.92	5.33	1 1 0	
4.87	1.25	5.83	4.20	1 0 1	
5.72	3.38	4.02	4.66		
DISLIKE			$\overline{X}$	DISLIKE > ROW MEAN	
1.33	2.22	3.25	2.19	0 1 1	
0.06	0.17	2.67	0.95	0 0 1	
1.63	4.75	0.83	2.21	0 1 0	
1.11	2.27	2.50	1.91		
SIMILARITY			$\overline{X}$	SIMILARITY > ROW MEAN	
4.93	3.44	3.04	3.93	1 0 0	
4.50	5.00	1.83	3.69	1 1 0	
2.87	1.92	3.33	2.75	1 0 1	
4.14	3.19	2.81	3.51		

highest in each row) and the absence of a reflexive dislike tie. This finding is not tautological, since CONCOR aggregates persons on the basis of choices made by and about all other members, not simply on the basis of mutual ties.

We now turn to the relations among blocks. Block 1 receives like and similarity ties from each block, but does not reciprocate these ties. Members of Block 1 dislike Blocks 2 and 3, who are in turn mutually antagonistic. This asymmetry of choice suggests a social hierarchy in which Block 1 is superordinate and Blocks 2 and 3 subordinate. This pattern of cliques within an overall hierarchy is exactly that predicted by Homans (1950) and Davis (1970). The superordinate position of Block 1 is supported by SYMLOG ratings, in which Block 1 was rated highest on the *P-N* dimension and relatively upward. Bales, Cohen, and Williamson (1979, Part 5) describe the *UP* type as popular and as favoring social success.

Further insight into the structure of the group can be gained from principal components analysis. Schwartz (1976) conjectures that the behavior of CONCOR in partitioning individuals into blocks resembles the application of a sign criterion to the first eigenvector of a suitably treated first correlation matrix M_1 (but see Arabie, Boorman, and Levitt, 1978). When the data are analyzed according to a variant of the procedure Schwartz advocates, the results are as expected (see Figure 2). The first eigenvector separates Block 3 from Blocks 1 and 2, as did the first CONCOR split, and the second eigenvector separates Block 1 from Block 2, as did the second CONCOR split. Again, the block members are tightly clustered. The overall correspondence with the results of multidimensional scaling is striking.

The plot also illuminates the positions of individuals. Person *g*, for example, is nearly as close to the members of Block 1 (leaders) as she is to Block 2 (onlookers). Recall that *g* made attempts at leadership during the first half of the sessions but was rebuffed. Person *c*, on the other hand, is more distant from the others, having received the highest dislike rating of any group member. The members of Block 1 form a small, compact cluster, suggesting a unified leadership group.

When the SYMLOG dimensions are regressed on the eigenvectors (Rabinowitz, 1975, pp. 374–378; Kruskal and Wish, 1978), the standardized regression weights are used to locate the SYMLOG

Figure 2. Eigenvector Plot, with SYMLOG Dimensions Superimposed

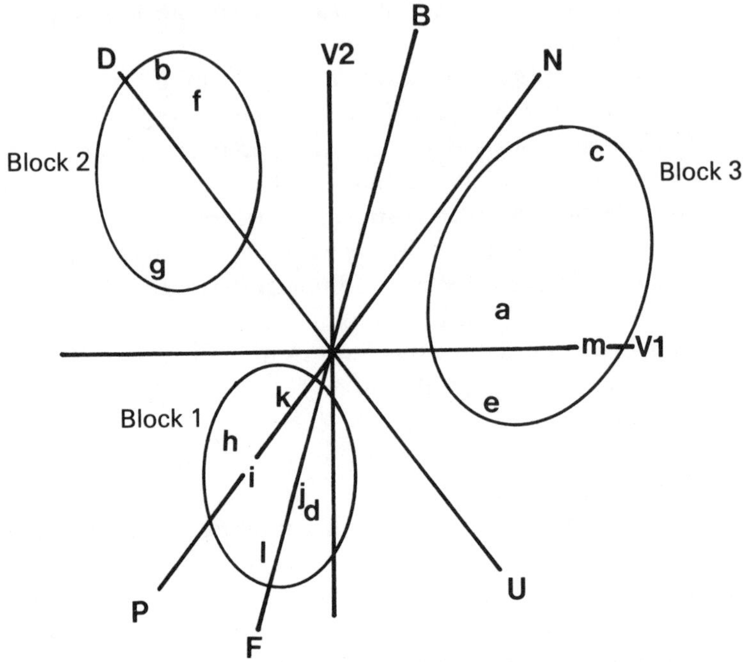

Note: Blocks defined by CONCOR are circled.

dimensions in the eigenvector space, as in Figure 2 and Table 3. The R^2 values for *UD* and *FB* are not large, but the value for *PN* is substantial. The *PN* dimension will be most adequately represented in the eigenvector space, the *FB* dimension next, and the *UD* dimension least adequately. This indicates that the sociometric judgments, like, dislike, and similarity of others to self, are most heavily influenced by differences in positive and negative affect, and least influenced by interpersonal dominance in the group.

Although the SYMLOG dimensions do not follow the eigenvectors, their superimposition nevertheless yields interpretable results. Block 1 is located near the *P* and *F* poles, and slightly toward *U*. Bales (1970, p. 209) characterizes the *UPF* type in terms of "leadership." Block 2 is toward the *D* pole, and Block 3 is high on both *N* and *B*. These placements are in accord with the substantive descriptions

Table 3. Beta Weights from Multiple Regression of SYMLOG Dimensions
on Eigenvectors of the First Correlation Matrix M_1

	EV1	EV2	EV3	R^2
UD	.27	−.37	.23	.26
PN	−.46	−.59	.21	.61
FB	−.18	−.58	−.28	.44

above. Finally, person c, who was most disliked overall, is placed closest to the N pole.

Up to this point, the blockmodel and the scalings have been based on sociometric data. The blocks identified have members who share behavioral attributes as well as position in a relational space. The pairwise similarity ratings are now used to show how group members themselves perceive the structure of the group in terms of similarity. The sociometric ratings differ from these data in that they tend to be egocentric; that is, judgments of liking, disliking, and other-self similarity use ego as a reference point. The pairwise similarity ratings are closer to affective neutrality.

The pairwise similarity matrices were combined into a 12 × 13 × 13 array and were submitted to the metric multidimensional scaling routine INDSCAL (Carroll and Chang, 1970; Carroll, 1972). INDSCAL not only produces a representation of rated objects in an n = dimensional space, but also reports the relative weighting of dimensions by each participant who makes judgments of similarity. Dimensions derived from INDSCAL may not be rotated and frequently have been found to be directly interpretable (Wish, Deutsch, and Kaplan, 1976; Kruskal and Wish, 1978).

The three-dimensional INDSCAL solution accounts for 52 percent of the variance in the similarity ratings. The first two of these dimensions, presented in Figure 3, largely retain the communality of block position, and the configuration is roughly similar to the KYST and principal components results. Person g is outside Block 2 and is located immediately adjacent to Block 1. Recall that g was assigned to Block 1 at midterm, and that she became much more like the members of Block 2 in the final weeks of the group. Evidently, this change was not so salient to the members of the group in their similarity ratings as it was in their sociometric choices. In view of the independence of

Figure 3. Dimensions of a Three-Dimensional INDSCAL Solution

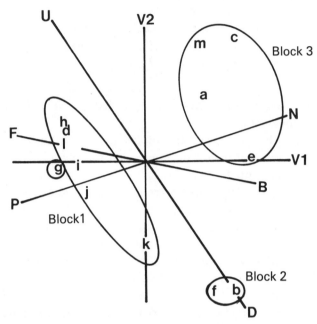

Note: SYMLOG dimensions are superimposed. Blocks defined by CONCOR are circled. SYMLOG dimensions are located with reference to results from multiple regression.

the sociometric and similarity data, however, the convergence of these results is striking.

The superimposition of the SYMLOG dimensions on the INDSCAL space after multiple regression allows further interpretation of the similarity space. R^2 values are larger for the regression of the SYMLOG dimensions on the INDSCAL dimensions than for the eigenvectors of M_1 (see Tables 3 and 4). This indicates that the SYMLOG dimensions correspond more closely to the similarity space than to the sociometric space. This is not surprising, since both the SYMLOG and pairwise similarity ratings are affectively neutral, while the sociometric ratings are both affective and egocentric. In similarity space, group members see Blocks 1 and 3 as differing on a *PF-NB* continuum, whereas Block 2 is strikingly closer to *D*. These

Table 4. Beta Weights from Multiple Regression of SYMLOG Dimensions on Dimensions Derived from INDSCAL of Pairwise Similarity Matrix

	IV1	IV2	IV3	R^2
UD	−.48	.67	−.33	.75
PN	−.75	−.28	−.25	.62
FB	−.35	.07	.81	.91

findings support the results of Table 1, but here they demonstrate the psychological reality of the SYMLOG dimensions. The correspondence of the SYMLOG and INDSCAL results indicates that group members perceive the similarity of persons in terms of the SYMLOG dimensions.

Finally, there is some evidence that blocks tend to weight the dimensions differently when their members judge similarity. Block 1 tends to emphasize Dimension 1 more heavily than Dimension 2, while for Blocks 2 and 3, the opposite pattern holds. Although a one-way analysis of variance is marginally insignificant ($F = 2.97$, $df = 2,9$, $p > .1$) due to small sample size, a measure-of-effect size (Cohen's $f = .87$; Cohen, 1969) is large. This suggests that blocks, in addition to being viewed as different, view similarity in different terms.

Discussion: Spatial Representations and Blockmodels

In choosing between these methods, one must judge the adequacy of metric distance to represent social distance, or the relational phenomena recorded in the original data. The main weakness of spatial representations is that they do not record meaningful and sociologically significant asymmetries in the data. In this case, the analogy to physical distance may be misleading. An essential property of metric space is symmetry (McFarland and Brown, 1973), while it is the asymmetries of power, status, affect, and so on that distinguish social distance (Levine, Carter, and Gorman, 1976, p. 839). Insofar as relational measures tap these sociological variables, spatial representations will be to some degree inadequate (but see Jones, in press).

For blockmodel analysis, the chief weakness of spatial representations is that the network structure of the original data is not recoverable. Conversely, a major advantage of blockmodel analysis is its ability to demonstrate the specific, concrete relations among blocks, across multiple criteria. Blockmodel analysts return to the original, nonsymmetrical matrices, preserving asymmetries for analysis.

However, detail is sacrificed in the reduction of the original relational matrices to binary form, and in the discrete assignment of individuals to blocks. It is here that spatial representations provide a useful complement to blockmodels, by demonstrating the marginality or centrality of given individuals to given blocks, and the overall spatial configuration of blocks. Nevertheless, the loss of detail in blockmodel representations is partially offset by the demonstration of an overall pattern of cliques within hierarchy, a pattern that would not have been discernible from the spatial representations alone. The key to this result lies in defining a new level of analysis, relations among aggregates, and in seeking regularities at this level.

These methods have different analytical strengths, which can best be seen as complementary. The results discussed in this paper would not be discoverable by either method alone; indeed, the most interesting findings come directly from a combination of approaches.

With regard to the field of small group research, several lines of future investigation seem fruitful. First, blockmodeling could be extended to a wider sample of self-analytical groups, with a view toward discovering typical structures. Second, behavioral data, rather than sociometric or similarity ratings, could be used as the basis of analysis. Third, the development of structure could be traced across time. Finally, if a typical structure can be demonstrated for this type of group, it can be used as a frame within which to locate more microscopic analyses of social interaction. Blockmodels provide a convenient operational context within which the structural and interactional dimensions of social groups can be integrated.

On The Delineation of Small Group Structures

Patrick Doreian

The nature and dynamics of social relationships, the constraints they impose on some behaviors, and the facilitation they provide for other behaviors are enduring topics for theoretical and empirical research. Examples abound: the dynamics of task-oriented groups (Bales and others, 1951), the clique structure of small groups (Doreian, 1969), overlapping group membership (Arabie, 1977), social status and social interaction (Berger and others, 1977), the structure of social networks (Holland and Leinhardt, 1976), the structure of scientific communities (Mullins and others, 1977), the diffusion of innovation (Coleman and others, 1966), urban networks (Mitchell, 1969), interlocking corporate directorates (Levine, 1972), the duality of individuals and groups (Breiger, 1974), the economic structure of production (Carter, 1967). These examples constitute a diverse, if not exhaustive, set of substantive and empirical areas, but they have several characteristics in common. Each involves a set or sets of social entities and each defines relations within or between these sets.

Given this abstract communality, it is not surprising to find that those areas of mathematics grounded in set theory are frequently used to represent and analyze social phenomena. With regard to graph theory, which has been used extensively, the material in Harary, Norman, and Cartwright (1965) has proved to be a valuable resource. The uses of categories and functors (Lorrain and White, 1971), of Boolean algebra (Bonacich, 1978), and of blockmodels (White, Boorman, and Breiger, 1976) illustrate the ways in which set theory may serve as a foundation for the analysis of social structure.

In an entirely different context, Atkin (1972) has proposed the use of algebraic topology to represent and analyze social phenomena. His interest extends to both local and global connectivity patterns. Although this connectivity has been explored previously by Kapferer (1969) and Doreian (1974), this chapter will compare the Atkin approach to other methods while using a data set common to all of them. These comparisons demonstrate the utility of Atkin's work and suggest that the language of algebraic topology is a very rich language for structural analysis.

The Data

The data used here were first gathered by Davis and others (1941) and reanalyzed by Homans (1950). Of particular concern are the subsequent examinations by White, Boorman, and Breiger (1976) and Breiger, Boorman, and Arabie (1975), who use blockmodeling; by Breiger (1974), who uses graph theory and associated matrix algebra; and by Phillips and Conviser (1972), who use information theory.

The data are taken from a group of 18 women as they participated in 14 activities or events. Their participation is shown in the matrix of Table 1. If $\Lambda = [\lambda_{ij}]$ denotes this matrix, then $\lambda_{ij} = 1$ if the i-th woman participates in the j-th event, and $\lambda_{ij} = 0$ otherwise. The women are denoted by W_i and the events by E_j. The set of all events is denoted by E and the set of all women by W.

Constructing Simplicial Complexes*

What are the binary relations between the two finite sets W and E? If λ is the relation "participated in," then $W_i \lambda E_j$ indicates that W_i participated in event E_j and $\lambda \subseteq W \times E$ (the Cartesian product of W and

*This section is directly adapted from Atkin (1976).

Table 1. Incidence Matrix for Participation in Event Data

		E_1	E_2	E_3	E_4	E_5	E_6	E_7	E_8	E_9	E_{10}	E_{11}	E_{12}	E_{13}	E_{14}
Eleanor	(W_1)	0	0	0	0	1	1	1	1	0	0	0	0	0	0
Brenda	(W_2)	1	0	1	1	1	1	1	1	0	0	0	0	0	0
Dorothy	(W_3)	0	0	0	0	0	0	0	1	1	0	0	0	0	0
Verne	(W_4)	0	0	0	0	0	0	1	1	1	0	0	1	0	0
Flora	(W_5)	0	0	0	0	0	0	0	0	1	0	1	0	0	0
Olivia	(W_6)	0	0	0	0	0	0	0	0	1	0	1	0	0	0
Laura	(W_7)	1	1	1	0	1	1	1	1	0	0	0	0	0	0
Evelyn	(W_8)	1	1	1	1	1	1	0	1	1	0	0	0	0	0
Pearl	(W_9)	0	0	0	0	0	1	0	1	1	0	0	0	0	0
Ruth	(W_{10})	0	0	0	0	1	0	1	1	1	0	0	0	0	0
Sylvia	(W_{11})	0	0	0	0	0	0	1	1	1	1	0	1	1	1
Katherine	(W_{12})	0	0	0	0	0	0	0	1	1	1	0	1	1	1
Myrna	(W_{13})	0	0	0	0	0	0	0	1	1	1	0	1	0	0
Theresa	(W_{14})	0	1	1	1	1	1	1	1	1	0	0	0	0	0
Charlotte	(W_{15})	0	0	1	1	1	0	1	0	0	0	0	0	0	0
Frances	(W_{16})	0	0	1	0	1	1	0	1	0	0	0	0	0	0
Helen	(W_{17})	0	0	0	0	0	0	1	1	0	1	1	1	0	0
Nora	(W_{18})	0	0	0	0	0	1	1	0	1	1	1	1	1	1

Source: Breiger, 1974, p. 186; Homans, 1950, p. 83.

E). The inverse relation λ^{-1} is defined by having $E_j \, \lambda^{-1} \, W_i$, or $(E_j,$ $W_i) \, \epsilon \, \lambda^{-1}$. Table 1 contains the incidence matrix Λ for λ. The incidence matrix for λ^{-1} is simply Λ' where the $'$ denotes transposition.

Let there be at least one $W_i \, \epsilon \, W$ such that a subset of $(p + 1)$ elements of E are λ-related to the element W_i. Such a subset of E will be called a p-simplex. If the members of this simplex are E_1, $E_2, \ldots, E_{p+1}$, then the simplex can be written

$$W_i = <E_1, E_2, \ldots, E_{p+1}>$$

or as

$$W_i = \sigma_p$$

and we refer to p as the dimension of σ_p.

To illustrate these ideas, consider W_1. Examination of the first row of Λ reveals that there are four events such that $W_1 \, \lambda \, E_j$. These events are E_2, E_4, E_8, and E_{12}. The suffixes denote the event numbers as displayed in Table 1. If the events were numbered according to membership in σ_3, the suffixes would be 1, 2, 3, and 4, with $p = 3$. Symbolically, $W_1 = <E_2, E_4, E_8, E_{12}>$ or $W_1 = \sigma_3$. Any subset of σ_p will have all its members in λ-relation to W_i and will be, therefore, another simplex. If the simplex has $q + 1$ members, with $q \leqslant p$, then it is denoted by σ_q. This q-simplex is called a face of σ_p and is denoted by $\sigma_q \leqslant \sigma_p$. In our example, $<E_2, E_4, E_8>$, a 2-simplex, is called σ_2 and is a face of W_1. Each $W_i \, \epsilon \, W$ identifies a p-simplex and all the faces of that simplex. The set of all the simplexes identified by the $\{W_i \, \epsilon \, W\}$ is called a simplicial complex K. More precisely, it is denoted by $K_W \, (E{:}\lambda)$, which conveys that E is the vertex set for K, λ is the relation used to construct K, and W is the other set for λ-relatedness. The vertexes of K, which are the elements E_i of E $(i = 1, 2, \ldots n)$, are identified as the o-simplexes. These are denoted by $\sigma_o^{\,i} = <E_i>$. The largest value, say N, of p such that there is $\sigma_p \, \epsilon \, K$, is called the dimension of K. This is denoted by $\dim K = N$. Table 2 gives a listing of the p-simplexes in $K_W \, (E, \lambda)$. This list is defined only in terms of the rows of Λ. Each p-simplex identifies all of its faces that are not listed in the Table. The *Notation* column gives the σ_p for each simplex. (An examination of this column reveals that $\dim K = 7$.)

Table 2. A Listing of the p-Simplexes in K_w $(E:\lambda)$

Simplex	Notation	Label
$<E_2, E_4, E_8, E_{12}>$	σ_3	W_1
$<E_2, E_4, E_7, E_8, E_{10}, E_{12}, E_{13}>$	σ_6	W_2
$<E_6, E_{12}>$	σ_1	W_3
$<E_4, E_5, E_6, E_{12}>$	σ_3	W_4
$<E_1, E_6>$	σ_1	W_5
$<E_1, E_6>$	σ_1	W_6
$<E_2, E_3, E_4, E_7, E_8, E_{10}, E_{12}>$	σ_6	W_7
$<E_2, E_3, E_6, E_7, E_8, E_{10}, E_{12}, E_{13}>$	σ_7	W_8
$<E_6, E_8, E_{12}>$	σ_2	W_9
$<E_2, E_4, E_6, E_{12}>$	σ_3	W_{10}
$<E_4, E_5, E_6, E_9, E_{11}, E_{12}, E_{14}>$	σ_6	W_{11}
$<E_5, E_6, E_9, E_{11}, E_{12}, E_{14}>$	σ_5	W_{12}
$<E_5, E_6, E_9, E_{12}>$	σ_3	W_{13}
$<E_2, E_3, E_4, E_6, E_7, E_8, E_{12}, E_{13}>$	σ_7	W_{14}
$<E_2, E_4, E_7, E_{13}>$	σ_3	W_{15}
$<E_2, E_7, E_8, E_{12}>$	σ_3	W_{16}
$<E_1, E_4, E_5, E_9, E_{12}>$	σ_4	W_{17}
$<E_1, E_4, E_5, E_6, E_8, E_9, E_{11}, E_{14}>$	σ_7	W_{18}

Delineating Social Structure by Use of Q-Connectivity

Each row of Λ represents some simplex, say $\sigma_p \in K$, and K is the simplicial complex defined by Λ. Consider Row i and Row j. Let the simplexes that these rows represent be σ_r and σ_s respectively. In general, if there are n actors and m events, then the (i, j) entry of the $(n \times n)$ matrix $\Lambda\Lambda'$ will be the number of 1's common to Row i and Row j. Alternatively put, the (i,j) entry is the number $(q + 1)$ where q is the highest dimension of a face σ_q shared by both σ_r and σ_s. At a later point in his work, Atkin is concerned with loops. If a loop has $q + 1$ links in it, there will be q distinct points in the loop. Hence, q is used as the dimension of a set of $q + 1$ elements. (In a loop two of these points will be identical.) Let U be the $(n \times n)$ matrix with 1's everywhere. Then the matrix $\Lambda\Lambda' - U$ has a precise interpretation:

1. The values in the main diagonal are the dimensions of the n primary simplexes defined by Λ.
2. The values off the main diagonal give the highest dimensions of shared faces for each pair of primary simplexes.

The matrix $\Lambda\Lambda'$ and hence the matrix $\Lambda\Lambda' - U$ are symmetrical. Table 3 gives the lower triangle of the values of $\Lambda\Lambda' - U$. The diagonal values give the dimensions of the 18 simplexes defined by Λ. For example, the (2, 2) entry is 6, and in Table 2 we see that W_2 is a 6-simplex. If an entry of $\Lambda\Lambda'$ is 0, indicating that there is no shared face, the corresponding entry in $\Lambda\Lambda' - U$ is -1. This has been denoted by $-$ in Table 3. The off-diagonal entries give the dimensions of shared faces. For example, the (W_8, W_7) entry is 5, indicating that W_8 and W_7 share a 5-simplex as a common face. This 5-simplex is $<E_2, E_3, E_7, E_8, E_{10}, E_{12}>$.

Atkin defines a chain of q-connections in the following way: Two simplexes σ_r and σ_s in K are said to be joined by a chain of connection if there is a finite sequence of simplexes σ_{α_1}, σ_{α_2}, $\ldots$, σ_{α_n} such that (1) $\sigma_{\alpha_1} \leqslant \sigma_r$, (2) $\sigma_{\alpha_n} \leqslant \sigma_s$, and (3) σ_{α_i} and $\sigma_{\alpha_{i+1}}$ share a common face, say σ_{β_i}, where $i = 1, \ldots, n - 1$. Further, if q is the least of the integers, $\alpha_1, \beta_1, \ldots, \beta_{n-1}, \alpha_n$, then the sequence of simplexes is a chain of q-connection. A description of the chains of q-connection provides a statement of the q-connectivity of K. For example, consider only W_3, W_4, W_5, and W_9. If these are the only primary p-simplexes, they can be geometrically represented as in Figure 1. Consider $W_4, <E_4, E_5, E_6, E_{12}>$, and $W_9, <E_6, E_8, E_{12}>$. W_4 and W_9 have $<E_6, E_{12}>$ as a common face and are thereby 1-connected. W_4 and W_3, $<E_6, E_{12}>$, also have $<E_6, E_{12}>$ as a common face and are 1-connected. W_4 and $W_5, <E_1, E_6>$, have only $<E_6>$ as a common face and are 0-connected.

Now consider W_2 and W_6 as simplexes of K. They share no common face. However, W_6 is 1-connected to W_{18} (they share $<E_1, E_6>$), and W_{18} is 1-connected to W_2 (they share $<E_4, E_8>$). So there is a chain, $W_2 \overset{1}{\text{---}} W_{18} \overset{1}{\text{---}} W_6$, of 1-connectivity between W_2 and W_6. Note that W_2 and W_{18} share $<E_4, E_8>$ and so are 1-connected (in a single step).

Consider W_8 and W_{15}. In terms of a single step they are 2-connected, since they share $<E_2, E_7, E_{13}>$. However, W_8 is 5-connected to W_2, and W_2 is 3-connected to W_{15}. As a two-step chain we have $W_8 \overset{5}{\text{---}} W_2 \overset{3}{\text{---}} W_{15}$ and so W_8 and W_{15} are 3-connected, since 3 is the lesser of 5 and 3.

The matrix $\Lambda\Lambda' - U$ can be used to find the chains of q-connection for K. This problem is exactly that of finding paths of

Table 3. Values of $\Lambda\Lambda' - U$

	W_1	W_2	W_3	W_4	W_5	W_6	W_7	W_8	W_9	W_{10}	W_{11}	W_{12}	W_{13}	W_{14}	W_{15}	W_{16}	W_{17}	W_{18}
W_1	3																	
W_2	3	6																
W_3	0	0	1															
W_4	-1	-1	-1	3														
W_5	-1	-1	0	0	-1													
W_6	-1	-1	0	-1	-1	1												
W_7	3	5	0	-1	-1	-1	6											
W_8	2	5	-1	2	0	0	5	7										
W_9	-1	-1	-1	3	0	0	-1	2	2									
W_{10}	2	2	-1	2	0	0	2	2	-1	3								
W_{11}	-1	-1	-1	2	0	0	-1	-1	-1	2	6							
W_{12}	0	0	-1	2	0	0	0	-1	-1	-1	5	5						
W_{13}	0	0	-1	2	0	0	0	-1	-1	-1	3	3	3					
W_{14}	3	5	1	0	0	0	5	6	2	3	2	-1	-1	7				
W_{15}	-1	3	-1	0	-1	-1	2	2	-1	0	0	-1	0	3	3			
W_{16}	2	3	0	2	0	0	3	3	-1	-1	0	0	2	3	1	3		
W_{17}	-1	-1	0	2	-1	0	0	0	0	-1	3	2	2	1	0	0	4	
W_{18}	-1	-1	0	2	-1	-1	-1	-1	-1	-1	5	4	2	2	0	0	3	7

Note: All minus signs indicate −1 (or no shared faces).

Figure 1. Four Illustrative p-Simplexes

level n for a valued graph, as outlined by Doreian (1974) and modified by Peay (1976). Their algorithm can be applied directly to $\Lambda\Lambda' - U$.

For each value of q, where $0 \leqslant q \leqslant N$, it is possible to identify those pieces of K that are q-connected. We define a relation μ_q as (σ_r, σ_s) $\epsilon\ \mu_q$ if and only if σ_r is q-connected to σ_s. One can straightforwardly show that μ_q is an equivalence relation and thereby partitions the set of simplexes $\{\sigma_p\}$, where $p \geqslant q$. At any value of q we can determine the number of equivalence classes in the partition defined by μ_q. This number is denoted by Q_q.

Consider again $\Lambda\Lambda'$. Breiger (1974) used this matrix in his exploration of the duality of people and groups. The diagonal entries of this matrix are, of course, the row sums of Λ. The matrix $\Lambda\Lambda' - U$ is simply Breiger's $\Lambda\Lambda'$ with 1 subtracted from each entry so that the terms in the matrix express the dimensions of the simplexes. By inspection, dim$K = N = 7$; there are no simplexes σ_q such that $q > 7$. Consider $q = 7$. Examination of the main diagonal of $\Lambda\Lambda' - U$ shows there are three 7-simplexes: W_8, W_{14}, and W_{18}. Since there are no chains of 7-connection, there are three equivalence classes, each consisting of a single 7-simplex. This means that $Q_7 = 3$.

Consider $q = 6$. In addition to the three 7-simplexes already discussed, we now have three 6-simplexes: W_2, W_7, and W_{11}. Use of the Doreian-Peay algorithm shows W_8 and W_{14} to be 6-connected. The simplexes W_2, W_7, W_8, and W_{11} are mutually 6-disconnected, and none of them is 6-connected with W_8 or W_{14}. Hence $Q_6 = 5$.

When $q = 5$, the equivalence class structure changes considerably. There is only one 5-simplex, W_{12}, to be added to the set of higher dimensional simplexes. Use of the Doreian-Peay algorithm reveals that W_2, W_7, W_8, and W_{14} are all mutually 5-connected (each in a one-step chain) and so are in one equivalence class. Similarly, W_{11}, W_{12}, and W_{18} constitute another equivalence class, although W_{12} and

W_{18} are not 5-connected in one step. Diagramatically, the 5-connection is shown in Figure 2, where $Q_5 = 2$ and single lines represent the 5-connection. Double lines indicate the link for $q = 6$.

Figure 2. 5-Connectivity for $K_W(E:\lambda)$

// indicates link present for q = 6.

When $q = 4$, there is little change in the connectivity of the structure. W_{17} is a 4-simplex and is added to the other seven p-simplexes for $p \geqslant 5$. This additional simplex is not connected to either of the two ($q = 5$) equivalence classes. Further, no member of one equivalence class is 4-connected to any member of the other equivalence class, and vice versa. Thus $Q_4 = 3$.

For $q = 3$, there are six 3-simplexes, $\{W_1, W_4, W_{10}, W_{13}, W_{15}, W_{16}\}$, to be included in the analysis of 3-connectivity. At this level, there are two equivalence classes. The new simplexes are split between the two $q = 4$ equivalence classes, and W_{17} is drawn into one of them. Hence $Q_3 = 2$.

For $q = 2$, the single 2-simplex, W_9, is added to the previous simplexes. Chains of 2-connection appear between the ($q = 3$) equivalence classes and, since W_9 is not disconnected, $Q_2 = 1$. When $q = 1$, all of the simplexes are considered, and all belong to one equivalence class. Thus $Q_1 = 1$ and, trivially, $Q_0 = 1$. Table 4 summarizes the q-connectivity of $K_W (E:\lambda)$.

Figure 3 provides a diagrammatic presentation of the q-connectivity for $q \leqslant 5$. To avoid clutter, only five 1-connections have been drawn. These 1-connections join Flora (W_5), Olivia (W_6), Helen (W_{17}), and Nora (W_{18}) in one equivalence class. These are the only connections these women have to the entire structure. Dorothy (W_3) is 1-connected to both of the equivalence classes ($q = 3$).

As previous investigators have found, the group of 18 women essentially splits into two subgroups: $G_1 = \{$Evelyn, Theresa, Laura,

Table 4. q-Connectivity for $K_W(E{:}\lambda)$

q	Simplexes	Equivalence Classes	Q_q
7	3	$\{W_8\}$, $\{W_{14}\}$, $\{W_{18}\}$	3
6	6	$\{W_2\}$, $\{W_7\}$, $\{W_8, W_{14}\}$, $\{W_{11}\}$, $\{W_{18}\}$	5
5	7	$\{W_2, W_7, W_8, W_{14}\}$, $\{W_{11}, W_{12}, W_{18}\}$	2
4	8	$\{W_2, W_7, W_8, W_{14}\}$, $\{W_{11}, W_{12}, W_{18}\}$, $\{W_{17}\}$	3
3	14	$\{W_1, W_2, W_7, W_8, W_{10}, W_{14}, W_{15}, W_{16}\}$ $\{W_4, W_{11}, W_{12}, W_{13}, W_{17}, W_{18}\}$	2
2	15	$\{W_1, W_2, W_7, W_8, W_9, W_{10}, W_{14}, W_{15}, W_{16},$ $W_4, W_{11}, W_{12}, W_{13}, W_{17}, W_{18}\}$	1
1,0	18	$\{\text{All}\}$	1

Figure 3. Connectivity for $K_W(E{:}\lambda)$

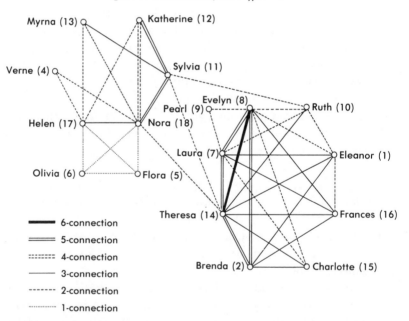

Brenda, Charlotte, Frances, Eleanor, Ruth, Pearl$\}$ and $G_2 = \{$Sylvia, Nora, Katherine, Helen, Verne, Myrna$\}$. By examining the various levels of q-connectivity or, equivalently, by looking at the values of Q_q for various q, one can discern the internal structuring of these groups. Each of the subgroups can be viewed as having a core and a periphery, with higher connectivity within the core, lower connectivity with the periphery. Evelyn, Theresa, Laura, and Brenda constitute the core of G_1, and within this core Evelyn and Theresa are most closely connected. Sylvia, Nora, and Katherine form the core of G_2, and Sylvia is the central core member. Pearl is 2-connected to two members of G_1, and both Olivia and Flora are 1-connected to G_2. Several 1-connectivities join members of the two subgroups. Dorothy (not included in Figure 3) is 1-connected to both G_1 and G_2. As a descriptive device, the Q-analysis presented here yields a clear and interpretable structure of the group of 18 women. This structure can now be compared with the structures obtained from other analyses.

Comparison with Other Procedures

In the original study, Davis and his colleagues (1941) identified two *cliques*. (Because the term *clique* has since taken on a more restricted meaning in graph-theoretic approaches to social structure, I will use the term *subgroup* in discussing this work.) Davis's subgroups were described as having a core, a set of primary members, and a set of secondary members. The primary subgroup was {Evelyn, Theresa, Laura, Brenda, Charlotte, Frances, Eleanor, Pearl, Ruth}. The secondary subgroup was {Sylvia, Nora, Helen, Katherine, Myrna, Ruth, Olivia, Flora, Dorothy}. In his reanalysis of these data, Homans (1950) also found two subgroups: {Evelyn, Theresa, Laura, Brenda, Charlotte, Frances, Eleanor} and {Sylvia, Nora, Katherine, Helen}, with Pearl, Ruth, Verne, Dorothy, Olivia, and Flora belonging to neither group. Homans describes the two groups as frayed at the edges. This fraying effect can be understood to arise from lower levels of q-connectivity.

With the exception of Ruth and Pearl, our subgroup G_1 is Homans's first subgroup. Moreover, for $q \geqslant 3$, our G_1 is a clearly distinct subgroup in which Ruth is connected to Theresa. Both Theresa and Ruth are 2-connected to separate members of G_2, and this, at first sight, puts Ruth and Theresa on the boundary of G_1. However, the connections of these two women to the rest of G_1 are markedly different. Theresa is clearly in the core, whereas most of Ruth's connections are at a level of 2-connectivity. While Ruth's connection to G_1 is much weaker, she can still be included in G_1.

There is no difference between G_1 and Davis's primary subgroup. However, for $q \geqslant 3$, it is clear that Pearl is not part of G_1. She is 2-connected to only two members of G_1, although these two members are part of the core of G_1. The three analyses are quite consistent in terms of G_1. In the present study, Ruth is included in G_1, as she is by Davis and his colleagues. Pearl is not excluded from G_1 as she is in Homans's analysis, but she is very tenuously connected to G_1. The core of G_1 as described here is the same core described by Davis, who, however, distinguishes the other members of the subgroup as primary and secondary. This distinction is not made here.

Things are less clear in G_2, since this subgroup has much less internal q-connectivity structure than G_1. In this area, there is considerable variance between the present analysis and that of Davis and his colleagues. This analysis indicates that Ruth, Olivia, Flora, and Dorothy should not be included in the second subgroup. Homans arrives at the same conclusion. According to Davis, Ruth belongs to both subgroups; indeed, she constitutes their overlap. Given the sharp distinction between G_1 and G_2 at the level of 3-connectivity, it seems preferable to see her as part of G_1, but as one of two persons linking the group to G_2. If we focus strictly on $q \geqslant 3$, then the membership of G_1 is $\{$ Evelyn, Theresa, Laura, Brenda, Charlotte, Frances, Eleanor, Ruth$\}$, while the membership of G_2 is $\{$ Sylvia, Nora, Katherine, Helen, Myrna$\}$. Apart from the inclusion of Ruth in G_1 and the inclusion of Myrna in G_2, the subgroup structure is that described by Homans. I note that both Ruth and Myrna are 3-connected to their respective groups by a single link.

The application of blockmodeling to these data (Breiger, Boorman, and Arabie, 1975) yielded a partition of the 18 women into two subgroups. The first subgroup, $\{$Evelyn, Theresa, Laura, Brenda, Charlotte, Frances, Eleanor, Ruth$\}$, is exactly the subgroup identified at the level of 3-connectivity. The remaining 10 women form the other subgroup identified by use of CONCOR. This set is a mixture of our G_2 (identified at a level of 3-connectivity) and women who do not genuinely belong to either group. If we consider 2-connectivity, Pearl would be added to our G_1, but the blockmodeling procedures place her in the other subgroup.

Schwartz (1976) has observed that blockmodeling creates a partition among the men of the Bank Wiring Room (Homans, 1950), when there are grounds for concluding that three of the men belong to neither of the two subgroups identified by Homans. Indeed, Homans reaches the same conclusion. It would appear, in the present case, that blockmodeling is insensitive to some of the variations in the strength of the social relations being analyzed. However, q-connectivity records these variations.

The use of information theory (Phillips and Conviser, 1972) creates a misleading partition of the group. Whereas the analyses of Davis and others, Homans, Breiger, and the present author basically agree on the subgroup structure and differ only in the frayed region discussed by Homans, the outcome of the procedure proposed by Phillips and Conviser is quite different. Group structure is clouded by including Verne and Myrna of G_2 in G_1 and by including Dorothy, Olivia, and Flora, who do not belong to either group, in G_2.

Breiger's partition (1974, p. 188) is the closest to the one obtained here; it is, except for Olivia and Flora, the same as the one found for q-connectivity with $q \geqslant 3$. This should not be too surprising, since both approaches make use of the matrix $\Lambda\Lambda'$. Perhaps the one criticism that can be lodged against Breiger has already been made by Breiger, Boorman, and Arabie (1975), who point out the ad hoc nature of some of his procedures. Breiger uses a dual structure, defined over the events, to eliminate those events which least discriminate among the women. He redefines Λ after these events have been removed and then computes the revised $\Lambda\Lambda'$. The present approach avoids these ad hoc decisions by dealing with a sequence of all q values. Breiger's use of the event × event matrix as a preliminary to the person × person matrix is a valuable contribution that, in principle, can be exploited by the use of a dual simplicial complex, or conjugate simplicial complex, in Atkin's terms.

The Dual Simplicial Complex

Breiger (1974, p. 183) uses the term *membership network analysis* to emphasize fundamental differences between his approach and the more conventional sociometric analyses. He rightly insists that membership in a group and social relations are both social ties and that, in the sociometric tradition, too much emphasis has been placed upon the latter. The individual and the group are dual, and this duality can be fruitfully pursued. From the perspective of social relations, individual actors are nodes in a network; from the perspective of memberships, these same actors are relations in the dual network of collectivities. In constructing the simplicial complex $K_W(E{:}\lambda)$, I took E to be the vertex set, λ the social relation, and W the reference set for λ-relatedness. The roles of W and E can be reversed. If W is the vertex set and λ^{-1} the social relation, E can be the reference set for λ^{-1}-relatedness. Thus $(E_j, W_i) \in \lambda^{-1}$ indicates that event E_j has W_i as a participant. In the same manner as before, I can construct the simplicial complex $K_E(W{:}\lambda^{-1})$, as shown in Table 5.

The incidence matrix for λ^{-1} is Λ', so if U is the (14×14) matrix with 1's everywhere, the matrix $\Lambda'\Lambda - U$ gives the q-connectivities of $K_E(W{:}\lambda^{-1})$. Table 6 shows the lower triangle of this symmetrical matrix. As before, the main diagonal of $\Lambda'\Lambda - U$ gives the dimensions of the individual simplexes, and the off-diagonal entries give the highest value of q for faces shared by the simplexes. Inspection of Table 5 reveals that $\dim K = 13$. For all values of $q \leqslant 13$, an analysis in terms of q-connectivity yields the structure shown in Table 7.

The structure of events could be analyzed in a manner parallel to the structural analysis of the people who constitute the social

Table 5. Simplexes of $K_E(W{:}\lambda^{-1})$

Simplex	Notation	Label
$< W_5, W_6, W_{17}, W_{18} >$	σ_3	E_1
$< W_1, W_2, W_7, W_8, W_{10}, W_{14}, W_{15}, W_{16} >$	σ_7	E_2
$< W_7, W_8, W_{14} >$	σ_2	E_3
$< W_1, W_2, W_4, W_7, W_{10}, W_{11}, W_{14}, W_{15}, W_{17}, W_{18} >$	σ_9	E_4
$< W_4, W_{11}, W_{12}, W_{13}, W_{17}, W_{18} >$	σ_5	E_5
$< W_3, W_4, W_5, W_6, W_8, W_9, W_{10}, W_{11}, W_{12}, W_{13}, W_{14}, W_{18} >$	σ_{11}	E_6
$< W_2, W_7, W_8, W_{14}, W_{15}, W_{16} >$	σ_5	E_7
$< W_1, W_2, W_7, W_8, W_9, W_{14}, W_{16}, W_{18} >$	σ_7	E_8
$< W_{11}, W_{12}, W_{13}, W_{17}, W_{18} >$	σ_4	E_9
$< W_2, W_7, W_8 >$	σ_2	E_{10}
$< W_{11}, W_{12}, W_{18} >$	σ_2	E_{11}
$< W_1, W_2, W_3, W_4, W_7, W_8, W_9, W_{10}, W_{11}, W_{12}, W_{13}, W_{14}, W_{16}, W_{17} >$	σ_{13}	E_{12}
$< W_2, W_8, W_{14}, W_{15} >$	σ_3	E_{13}
$< W_{11}, W_{12}, W_{18} >$	σ_2	E_{14}

Table 6. Lower Triangle of $K_E(W{:}\lambda^{-1})$

	E_1	E_2	E_3	E_4	E_5	E_6	E_7	E_8	E_9	E_{10}	E_{11}	E_{12}	E_{13}	E_{14}
E_1	3													
E_2	–	7												
E_3	–	2	2											
E_4	1	5	1	9										
E_5	1	–	–	3	5									
E_6	2	2	1	4	4	11								
E_7	–	5	2	3	–	1	5							
E_8	0	5	2	4	0	3	4	7						
E_9	1	–	–	2	4	3	–	0	4					
E_{10}	–	2	1	1	–	0	2	2	–	2				
E_{11}	0	–	–	1	2	2	–	0	2	–	2			
E_{12}	0	6	2	7	4	8	4	6	3	2	1	13		
E_{13}	–	3	1	2	–	1	3	2	–	1	–	2	3	
E_{14}	0	–	–	1	2	2	–	0	2	–	2	1	1	2

Table 7. q-Connectivity for $K_E(W{:}\lambda^{-1})$

q	Number of Simplexes	Equivalence Classes	Q_q
13, 12	1	$\{E_{12}\}$	1
11, 10	2	$\{E_{12}\}$, $\{E_6\}$	2
9	3	$\{E_4\}$, $\{E_6\}$, $\{E_{12}\}$	3
8	3	$\{E_4\}$, $\{E_6, E_{12}\}$	2
7	5	$\{E_2\}$, $\{E_4, E_6, E_{12}\}$, $\{E_8\}$	3
6	5	$\{E_2, E_4, E_6, E_8, E_{12}\}$	1
5	7	$\{E_2, E_4, E_6, E_7, E_8, E_{12}\}$, $\{E_5\}$	2
4	8	$\{E_2, E_4, E_6, E_7, E_8, E_5, E_9, E_{12}\}$	1
3	10	$\{E_2, E_4, E_5, E_6, E_7, E_8, E_9, E_{12}, E_{13}\}$, $\{E_1\}$	2
2, 1, 0	14	$\{$ All $\}$	

group. Unfortunately, Davis and others did not indicate the nature of the 14 events they recorded. It would have been interesting to see which kinds of events belong to the various equivalence classes and which activity types draw upon the same participants. In this way, the duality noted by Breiger could be further elaborated.

Conclusion

This chapter has sought to demonstrate the utility of some ideas drawn from algebraic topology, as suggested by Atkin, for

representing and analyzing social relational structures. These techniques were used to analyze a group of women and to delineate the
internal structure of the group. This description was reasonably
consistent with most of the previous analyses of this group's
structure. Differences among the other descriptions can be readily
incorporated into this analysis by considering different levels of
q-connectivity. In this sense, these algebraic topological ideas
constitute a more flexible and sensitive language for describing social
structural relations and the kinds of duality noted by Simmel (1955)
and by Breiger.

　　While the analysis in this chapter focuses upon the empirical
description of a small group, the language of algebraic topology can
be readily applied to all of the examples that introduce this chapter.
Further, this language could very likely be used to analyze role systems and other institutional structural relations. By restricting attention to the conventional analysis of group structure, I have not
displayed the real power of Atkin's ideas. The rich algebraic poten-
tials of his homology and homotopy theory have not been utilized.
These ideas are, however, expounded in Atkin (1976) and should
provide a rich resource for social scientists.

References

Abrahams, R. D. *The Changing Concept of the Negro Hero*. Bobbs-Merrill Reprint Series in Black Studies BC-4 (67389). Indianapolis: Bobbs-Merrill, 1962.

Anderberg, M. R. *Cluster Analysis for Applications*. New York: Academic Press, 1973.

Anderson, J. A. "Separate Sample Logistic Discrimination." *Biometrika*, 1972, *59*, 19–35.

Anderson, J. A. "Logistic Discrimination with Medical Applications." In T. Cacoullos (Ed.), *Discriminant Analysis and Applications*. New York: Academic Press, 1973.

Anderson, J. A. "Quadratic Logistic Discrimination." *Biometrika*, 1975, *62*, 149–154.

Anderson, T. W., and Bahadur, R. R. "Classification into Two Multivariate Normal Distributions with Different Covariance Matrices." *Annals of Mathematical Statistics*, 1972, *33*, 420–431.

Arabie, P. "Clustering Representations of Group Overlap." *Journal of Mathematical Sociology*, 1977, *4*, 113–128.

Arabie, P., Boorman, S. A., and Levitt, P. R. "Constructing Blockmodels: How and Why." *Journal of Mathematical Psychology*, 1978, *17*, 31–63.

Atkin, R. H. "From Cohomology in Physics to q-Connectivity in Social Science." *International Journal of Man-Machine Studies*, 1972, *4*, 139–167.

Atkin, R. H. "An Algebra for Patterns on a Complex, II." *International Journal of Man-Machine Studies*, 1976, *8*, 483–498.

Austin, M. P., and Greig-Smith, P. "The Application of Quantitative Methods to Vegetation Survey II." *Journal of Ecology*, 1968, *56*, 827–844.

Bacon, M. K., Barry, H., III, and Child, I. L. "A Cross-Cultural Study of Drinking: II. Relations to Other Features of Culture." *Quarterly Journal of Studies on Alcohol*, 1965, *3*, 29–48.

Badian, E. *Foreign Clientelae (264–70 B.C.)*. Oxford, England: Clarendon Press, 1958.

Baker, F. B. "Stability of Two Hierarchical Grouping Techniques. Case 1: Sensitivity to Data Errors." *Journal of the American Statistical Association*, 1974, *69*, 440–445.

Baker, F. B., and Hubert, L. J. "Measuring the Power of Hierarchical Cluster Analysis." *Journal of the American Statistical Association*, 1975, *70*, 31–38.

Baker, F. B., and Hubert, L. J. "A Graph-Theoretic Approach to Goodness-of-Fit in Complete-Link Hierarchical Clustering." *Journal of the American Statistical Association*, 1976, *71*, 870–878.

Bales, R. F. *Interaction Process Analysis*. Reading, Mass.: Addison-Wesley, 1950.

Bales, R. F. "Interaction Process Analysis." *International Encyclopedia of the Social Sciences*, 1968, *7*, 465–471.

Bales, R. F. *Personality and Interpersonal Behavior*. New York: Holt, Rinehart and Winston, 1970.

Bales, R. F., Cohen, S. P., and Williamson, S. A. *SYMLOG: A System for the Multiple Level Observation of Groups*. New York: Free Press, 1979.

Bales, R. F., and others. "Channels of Communication in Small Groups." *American Sociological Review*, 1951, *16*, 461–468.

Ball, G. H., and Hall, D. J. *ISODATA: A Novel Method of Data Analysis and Pattern Classification*. Menlo Park, Calif.: Stanford Research Institute, 1965.

Ball, G. H., and Hall, D. J. "A Clustering Technique for Summarizing Multivariate Data." *Behavioral Science*, 1967, *12*, 153–155.

Bartko, J. J., Strauss, J. S., and Carpenter, W. T. "An Evaluation of Taxonomic Techniques for Psychiatric Data." *Classification Society Bulletin*, 1971, *2*, 2–28.

Barton, A. H. "The Concept of Property Space in Social Research." In P. F. Lazarsfeld and M. Rosenberg (Eds.), *The Language of Social Research.* New York: Free Press, 1955.

Berge, C. *The Theory of Graphs and Its Applications.* New York: Wiley, 1962.

Berger, J., and others. *Status Characteristics and Social Interaction.* New York: Elsevier, 1977.

Bertin, P. *Semiologie Graphique [Graphic Semiology].* (2nd ed.) Paris: Gauthier-Villars, 1973.

Bhat, M. V., and Haupt, A. "An Efficient Clustering Algorithm." *IEEE Transactions on Systems, Man, and Cybernetics,* 1976, *6,* 61–64.

Bieba, A. M., and others. "Application of Multivariate Techniques to Analytical Data on Aegean Ceramics." *Archaeometry,* 1976, *18* (1), 59–74.

Bishop, Y.M.M., Fienberg, S. E., and Holland, P. W. *Discrete Multivariate Analysis: Theory and Practice.* Cambridge: MIT Press, 1975.

Blackwell, J. E. *The Black Community: Diversity and Unity.* New York: Dodd, Mead, 1975.

Blashfield, R. K. "Mixture Model Tests of Cluster Analysis: Accuracy of Four Agglomerative Hierarchical Methods." *Psychological Bulletin,* 1976, *83,* 377–388.

Blashfield, R. K. "A Consumer Report on Cluster Analysis Software. No. 3: Iterative Partitioning Methods." Unpublished report, University of Florida Medical School, 1977.

Blashfield, R. K., and Aldenderfer, M. S. "Computer Software Programs for Performing Iterative Partitioning Cluster Analysis." *Applied Psychological Measures,* 1978a, *2,* 533–541.

Blashfield, R. K., and Aldenderfer, M. S. "The Literature on Cluster Analysis." *Multivariate Behavioral Research,* 1978b, *13,* 271–295.

Bloch, M. *Seigneurie Française et Manoir Anglais [French Lordship and English Manor Houses].* Paris: Armand Colin, 1960.

Bloxom, B. "Individual Differences in Multidimensional Scaling." *Research Bulletin* (Princeton, Educational Testing Service), 1968.

Boas, F. *Indianische Sagen von der Nord-Pacifischen Küste Amerikas [Indian Legends of the North Pacific Coast of America].* Berlin: A. Asher, 1894.

Bock, R. D., and Husain, S. Z. "Factors of the Tele: A Preliminary Report." *Sociometry*, 1952, *15*, 206–219.

Bonacich, P. "Using Boolean Algebra to Analyze Overlapping Memberships." In K. F. Schuessler (Ed.), *Sociological Methodology 1979*. San Francisco: Jossey-Bass, 1978.

Boorman, S. A. "Metric Spaces of Complex Objects." Unpublished honors thesis, Applied Mathematics, Harvard University, 1970.

Boorman, S. A. "A Combinatorial Optimization Model for Transmission of Job Information Through Contact Networks." *Bell Journal of Economics*, 1975, *6*, 216–249.

Boorman, S. A. "Informational Optima in a Formal Hierarchy: Calculations Using the Semigroup." *Journal of Mathematical Sociology*, 1977, *5*, 129–147.

Boorman, S. A., and Arabie, P. "Structural Measures and the Method of Sorting." In R. N. Shepard, A. K. Romney, and S. B. Nerlove (Eds.), *Multidimensional Scaling: Theory and Applications in the Behavioral Sciences*. Vol. 1. New York: Seminar Press, 1972.

Boorman, S. A., and Arabie, P. "Algebraic Approaches to the Comparison of Concrete Social Structures Represented as Networks: Reply to Bonacich." *American Journal of Sociology*, 1980, *86*, 166–174.

Boorman, S. A., and White, H. C. "Social Structure from Multiple Networks. II: Role Structures." *American Journal of Sociology*, 1976, *81*, 1384–1446.

Borg, I. "Geometric Representations of Individual Differences." In J. C. Lingoes, I. Borg, and E. E. Roskam (Eds.), *Geometric Representations of Relational Data*. 2nd ed. Ann Arbor: Mathesis Press, 1979.

Borg, I., and Lingoes, J. C. "A Direct Transformational Approach to Multidimensional Analysis of Three-Way Data Matrices." *Michigan Mathematical Psychology Program*, 1976, *1*, 1–33. Also in: *Zeitschrift f. Sozial Psychologie* [*Journal for Social Psychology*], 1977, *8*, 98–114.

Borg, I., and Lingoes, J. C. "What Weight Should Weights Have in the Analysis of Individual Differences?" *Quality and Quantity*, 1978, *12*, 223–237.

Boyce, A. J. "A Comparative Study of Some Numerical Methods." In A. J. Cole (Ed.), *Numerical Taxonomy* (Proceedings of the Colloquium in Numerical Taxonomy, University of St. Andrews).

London: Academic Press, 1969.

Boyd, J. P. "The Universal Semigroup of Relations." *Social Networks*, 1979/80, *2*, 91–117.

Boyle, R. P. "Algebraic Systems for Normal and Hierarchical Sociograms." *Sociometry*, 1969, *32*, 99–118.

Breiger, R. L. "The Duality of Persons and Groups." *Social Forces*, 1974, *53*, 181–190.

Breiger, R. L. "Career Attributes and Network Structure: A Blockmodel Study of a Biomedical Research Specialty." *American Sociological Review*, 1976, *41*, 117–135.

Breiger, R. L. "Toward an Operational Theory of Community Elite Structures." *Quality and Quantity*, 1979, *13*, 21–57.

Breiger, R. L. "Structures of Economic Interdependence Among Nations." In P. M. Blau and R. K. Merton (Eds.), *Continuities in Structural Inquiry*. Beverly Hills: Sage, in press.

Breiger, R. L., Boorman, S. A., and Arabie, P. "An Algorithm for Clustering Rational Data, with Applications to Social Network Analysis and Comparison with Multidimensional Scaling." *Journal of Mathematical Psychology*, 1975, *12*, 328–383.

Breiger, R. L., and Ennis, J. G. "Personae and Social Roles: The Network Structure of Personality Types in Small Groups." *Social Psychology Quarterly*, 1979, *42*, 262–270.

Brown, M. A., and Blin-Stoyle, A. E. "A Sample Analysis of British Middle and Late Bronze Age Material, Using Optical Spectrometry." *Archaeometry*, 1959, *2*, 188–208 and supplement.

Cacoullos, T. *Discriminant Analysis and Applications*. New York: Academic Press, 1973.

Campbell, D. T. "A Rationale for Weighting First, Second, and Third Sociometric Choices." *Sociometry*, 1954, *17*, 242–243.

Carrington, P. J., Heil, G. H., and Berkowitz, S. D. "A Goodness-of-Fit Index for Blockmodels." *Social Networks*, 1979/80, *2*, 219–234.

Carroll, J. D. "The Nature of the Data, or How to Choose a Correlation Coefficient." *Psychometrika*, 1961, *26*, 347–372.

Carroll, J. D. "Individual Differences and Multidimensional Scaling." In A. K. Romney, R. N. Shepard, and S. B. Nerlove (Eds.), *Multidimensional Scaling: Applications*. Vol. II. New York: Seminar Press, 1972.

Carroll, J. D., and Arabie, P. "Multidimensional Scaling." *Annual Review of Psychology*, 1980, *31*, 607–649.

Carroll, J. D., and Chang, J. J. "Analysis of Individual Differences in Multidimensional Scaling via an *N*-Way Generalization of 'Eckart-Young' Decomposition." *Psychometrika*, 1970, *35*, 283–320.

Carroll, J. D., and Chang, J. J. "IDIOSCAL (Individual Differences In Orientation SCALing): A Generalization of INDSCAL allowing IDIOsyncratic Refence Systems As Well As an Analytical Approximation to INDSCAL." Paper presented at 1972 Psychometric Society Meeting, Princeton, March 1972.

Carter, A. P. *Structural Change in the American Economy.* Cambridge: Harvard University Press, 1967.

Catling, H. W., and Millett, A. "A Study of the Inscribed Stirrup Jars from Thebes." *Archaeometry*, 1965, *8*, 3–85.

Cattell, R. B. *Factor Analysis.* New York: Harper & Row, 1952.

Cattell, R. B. "The Data Box: Its Ordering of Total Resources in Terms of Possible Relational Systems." In R. B. Cattell (Ed.), *Handbook of Multivariate Experimental Psychology.* Chicago: Rand McNally, 1966a.

Cattell, R. B. "The Scree Test for the Number of Factors." *Multivariate Behavioral Research*, 1966b, *1* (2), 245.

Cattell, R. B., Coulter, M. A., and Tsujioka. "The Taxonometric Recognition of Types and Functional Emergents." In R. B. Cattell (Ed.), *Handbook of Multivariate Experimental Psychology.* Chicago: Rand McNally, 1966.

Cattell, R. B., and Jaspers, J. "A General Plasmode (No. 30-10-5-2) for Factor Analytic Exercises and Research." *Multivariate Behavioral Research Monographs*, 1967, *67* (3), 1–211.

Chaney, R. P. "Typology and Patterning: Spiro's Sample Reexamined." *American Anthropologist*, 1966, *68*, 1456–1470.

Chernoff, H. "The Use of Faces to Represent Points in *K*-Dimensional Space Graphically." *Journal of the American Statistical Association*, 1973, *68*, 361–368.

Clark, K. B. *Dark Ghetto: Dilemmas of Social Power.* New York: Harper & Row Torchbooks, 1967.

Clements, F. W. "Use of Cluster Analysis with Anthropological Data." *American Anthropologist*, 1954, *56*, 180–199.

Cleveland, W. S., and Lachenbruch, P. A. "A Measure of Divergence Among Several Populations." *Communications in Statistics*, 1974, *3* (3), 201–211.

Cliff, N., and Hamburger, C. D. "The Study of Sampling Errors in Factor Analysis by Means of Artificial Experiments." *Psychological Bulletin*, 1967, *68* (6), 430.

Clifford, A. H., and Preston, G. B. "The Algebraic Theory of Semigroups." Paper presented at meeting of American Mathematical Society, Providence, R.I., 1961.

Clifford, H. T., and Stephenson, W. *An Introduction to Numerical Classification*. New York: Academic Press, 1975.

Clunies-Ross, C. W., and Riffenburgh, R. H. "Geometry and Linear Discrimination." *Biometrika*, 1960, *47*, 185–189.

Cochran, W. G. "On the Performance of Linear Discriminant Function." *Technometrics*, 1964, *6* (2), 179–180.

Cochran, W. G., and Hopkins, C. E. "Some Classification Problems with Multivariate Qualitative Data." *Biometrics*, 1961, *17*, 10–31.

Coffin, J. L. "A Statistical Analysis of Driver's and Massey's 1957 Monograph *Comparative Studies of North American Indians*." Unpublished doctoral dissertation, Indiana University, 1973.

Cohen, J. *Statistical Power Analysis for the Behavioral Sciences*. New York: Academic Press, 1969.

Cohn, P. H. *Universal Algebra*. New York: Harper & Row, 1965.

Coleman, J. A., and others. *Medical Innovation*. Indianapolis: Bobbs-Merrill, 1966.

Cooley, W. W., and Lohnes, P. R. *Multivariate Data Analysis*. New York: Wiley, 1971.

Coombs, C. H. *A Theory of Data*. New York: Wiley, 1964.

Coombs, C. H., Coombs, L. C., and McClelland, G. H. "Preference Scales for Number and Sex of Children." *Population Studies*, 1975, *29*, 273–298.

Cormack, R. M. "A Review of Classification." *Journal of the Royal Statistical Society*, 1971, *134* (Series A), 321–367.

Couch, A. S. "Psychological Determinants of Interpersonal Behavior." Unpublished doctoral dissertation, Harvard University, 1960.

Cox, D. R. "Some Procedures Associated with the Logistic Response Curve." *Research Papers in Statistics: Festschrift for J. Neyman*. New York: Wiley, 1966.

Cox, D. R. *Analysis of Binary Data*. London: Methuen, 1976.

Cramer, H. *The Elements of Probability Theory and Some of Its Applications*. New York: Wiley, 1946.

Cronbach, L. J., and Gleser, G. C. "Assessing Similarity Between Profiles." *Psychological Bulletin*, 1953, *50*, 456–473.

Crowell, R. H., and Fox, R. H. *Introduction to Knot Theory*. Boston: Ginn, 1963.

Cunningham, K. M., and Ogilvie, J. C. "Evaluation of Hierarchical Grouping Techniques—A Preliminary Study." *Computer Journal*, 1972, *15*, 209–215.

Czekanowski, J. "Objektive Kriterien in der Ethnologie" [Objective Criteria in Ethnology]. *Korrespondenz-Blatt der Deutschen Gesellschaft für Anthropologie, Ethnologie und Urgeschichte [Correspondence Sheet for the German Society of Anthropology, Ethnology, and Primordial History]*, 1911, *42* (August–December), 1–5.

D'Andrade, R. G. "*U*-Statistic Hierarchical Clustering." *Psychometrika*, 1978, *43*, 59–67.

Davis, A., and others. *Deep South*. Chicago: University of Chicago Press, 1941.

Davis, J. A. "Clustering and Hierarchy in Interpersonal Relations: Testing Two Graph Theoretical Models on 742 Sociomatrices." *American Sociological Review*, 1970, *35*, 843–851.

Davis, J. A., and Leinhardt, S. "The Structure of Positive Interpersonal Relations in Small Groups." In J. Berger, M. Zelditch, and B. Anderson (Eds.), *Sociological Theories in Progress*. Vol. 2. Boston: Houghton Mifflin, 1972.

Day, N. E., and Kerridge, D. G. "A General Maximum Likelihood Discriminant." *Biometrics*, 1967, *23*, 313–323.

Day, W.H.E. "Validity of Clusters Formed by Graph-Theoretic Cluster Methods." *Mathematical Biosciences*, 1977, *36*, 299–317.

Delabre, M., Bianchi, A., and Veron, M. "Étude Critique de Methodes de Taxonomic Numerique: Application à une Classification de Bacteries Agricoles" [Critical Study of Methods of Numerical Taxonomy: Application to a Classification of Agricultural Bacteria]. *Annals of Microbiology* (Institute Pasteur), 1973, *124A*, 489–506.

Demirmen, F. "Multivariate Procedures and Fortran IV Program for Evaluation and Improvement of Classifications." *Kansas State Geological Survey, Computer Contribution*, 1969, *31* (entire issue).

Dempster, A. P. "Tests for the Equality of Two Covariance Matrices in Relation to a Best Linear Discriminator Analysis." *Annals of Mathematical Statistics*, 1964, *35*, 190–199.

Devlin, S. J., Gnanadesikan, R., and Kettenring, J. R. "Robust Estimation of Covariance and Correlational Matrices." Unpublished manuscript, Bell Telephone Laboratories, Murray Hill, N.J., 1975.

Dewey, J. *Logic: The Theory of Inquiry.* New York: Holt, Rinehart and Winston, 1938.

Diday, E., and Simon, J. C. "Clustering Analysis." In K. S. Fu (Ed.), *Communication and Cybernetics 10: Digital Pattern Recognition.* Berlin: Springer-Verlag, 1976.

Dixon, W. J. *BMD–Biomedical Computer Programs.* Berkeley and Los Angeles: University of California Press, 1971.

Doreian, P. "A Note on the Detection of Cliques in Valued Graphs." *Sociometry,* 1969, *32,* 237–242.

Doreian, P. "On the Connectivity of Social Networks." *Journal of Mathematical Sociology,* 1974, *3,* 254–258.

Driver, H. E. "An Integration of Functional, Evolutionary, and Historical Theory by Means of Correlations." *Indiana University Publications in Anthropology and Linguistics,* 1956, *12,* 1–36.

Driver, H. E. "The Contribution of A. L. Kroeber to Culture Area Theory and Practice." *Indiana University Publications in Anthropology and Linguistics,* 1962, *18,* 1–28.

Driver, H. E. "Statistical Studies of Continuous Geographical Distributions." In R. Naroll and R. Cohen (Eds.), *A Handbook of Method in Cultural Anthropology.* Garden City, N.Y.: Natural History Press, 1970.

Driver, H. E. "Cross Cultural Studies." In J. J. Honigman (Ed.), *Handbook of Social and Cultural Anthropology.* Chicago: Rand McNally, 1972.

Driver, H. E., and Coffin, J. L. "Classification and Development of North American Indian Cultures: A Statistical Analysis of the Driver-Massey Sample." *Transactions of the American Philosophical Society,* 1975, *65* (3), 5–120.

Driver, H. E., and Kroeber, A. L. "Quantitative Expressions of Cultural Relationships." *University of California Publications in American Archaeology and Ethnology,* 1932, *31,* 211–256.

Driver, H. E., and Massey, W. C. "Comparative Studies of North American Indians." *Transactions of the American Philosophical Society,* 1957, *47,* 165–456.

Driver, H. E., and Schuessler, K. F. "Factor Analysis of Ethnographic Data." *American Anthropologist,* 1957, *59,* 655–663.

Driver, H. E., and Schuessler, K. F. "Correlational Analysis of Murdock's 1957 Ethnographic Sample." *American Anthropologist*, 1968, *69*, 332–352.

Driver, H. E., and others. "Statistical Classification of North American Indian Ethnic Units." *Ethnology*, 1972, *11*, 311–339.

Dubes, R. C., and Jain, A. K. "Validity Studies in Clustering Methodologies." *Pattern Recognition*, 1979, *11*, 235–254.

Duran, B. S., and Odell, P. L. *Cluster Analysis: A Survey*. Berlin: Springer-Verlag, 1974.

Ehrich, R. W., and Henderson, G. M. "Culture Area." *International Encyclopedia of the Social Sciences*, 1968, *3*, 563–568.

Eisenbeis, R. A., Gilbert, G. G., and Avery, R. B. "Investigating the Relative Importance of Individual Variables and Variable Subsets in Discriminant Analysis." *Communications in Statistics*, 1973, *2* (3), 205–219.

Erdös, P., and Rényi, A. "On Random Matrices II." *Studia Scientiarum Mathematicarum Hungarica* [*Studies of the Mathematical Sciences of Hungary*], 1968, *3*, 459–464.

Everitt, B. *Cluster Analysis*. London: Heinemann, 1974.

Farris, J. S. "On the Cophenetic Correlation Coefficient." *Systematic Zoology*, 1969a, *18*, 279–285.

Farris, J. S. "A Successive Approximation Approach to Character Weighting." *Systematic Zoology*, 1969b, *18*, 374–385.

Feger, H. "Die Erfassung Individueller Einstellungsstrukturen" [The Setting up of Individual Reference Structures]. *Zeitschrift f. Sozial Psychologie* [*Journal of Social Psychology*], 1974, *5*, 242–254.

Fienberg, S. E., and Lee, S. K. "On Small World Statistics." *Psychometrika*, 1975, *40*, 219–228.

Fisher, R. A. "The Use of Multiple Measurements in Taxonomic Problems." *Annals of Eugenics*, 1936, *7*, 179–188.

Fleiss, J. L., and Zubin, J. "On the Methods and Theory of Clustering." *Multivariate Behavioral Research*, 1969, *4*, 235–250.

Forgas, J. P. "Social Episodes and Social Structure in an Academic Setting: The Social Environment of an Intact Group." *Journal of Experimental Social Psychology*, 1978, *14*, 434–448.

Fowlkes, E. B., and McRae, J. E. "Graphical Techniques for Displaying Multidimensional Clusters." Unpublished paper, Bell Telephone Laboratories, Murray Hill, N.J., 1977.

Friedman, H. P., and Rubin, J. "On Some Invariant Criteria for

Grouping Data." *Journal of the American Statistical Association*, 1967, *62*, 1159-1179.

Giacomelli, F., and others. "Subpopulations of Blood Lymphocytes Demonstrated by Quantitative Cytochemistry." *Journal of Histochemistry and Cytochemistry*, 1971, *19*, 426-433.

Gilbert, E. S. "On Discrimination Using Qualitative Variables." *Journal of the American Statistical Association*, 1968, *63*, 1399-1412.

Gilbert, E. S. "The Effect of Unequal Variance-Covariance Matrices on Fisher's Linear Discriminant Function." *Biometrics*, 1969, *25*, 505-516.

Gnanadesikan, R. *Methods of Statistical Data Analysis of Multivariate Observations*. New York: Wiley, 1977.

Gnanadesikan, R., Kettenring, J. R., and Landwehr, J. M. "Interpreting and Assessing the Results of Cluster Analysis." Paper presented at Institute for Scientific Information meeting, Philadelphia, 1977.

Goodman, L. A. "A New Model for Scaling Response Patterns." *Journal of the American Statistical Association*, 1975, *70*, 755-768.

Goodman, L. A., and Kruskal, W. H. "Measures of Association for Cross-Classifications, I." *Journal of the American Statistical Association*, 1954, *49*, 723-764.

Goodman, L. A., and Kruskal, W. H. "Measures of Association for Cross-Classifications, II." *Journal of the American Statistical Association*, 1959, *54*, 123-163.

Goodman, L. A., and Kruskal, W. H. "Measures of Association for Cross-Classifications, III." *Journal of the American Statistical Association*, 1963, *58*, 310-364.

Gouldner, A. W., and Peterson, R. A. *Notes on Technology and the Moral Order*. Indianapolis: Bobbs-Merrill, 1962.

Gower, J. C. "Some Distance Properties of Latent Root and Vector Methods Used in Multivariate Analysis." *Biometrika*, 1966, *53*, 325-338.

Gower, J. C. "A Survey of Numerical Methods Useful in Taxonomy." *Acarologia*, 1969, *11*, 357-375.

Gower, J. C. "A General Coefficient of Similarity and Some of Its Properties." *Biometrics*, 1971, *27*, 857-874.

Gower, J. C. "Generalized Procrustes Analysis." *Psychometrika*, 1975, *40*, 33-51.

Gower, J. C., and Ross, G.J.S. "Minimum Spanning Trees and Single Linkage Cluster Analysis." *Applied Statistics*, 1969, *18*, 54–64.

Green, P. E., and Carroll, J. D. *Mathematical Tools for Applied Multivariate Analysis*. New York: Academic Press, 1976.

Green, P. E., and Rao, V. R. *Applied Multidimensional Scaling*. New York: Holt, Rinehart and Winston, 1972.

Green, V. M. "The Confrontation of Diversity Within the Black Community." *Human Organization*, 1970, *29*, 267–272.

Griffith, B. C., Maier, V. L., and Miller, A. J. "Describing Communications Networks Through the Use of Matrix-Based Measures." Unpublished paper, Graduate School of Library Science, Drexel University, 1973.

Guilford, J. P. *Fundamental Statistics in Psychology and Education*. (4th ed.) New York: McGraw-Hill, 1965.

Gulliksen, H., and Gulliksen, D. *Attitudes of Different Groups Toward Work, Aims, Goals and Activities*. Multivariate Behavioral Research Monographs. Austin, Tex.: Society of Multivariate Experimental Psychology, 1972.

Guttman, L. "Order Analysis of Correlation Matrices." In R. B. Cattell (Ed.), *Handbook of Multivariate Experimental Psychology*. Chicago: Rand McNally, 1966.

Guttman, L. "A General Nonmetric Technique for Finding the Smallest Coordinate Space for a Configuration of Points." *Psychometrika*, 1968, *33*, 469–506.

Guttman, L. *The Facet Approach to Theory Development*. Mimeographed. Tel Aviv, Israel: Hebrew University, 1970.

Haberman, S. J. "Maximum Likelihood Estimates in Exponential Response Models." *Annals of Statistics*, 1977, *5*, 815–841.

Hammond, N., Harbottle, G., and Gazard, T. "Neutron Activation and Statistical Analysis of Maya Ceramics and Clays from Lubaantun, Belize." *Archaeometry*, 1976, *18* (2), 147–168.

Han, C.-P. "A Note on Discrimination in the Case of Unequal Covariance Matrices." *Biometrika*, 1968, *55*, 586–587.

Hannerz, U. *Soulside: Inquiries into Ghetto Culture and Community*. New York: Columbia University Press, 1969.

Harary, F., Norman, R. Z., and Cartwright, D. *Structural Models: An Introduction to the Theory of Directed Graphs*. New York: Wiley, 1965.

Harbottle, G. "Activation Analysis Study of Ceramics from the Copacha (Colima) and Openo (Michoacan) Phases of West Mexico." *American Antiquity*, 1975, *40* (4), 453–458.

Harman, H. H. *Modern Factor Analysis.* (1st ed.) Chicago: University of Chicago Press, 1960.

Harman, H. H. *Modern Factor Analysis.* (2nd ed.) Chicago: University of Chicago Press, 1967.

Hartigan, J. A. "Representation of Similarity Matrices by Trees." *Journal of American Statistical Association*, 1967, *62*, 1140–1158.

Hartigan, J. A. *Clustering Algorithms.* New York: Wiley, 1975a.

Hartigan, J. A. "Printer Graphics for Clustering." *Journal of Statistical and Computer Simulation*, 1975b, *4*, 187–213.

Hartigan, J. A. "Asymptotic Distributions for Clustering Criteria." Paper presented at annual meeting of Classification Society, Hanover, N.H., June 1977a.

Hartigan, J. A. "Distribution Problems in Clustering." In J. Van Ryzin (Ed.), *Classification and Clustering.* New York: Academic Press, 1977b.

Hayashi, C. "On the Prediction of Phenomena from Qualitative Data and the Quantification of Qualitative Data from the Mathematico-Statistical Point of View." *Annals of the Institute of Statistical Mathematics*, 1952, *3*, 69–98.

Heil, G. H., and White, H. C. "An Algorithm for Finding Simultaneous Homomorphic Correspondences Between Graphs and Their Image Graphs." *Behavioral Science*, 1976, *21*, 26–35.

Henderson, D. M. "A Study of the Effects of Family Structure and Poverty on Negro Adolescents from the Ghetto." Unpublished doctoral dissertation, University of Pittsburgh, 1967.

Hickman, J. M. "Dimensions of a Complex Concept: Method Exemplified." *Human Organization*, 1962, *21*, 214–218.

Hill, M. O. "Correspondence Analysis: A Neglected Multivariate Method." *Journal of the Royal Statistical Society*, 1974, *23*, 340–354.

Hodson, R. R., Kendall, D. G., and Tauter, P. (Eds.) *Mathematics in the Archaeological and Historical Sciences.* Chicago: Aldine-Atherton, 1971.

Holland, P. W. "Analyzing Sociometric Data." In B. B. Wolman (Ed.), *International Encyclopedia of Neurology, Psychiatry, Psychoanalysis, and Psychology.* New York: D. Van Nostrand, 1977.

Holland, P. W., and Leinhardt, S. "The Structural Implications of Measurement Error in Sociometry." *Journal of Mathematical Sociology*, 1973, *3*, 85–111.

Holland, P. W., and Leinhardt, S. "Local Structure in Social Networks." In D. Heise (Ed.), *Sociological Methodology 1977*. San Francisco: Jossey-Bass, 1976.

Hollister, L. E., Overall, J. E., and Shelton, J. " Amitriptyline, Perphenazine and Amitriptyline-Perphenazine in Different Depressive Syndromes." *Archives of General Psychiatry*, 1967, *17*, 486–493.

Holzinger, K. H., and Harman, H. H. *Factor Analysis*. Chicago: University of Chicago Press, 1941.

Homans, G. C. *The Human Group*. New York: Harcourt Brace Jovanovich, 1950.

Horan, C. B. "Multidimensional Scaling: Combining Observations When Individuals Have Different Perceptual Structures." *Psychometrika*, 1969, *34*, 139–165.

Horn, J. L. "On Subjectivity in Factor Analysis." *Educational and Psychological Measurement*, 1967, *27* (4), 811.

Hubert, L. J. "Monotone Invariant Clustering Procedures." *Psychometrika*, 1973, *38*, 47–62.

Hubert, L. J. "Approximate Evaluation Techniques for the Single-Link and Complete-Link Hierarchical Clustering Procedures." *Journal of the American Statistical Association*, 1974, *69*, 698–704.

Hubert, L. J. "Generalized Concordance." *Psychometrika*, 1979, *44*, 135–142.

Hubert, L. J., and Baker, F. B. "An Empirical Comparison of Baseline Models for Goodness-of-Fit in *R*-Diameter Hierarchical Clustering." In J. Van Ryzin (Ed.), *Classification and Clustering*. New York: Academic Press, 1977.

Hubert, L. J., and Baker, F. B. "Applications of Combinatorial Programming to Data Analysis: The Traveling Salesman and Related Problems." *Psychometrika*, 1978a, *43*, 81–91.

Hubert, L. J., and Baker, F. B. "Evaluating the Conformity of Sociometric Measurements." *Psychometrika*, 1978b, *43*, 31–41.

Hubert, L. J., and Levin, J. R. "Evaluating Object Set Partitions: Free Sort Analysis and Some Generalizations." *Journal of Verbal Learning and Verbal Behavior*, 1976a, *15*, 459–470.

Hubert, L. J., and Levin, J. R. "A General Statistical Framework for Assessing Categorical Clustering in Free Recall." *Psychological Bulletin*, 1976b, *83*, 1072–1080.

Hubert, L. J., and Schultz, J. "Quadratic Assignment as a General Data Analysis Strategy." *British Journal of Mathematical and Statistical Psychology*, 1976, *29*, 190–241.

Hudson, H. C. "Dimensionality Among Intertrait Relationships in North American Indian Ethnic Units." Unpublished doctoral dissertation, Indiana University, 1979.

Humphreys, L. G., and others. "Capitalization on Chance in Rotation of Factors." *Educational and Psychological Measurement*, 1969, *29* (2), 259.

Hung, A. Y., and Dubes, R. C. "An Introduction to Multi-Class Pattern Recognition in Unstructured Situations." *Interim Science Report No. 12*, Division of Engineering Research, Michigan State University, East Lansing, 1970.

Hutchinson, J. W., and Roberts, J. M. "Expressive Constraints on Driver Re-Education in Psychological Aspects of Driver Behavior." *Institute for Road Safety Research*, 1972, *2* (Section II), 1–12.

Hutchinson, M., Johnstone, K. I., and White, D. R. "The Taxonomy of Certain Thiofacilli." *Journal of General Microbiology*, 1965, *41*, 357–366.

Hymes, D. *The Use of Computers in Anthropology*. Paris: Mouton, 1965.

Jackson, D. N. "Comparison of Classifications." In A. J. Cole (Ed.), *Numerical Taxonomy*. New York: Academic Press, 1969.

Jardine, N., and Sibson, R. "The Construction of Hierarchic and Non-Hierarchic Classifications." *Computer Journal*, 1968, *11*, 177–184.

Jardine, N., and Sibson, R. *Mathematical Taxonomy*. New York: Wiley, 1971.

Johnson, A. E., and Johnson, A. S. "*K*-Means and Temporal Variability in Kansas City Hopewell Ceramics." *American Antiquity*, 1975, *40* (3), 283–295.

Johnson, N., and Sanday, P. "Subculture Variations in an Urban Poor Population." *American Anthropologist*, 1971, *73*, 128–143.

Johnson, P. O. "The Quantification of Qualitative Data in Discriminant Analysis." *Journal of the American Statistical Association*, 1950, *45*, 65–76.

Johnson, S. C. "Hierarchical Clustering Schemes." *Psychometrika*, 1967, *32*, 241–254.

Jones, K. J. "Problems of Grouping Individuals and the Method of Modality." *Behavioral Science*, 1968, *13*, 496–511.

Jones, L. E. "Construal of Social Environments: Multidimensional Models of Interpersonal Perception and Attraction." In N. Hirschberg (Ed.), *Multivariate Models in the Social Sciences*. Hillsdale, N.J.: Erlbaum, in press.

Jones, L. E., and Young, F. W. "The Structure of a Social Environment: A Longitudinal Individual Differences Scaling of an Intact Group." *Journal of Personality and Social Psychology*, 1972, *24*, 108–121.

Jöreskog, K. G. "A General Approach to Confirmatory Maximum Likelihood Factor Analysis." *Psychometrika*, 1969, *34*, 183–202.

Jorgensen, J. G. *Salish Language and Culture*. Bloomington: Indiana University Press, 1969.

Kaiser, H. F. "The Varimax Criterion for Analytic Rotation in Factor Analysis." *Psychometrika*, 1958, *23* (3), 187–200.

Kapferer, B. "Norms and the Manipulation of Relationships in a Work Context." In J. C. Mitchell (Ed.), *Social Networks in Urban Situations*. Manchester, England: Manchester University Press, 1969.

Kapsis, R. W. "Black Ghetto Diversity and Anomie: A Sociopolitical View." *American Journal of Sociology*, 1978, *83*, 1132–1153.

Kay, M. "Social Distance Among Central Missouri Hopewell Settlements: A First Approximation." *American Antiquity*, 1975, *40* (3), 64–71.

Kendall, M. G. *A Course in Multivariate Analysis*. London: Charles Griffin, 1957.

Kendall, M. G. "Discrimination and Classification." In P. R. Krishnaiah (Ed.), *Multivariate Analysis*. New York: Academic Press, 1966.

Kendall, M. G., and Stuart, A. *The Advanced Theory of Statistics*. (3rd ed.) New York: Hafner Press, 1976.

Kim, K. H., and Roush, F. W. "Two-Generator Semigroups of Binary Relations." *Journal of Mathematical Psychology*, 1978, *17*, 236–246.

King, B. F. "Step-Wise Clustering Procedures." *Journal of the American Statistical Association*, 1967, *62*, 86–101.

Köbben, A.J.F. "Comparativists and Non-Comparativists." In R.

Naroll and R. Cohen (Eds.), *A Handbook of Method in Cultural Anthropology*. Garden City, N.Y.: Natural History Press, 1970.

Koopmans, T. C. *Three Essays on the State of Economic Science*. New York: McGraw-Hill, 1957.

Kozelka, R. M., and Roberts, J. M. "A New Approach to Non-Zero Concordance in Explorations." In P. Kay (Ed.), *Mathematical Anthropology*. Cambridge: MIT Press, 1971.

Kroeber, A. L. "Cultural and Natural Areas of Native North America." *University of California Publications in American Archaeology and Ethnology*, 1939, *38*, 1–242.

Kruskal, J. B. "Multidimensional Scaling by Optimizing Goodness-of-Fit to a Nonmetric Hypothesis." *Psychometrika*, 1964a, *29*, 1–27.

Kruskal, J. B. "Non-Metric Multidimensional Scaling: A Numerical Method." *Psychometrika*, 1964b, *29*, 115–129.

Kruskal, J. B., and Wish, M. *Multidimensional Scaling*. Beverly Hills: Sage, 1978.

Kruskal, J. B., Young, F. W., and Seery, J. B. "How to Use KYST: A Very Flexible Program to Do Multidimensional Scaling and Unfolding." Unpublished manuscript, Bell Laboratories, 1973.

Krzanowski, W. J. "Discrimination and Classification Using Both Binary and Continuous Variables." *Journal of the American Statistical Association*, 1975, *70*, 782–790.

Krzanowski, W. J. "The Performance of Fisher's Linear Discriminant Function Under Non-Optimal Conditions." *Technometrics*, 1977, *19*, 191–200.

Laberge, S. "Étude de la Variation des Pronoms Définis et Indéfinis dans le Français Parlé à Montréal" [Study of the Variation of Definite and Indefinite Pronouns in Spoken French in Montreal]. Unpublished doctoral dissertation, Université de Montréal, 1977.

Lachenbruch, P. A. "On Expected Probabilities of Misclassification in Discriminant Analysis, Necessary Sample Size and a Relation with the Multiple Correlation Coefficient." *Biometrics*, 1968, *24*, 823–834.

Lachenbruch, P. A. "Some Results in Multiple Group Discriminant Problems." In T. Cacoullos (Ed.), *Discriminant Analysis and Application*. New York: Academic Press, 1973.

Lachenbruch, P. A. *Discriminant Analysis*. New York: Hafner Press, 1975a.

Lachenbruch, P. A. "Zero-Mean Difference Discrimination and the Absolute Linear Discriminant Function." *Biometrika*, 1975b, *62* (2), 397-401.

Lachenbruch, P. A., and Mickey, M. R. "Estimation of Error Rates in Discriminant Analysis." *Technometrics*, 1968, *10* (1), 1-11.

Lachenbruch, P. A., Sneeringer, C., and Revo, L. T. "Robustness of the Linear and Quadratic Discriminant Function to Certain Types of Non-normality." *Communications in Statistics*, 1973, *1* (1), 39-56.

Lambert, J. M., and Williams, W. T. "Multivariate Methods in Plant Ecology: IV. Nodal Analysis." *Journal of Ecology*, 1962, *50*, 775-802.

Lance, G. N., and Williams, W. T. "A General Theory of Classificatory Sorting Strategies: I. Hierarchical Systems." *Computer Journal*, 1967, *9*, 373-380.

Landau, H. G. "On Dominance Relations and the Structure of Animal Societies: I. Effect of Inherent Characteristics." *Bulletin of Mathematical Biophysics*, 1951, *13*, 1-19.

Landau, H. G. "Development of Structure in a Society with a Dominance Relation When New Members Are Added Successively." *Bulletin of Mathematical Biophysics*, 1965, *27* (Special Issue), 151-160.

Landwehr, J. M. "Approximate Confidence Regions from Cluster Analysis." Unpublished doctoral dissertation, University of Chicago, 1972.

Laumann, E. O., and Pappi, F. U. *Networks of Collective Action*. New York: Academic Press, 1976.

Lawley, D. N., and Maxwell, A. E. *Factor Analysis as a Statistical Method*. London: Butterworths, 1963.

Lenstra, J. K. "Clustering a Data Array and the Traveling Salesman Problem." *Operations Research*, 1974, *22*, 413-414.

Levine, D. D., Carter, E. B., and Gorman, E. M. "Simmel's Influence on American Sociology, I." *American Journal of Sociology*, 1976, *81*, 813-845.

Levine, J. H. "The Sphere of Influence." *American Sociological Review*, 1972, *37*, 14-27.

Lewis, H. "Culture of Poverty? What Does It Matter?" In E. B. Leacock (Ed.), *Culture of Poverty: A Critique*. New York: Simon & Schuster, 1971.

Liebow, E. *Tally's Corner: A Study of Negro Streetcorner Men.* Boston: Little, Brown, 1967.

Ling. R. F. "An Exact Probability Distribution on the Connectivity of Random Graphs." *Journal of Mathematical Psychology,* 1975, *12*, 90–98.

Lingoes, J. C. "An IBM-7090 Program for Guttman-Lingoes Smallest Space Analysis, I." *Behavioral Science,* 1965, *10*, 183–184.

Lingoes, J. C. *The Guttman-Lingoes Nonmetric Program Series.* Ann Arbor: Mathesis Press, 1973.

Lingoes, J. C. "A Neighborhood Preserving Transformation for Fitting Configurations." Paper presented at U.S.-Japan Conference on Multidimensional Scaling, La Jolla, Calif., August 1975.

Lingoes, J. C., and Borg, I. "Optimal Solutions for Dimension and Vector Weights in PINDIS." *Michigan Mathematical Psychology Program,* 1976a, *4*, 1–19.

Lingoes, J. C., and Borg, I. "**P**rocrustean **IN**dividual **DI**fference Scaling: A Direct Transformational Approach to Multidimensional Analysis of Three-Way Data Matrices." *Journal of Marketing Research,* 1976b, *13*, 406–407.

Lingoes, J. C., and Borg, I. "A Direct Procrustean Analysis of Individual Differences Scaling Using Increasingly Complex Transformations." *Psychometrika,* 1978, *43*, 491–519.

Lingoes, J. C., and Roskam, E. "A Mathematical and Empirical Analysis of Two Multidimensional Scaling Algorithms." *Psychometric Monographs,* 1973, *38*, 1–93.

Lingoes, J. C., and Schönemann, P. H. "Alternative Measures of Fit for the Schönemann-Carroll Matrix Fitting Algorithm." *Psychometrika,* 1974, *39*, 423–427.

Linhart, H. "Techniques for Discriminant Analysis with Discrete Variables." *Metrika,* 1959, *2*, 138–149.

Lorr, M., and Radhakrishnan, B. K. "A Comparison of Two Methods of Cluster Analysis." *Educational and Psychological Measurement,* 1967, *27*, 47–53.

Lorrain, F., and White, H. C. "Structural Equivalence of Individuals in Social Networks." *Journal of Mathematical Sociology,* 1971, *1*, 49–80.

Luce, R. D. "Connectivity and Generalized Cliques in Sociometric Group Structure." *Psychometrika,* 1950, *15*, 169–190.

Luce, R. D., and Galanter, E. "Psychophysical Scaling." In R. D. Luce, R. R. Bush, and E. Galanter (Eds.), *Handbook of Mathematical Psychology*. Vol. 1. New York: Wiley, 1963.

McCormick, W. T., Jr., Schweitzer, P. J., and White, T. W. "Problem Decomposition and Data Reorganization by a Clustering Technique." *Operations Research*, 1972, *20*, 993–1009.

McFarland, D. D., and Brown, D. J. "Social Distance as a Metric: A Systematic Introduction to Smallest Space Analysis." In E. O. Laumann (Ed.), *Bonds of Pluralism*. New York: Wiley, 1973.

McIntyre, R. M., and Blashfield, R. K. "A Nearest-Centroid Technique for Evaluating the Minimum Variance Cluster Procedure." *Multivariate Behavioral Research*, 1980, *15*, 225–238.

McKay, R. J. "Simultaneous Procedures in Discriminant Analysis Involving Two Groups." *Technometrics*, 1976, *18* (1), 47–53.

MacQueen, J. B. "Some Methods for Classification and Analysis of Multivariate Observations." *Proceedings of the Fifth Berkeley Symposium on Mathematical Statistics and Probability, I*, 1967, 281–297.

McQuitty, L. L., and Clark, J. A. "Clusters from Iterative, Intercolumnar Correlational Analysis." *Educational and Psychological Measurement*, 1968, *28*, 211–238.

MacRae, D., Jr. "Direct Factor Analysis of Sociometric Data." *Sociometry*, 1960, *23*, 360–371.

MacRae, D., Jr. *Issues and Parties in Legislative Analysis: Methods of Statistical Analysis*. New York: Harper & Row, 1970.

Marks, S., and Dunn, O. J. "Discriminant Functions When Covariance Matrices Are Unequal." *Journal of the American Statistical Association*, 1974, *69*, 555–559.

Maroy, J. P., and Peneau, J. P. "Typologies en Architecture." First International Symposium on Data Analysis and Informatics (Versailles). Vol II. Rocquencourt, France: Institut de Recherché d'Informatique et d'Automatique [Office of Research for Computerized Information], 1977.

Marriot, F.H.C. "Practical Problems in a Method of Cluster Analysis." *Biometrics*, 1971, *27*, 501–514.

Matula, D. W. "Graph Theoretic Techniques for Cluster Analysis Algorithms." In J. Van Ryzin (Ed.), *Classification and Clustering*. New York: Academic Press, 1977.

Mehrabian, A. *Basic Dimensions for a General Psychological Theory*. Cambridge, Mass.: Oelgeschlager, Gunn & Hain, 1980.

Michaelis, J. "Simulation Experiments with Multiple Group Linear and Quadratic Discriminant Analysis." In. T. Cacoullos (Ed.), *Discriminant Analysis and Applications.* New York: Academic Press, 1973.

Milligan, G. W., and Issac, P. O. "The Validation of Four Ultrametric Clustering Algorithms." *Pattern Recognition,* 1980, *12,* 41–50.

Mitchell, J. C. *Social Networks in Urban Situations.* Manchester, England: Manchester University Press, 1969.

Morf, M. E., Miller, C. E., and Syrotrick, J. M. "A Comparison of Cluster Analysis and Q-Factor Analysis." *Journal of Clinical Psychology,* 1976, *32,* 59–64.

Morrison, D. G. "Measurement Problems in Cluster Analysis." *Management Science,* 1967, *13* (Series B), 775–780.

Moss, W. W. "Experiments with Various Techniques of Numerical Taxonomy." *Systematic Zoology,* 1968, *17,* 31–47.

Mulaik, S. H. *The Foundations of Factor Analysis.* New York: McGraw-Hill, 1972.

Mullins, N. C., and others. "The Group Structure of Two Scientific Specialties: A Comparative Study." *American Sociological Review,* 1977, *42,* 552–562.

Murdock, G. P. "World Ethnographic Sample." *American Anthropologist,* 1957, *59,* 644–687.

Murdock, G. P. *Ethnographic Atlas.* Pittsburgh: University of Pittsburgh Press, 1967.

Nadel, S. F. *The Theory of Social Structure.* London: Cohen and West, 1957.

Naroll, R. "What Have We Learned from Cross-Cultural Surveys?" *American Anthropologist,* 1970, *72,* 1227–1288.

Neel, J. V., Rothhammer, F., and Lingoes, J. C. "The Genetic Structure of a Tribal Population, the Yanomama Indians: X. Agreement Between Representations of Village Distances Based on Different Sets of Characteristics." *American Journal of Human Genetics,* 1974, *26,* 281–303.

Neumann, G. K. "Archaeology and Race in the American Indians." In J. B. Griffin (Ed.), *Archaeology of Eastern United States.* Chicago: University of Chicago Press, 1952.

Newcomb, T. M. *The Acquaintance Process.* New York: Holt, Rinehart and Winston, 1961.

Nie, N. H., and others. *SPSS: Statistical Package for the Social Sciences.* (2nd ed.) New York: McGraw-Hill, 1975.

Nunnally, J. C. *Psychometric Theory.* New York: McGraw-Hill, 1967.

Osgood, C. E. "Semantic Differential Technique in the Comparative Study of Cultures." *American Anthropologist*, 1964, *66*, 171–200.

Osgood, C. E., Suci, G. J., and Tannenbaum, P. H. *The Measurement of Meaning.* Urbana: University of Illinois Press, 1957.

Paykel, E. S. "Correlates of Depressive Typology." *Archives of General Psychiatry*, 1972, *120*, 146–156.

Peay, E. R. "Nonmetric Grouping: Clusters and Cliques." *Psychometrika*, 1975, *40*, 297–313.

Peay, E. R. "A Note Concerning 'On the Connectivity of Social Networks.'" *Journal of Mathematical Sociology*, 1976, *4*, 319–321.

Penrose, L. S. "Distance, Size and Shape." *Annals of Eugenics*, 1954, *18*, 337–343.

Phillips, D. B., and Conviser, R. H. "Measuring the Structure and Boundary Properties of Groups: Some Uses of Information Theory." *Sociometry*, 1972, *35* (2), 235–254.

Prag, A., and others. "Hellenistic Glazed Wares from Athens and Southern Italy: Analytical Techniques and Implications." *Archaeometry*, 1974, *16* (2), 153–187.

Prothro, E. T. "Patterns of Permissiveness Among Preliterate Peoples." *Journal of Abnormal and Social Psychology*, 1960, *51*, 151–154.

Rabinowitz, G. B. "An Introduction to Nonmetric Multidimensional Scaling." *American Journal of Political Science*, 1975, *19*, 343–390.

Rainwater, L. *Behind Ghetto Walls: Black Family Life in a Federal Slum.* Hawthorne, N.Y.: Aldine, 1974.

Rao, C. R. *Advanced Statistical Methods in Biometric Research.* New York: Wiley, 1952.

Rao, C. R. "Inference on Discriminant Function Coefficients." In R. C. Bose and others (Eds.), *Essays in Probability and Statistics.* Chapel Hill: University of North Carolina and Statistical Publishing Society, 1970.

Raskin, A., and Crook, T. H. "The Endogeneous-Neurotic Distinction as a Predictor of Response to Antidepressant Drugs." *Psychological Medicine*, 1976, *6*, 59–70.

Redfield, R. *Tepoztlan*. Chicago: University of Chicago Press, 1930.

Redfield, R. *The Folk Culture of Yucatan*. Chicago: University of Chicago Press, 1941.

Rightmore, G. P. "Iron Age Skills from Southern Africa Reassessed by Multiple Discriminant Analysis." *American Journal of Physical Anthropology*, 1970, *33*, 147–168.

Roberts, J. M. "Kinsmen and Friends in Zuni Culture: A Terminological Note." *El Placio*, 1965, *72*, 38–43.

Roberts, J. M., and Chick, G. E. "Butler County Eight Ball: A Behavioral Space Analysis." In J. H. Goldstein (Ed.), *Sports, Games, and Play*. Hillsdale, N.J.: Erlbaum, 1979.

Roberts, J. M., Golder, T. V., and Chick, G. E. "Judgment, Oversight, and Skill: A Cultural Analysis of P-3 Pilot Error." *Human Organization*, 1980, *39* (1), 5–21.

Roberts, J. M., Hutchinson, J. W., and Carlson, G. S. "Traffic Control Decisions and Self-Testing Values: A Preliminary Note." *Traffic Engineering*, 1972, *42*, 42–48.

Roberts, J. M., Hutchinson, J. W., and Hanscom, F. "Driving Behavior and Self-Testing Attitudes." Unpublished manuscript, University of Pittsburgh, n. d.

Roberts, J. M., and Jones, D. "Significant Figures in a Black Community Organization." Unpublished manuscript, University of Pittsburgh, n. d.

Roberts, J. M., Kozelka, R. M., and Arth, M. J. "Some Highway Culture Patterns." *The Plains Anthropologist*, 1956, *3*, 3–14.

Roberts, J. M., and Kundrat, D. G. "Variation in Expressive Balances and Competence for Sports Car Rally Teams." *Urban Life*, 1978, *7* (2), 231–251.

Roberts, J. M., and Nattrass, S. M. "Women and Trapshooting: Competence and Expression in a Game of Physical Skill with Chance." In H. B. Schwartzman (Ed.), *Play and Culture*. West Point, N.Y.: Leisure Press, 1980.

Roberts, J. M., Strand, R. F., and Burmeister, E. "Preferential Pattern Analysis in Explorations." In P. Kay (Ed.), *Mathematical Anthropology*. Cambridge: MIT Press. 1971.

Roberts, J. M., Thompson, W. E., and Sutton-Smith, B. "Expressive Self-Testing in Driving." *Human Organization*, 1966, *25*, 54–63.

Roberts, J. M., and Wicke, J. O. "Flying and Expressive Self-Testing." *Naval War College Review*, 1971, *23*, 67–80.

Roberts, J. M., and others. "The Small Highway Business on U.S. 30 in Nebraska." *Economic Geography*, 1956, *32*, 139–152.

Rodman, H. "The Lower-Class Value Stretch." *Social Forces*, 1963, *42*, 205–215.

Rodman, H. *Lower-Class Families: The Culture of Poverty in Negro Trinidad.* New York: Oxford University Press, 1971.

Rodman, H. "Culture of Poverty: The Rise and Fall of a Concept." *American Sociological Review*, 1977, *25*, 867–876.

Roethlisberger, F. J., and Dickson, W. J. *Management and the Worker.* Cambridge: Harvard University Press, 1939.

Rogers, G., and Linden, J. D. "Use of Multiple Discriminant Function Analysis in the Evaluation of Three Multivariate Grouping Techniques." *Educational and Psychological Measurement*, 1973, *33*, 787–802.

Rohlf, F. J. "Methods of Comparing Classifications." *Annual Review of Ecology and Systematics*, 1974, *5*, 101–113.

Rohlf, F. J. "Representing Clusters as Solid Objects in a 3-Space." Paper presented at annual meeting of the Classification Society, Clemson University, Clemson, S.C., May 1978.

Rohlf, F. J., and Sokal, R. R. "Coefficients of Correlation and Distance in Numerical Taxonomy." *The University of Kansas Science Bulletin*, 1965, *45*, 3–27.

Romney, A. K., and D'Andrade, R. G. "Cognitive Aspects of English Kin Terms." *American Anthropologist*, 1964, *66*, 146–179.

Roskam, E., and Lingoes, J. C. "MINISSA-I: A Fortran IV (G) Program for the Smallest Space Analysis of Square Symmetric Matrices." *Behavioral Science*, 1970, *15*, 204–205.

Ross, I. C., and Harary, F. "A Description of Strengthening and Weakening Members of a Group." *Sociometry*, 1959, *22*, 139–147.

Rousseau, P. "Analyse de Données Binaires" [Analysis of Binary Data]. Unpublished doctoral dissertation, Université de Montréal, 1978.

Rousseau, P., and Sankoff, D. "Singularities in the Analysis of Binary Data." *Biometrika*, 1978a, *65*, 603–608.

Rousseau, P., and Sankoff, D. "A Solution to the Problem of Grouping Speakers." In D. Sankoff (Ed.), *Linguistic Variation Models and Methods.* New York: Academic Press, 1978b.

Rubin, J. "An Approach to Organizing Data in Homogeneous

Groups." *Systematic Zoology*, 1966, *15*, 169–182.

Rubin, J., and Friedman, H. P. *A Cluster Analysis and Taxonomy System for Grouping and Classifying Data*. New York: IBM, 1967.

Rummel, R. J. *Applied Factor Analysis*. Chicago: Northwestern University Press, 1970.

Russell, B. "Mathematical Logic as Based on the Theory of Types." *American Journal of Mathematics*, 1908, *30*, 222–262.

Sailer, L. D. "Structural Equivalence: Meaning and Definition, Computation, and Application." *Social Networks*, 1978, *1*, 73–90.

Sampson, S. F. "Crisis in a Cloister." University microfilms N. 69-5775. Ann Arbor: University of Michigan, 1969.

Sawyer, J., and LeVine, R. "Cultural Dimensions: A Factor Analysis of the World Ethnographic Sample." *American Anthropologist*, 1966, *68*, 708–731.

Schönemann, P. H. "An Algebraic Solution for a Class of Subjective Metrics Models." *Psychometrika*, 1972, *37*, 441–451.

Schönemann, P. H., and Carroll, R. M. "Fitting One Matrix to Another Under Choice of a Central Dilation and a Rigid Motion." *Psychometrika*, 1970, *35*, 245–255.

Schuessler, K. F. *Analyzing Social Data*. Boston: Houghton Mifflin, 1971.

Schuessler, K. F., and Driver, H. E. "A Factor Analysis of the 16 Primitive Societies." *American Sociological Review*, 1956, *21*, 493–499.

Schwartz, J. E. "An Examination of CONCOR and Related Methods for Blocking Sociometric Data." In D. R. Heise (Ed.), *Sociological Methodology 1977*. San Francisco: Jossey-Bass, 1976.

Scott, A. J., and Symons, M. J. "Clustering Methods Based on the Likelihood Ratio Criteria." *Biometrics*, 1971, *27*, 387–397.

Shepard, R. N. "The Analysis of Proximities: Multidimensional Scaling with an Unknown Distance Function, I." *Psychometrika*, 1962, *27*, 127–140.

Shepard, R. N., Romney, A. K., and Nerlove, S. B. *Multidimensional Scaling*. 2 vols. New York: Seminar Press, 1972.

Shotland, R. L. *University Communications Network: The Small World Method*. New York: Wiley, 1976.

Simmel, G. *Conflict and the Web of Group-Affiliations*. New York: Free Press, 1955.

Simmons, L. W. *The Role of the Aged in Primitive Society*. New Haven: Yale University Press, 1945.

Skinner, H. A. "A Multivariate Strategy for Classification Research." University of Western Ontario, Canada, Department of Psychology Bulletin 301, 1974.

Slagle, J. R., Chang, C. L., and Heller, S. R. "A Clustering and Data-Reorganizing Algorithm." *IEEE Transactions on Systems, Man, and Cybernetics*, 1975, *5*, 125–128.

Slater, P. E. *Microcosm: Structural, Psychological, and Religious Evolution in Groups.* New York: Wiley, 1966.

Smith, F. J., and Crano, W. D. "Global and Regional Analyses of the Ethnographic Atlas." *American Anthropologist*, 1977, *79*, 363–387.

Sneath, P.H.A. "A Comparison of Different Clustering Methods As Applied to Randomly Spaced Points." *Classification Society Bulletin*, 1966, *1*, 2–18.

Sneath, P.H.A. "A Significance Test for Clusters in UPGMA Phenograms Obtained from Squared Euclidean Distances." *Classification Society Bulletin*, 1977, *4*, 2–14.

Sneath, P.H.A., and Sokal, R. R. *Numerical Taxonomy.* San Francisco: W. H. Freeman, 1973.

Snygg, C. E. "Plotting High-Dimensional Data." Paper presented at annual meeting of the Classification Society, Clemson University, Clemson, S.C., May 1978.

Sokal, R. R., and Rohlf, F. J. "The Comparison of Dendrograms by Objective Methods." *Taxon*, 1962, *11*, 33–40.

Sokal, R. R., and Sneath, P.H.A. *Principles of Numerical Taxonomy.* San Francisco: W. H. Freeman, 1963.

Solomon, H. "Numerical Taxonomy." Unpublished paper, Stanford University Department of Statistics, 1970.

Sonquist, J. A., Baker, E. L., and Morgan, J. N. *Searching for Structure.* Ann Arbor: Institute of Social Research, University of Michigan, 1971.

Spiro, M. E. "A Typology of Social Structure and the Patterning of Social Institutions: A Cross-Cultural Study." *American Anthropologist*, 1965, *67*, 1097–1119.

Stevens, S. S. "On the Theory of Scales of Measurement." *Science*, 1946, *103*, 667–680.

Stevens, S. S. "Issues in Psychophysical Measurement." *Psychological Review*, 1971, *78*, 426–450.

Strauss, J. S., and others. "Use of the Biplot for the Classification of Psychiatric Disorders." Paper presented at annual meeting of the

Classification Society, Rochester, N.Y., May 1976.

Stringer, C. B. "Population Relationships of Later Pleistocene Hominids: A Multivariate Study of Available Crania." *Journal of Archaeological Science*, 1974, *1*, 317–342.

Strodtbeck, F. G. "Bales 20 Years Later: A Review Essay." *American Journal of Sociology*, 1973, *79*, 459–465.

Thompson, D'A. W. *On Growth and Form*. (2nd ed.) New York: Macmillan, 1948.

Thurstone, L. L. *Multiple Factor Analysis*. Chicago: University of Chicago Press, 1947.

Tissot, A. *Mémoire sur la Représentation des Surfaces, et les Projections des Cartes Géographiques [Notes on the Representation of Surfaces and Projections of Geographic Maps]*. Paris: Gauthier-Villars, 1881.

Tobler, W. R. "Map Transformations of Geographic Space." Unpublished doctoral dissertation, University of Washington, 1961.

Tobler, W. R. "D'Arcy Thompson and the Analysis of Growth and Form." *Michigan Academy of Science, Arts, and Letters*, 1963, *58*, 385–390.

Torgerson, W. S. *Theory and Methods of Scaling*. New York: Wiley, 1958.

Tryon, R. C., and Bailey, D. E. *Cluster Analysis*. New York: McGraw-Hill, 1970.

Tucker, L., and Lewis, C. "A Reliability Coefficient for Maximum Likelihood Factor Analysis." *Psychometrika*, 1973, *38*, 1–10.

Turner, D. W., and Tidmore, F. E. "Clustering with Chernoff-Type Faces." Paper presented at American Statistical Association meetings, Chicago, 1977.

Urbakh, V. Y. "Linear Discriminant Analysis: Loss of Discriminating Power When a Variate Is Omitted." *Biometrics*, 1971, *27*, 531–534.

Van Ryzin, J. *Classification and Clustering*. New York: Academic Press, 1977.

Voegelin, C., and Voegelin, F. *Anthropological Linguistics: Index to Languages of the World*. Vol. 7. Bloomington: Indiana University Press, 1966.

Walker, S. H., and Duncan, D. B. "Estimation of the Probability of an Event as a Function of Several Independent Variables." *Biometrika*, 1967, *54*, 167–179.

Ward, G. K. "A Systematic Approach to the Definition of Sources of Raw Material." *Archaeometry*, 1974, *16* (1), 41–53.

Ward, J. H. "Hierarchical Grouping to Optimize an Objective Function." *Journal of the American Statistical Association*, 1963, *58*, 236–244.

Ward, J. H., and Hook, M. E. "Application of a Hierarchical Grouping Procedure to a Problem of Grouping Profiles." *Educational and Psychological Measurement*, 1963, *23*, 69–81.

Weiner, J. M., and Dunn, O. J. "Elimination of Variates in Linear Discrimination Problems." *Biometrics*, 1966, *22*, 268–275.

Wherry, R. J., Sr., and Wherry, R. J., Jr. "Wherry-Wherry Hierarchical Factor Analysis." In R. J. Wherry, Sr., and J. Olivero (Eds.), *Computer Programs for Psychology*. Columbus: Ohio State University, 1971.

White, H. C. "Management Conflict and Sociometric Structure." *American Journal of Sociology*, 1961, *67*, 185–199.

White, H. C. *Chains of Opportunity*. Cambridge: Harvard University Press, 1970.

White, H. C., Boorman, S. A., and Breiger, R. L. "Social Structure from Multiple Networks: I. Blockmodels of Roles and Positions." *American Journal of Sociology*, 1976, *81*, 730–780.

Whiting, J. W., and Child, I. L. *Child Training and Personality: A Cross Cultural Study*. New Haven: Yale University Press, 1953.

Williams, M. D. *Community in a Black Pentecostal Church: An Anthropological Study*. Pittsburgh: University of Pittsburgh Press, 1974.

Williams, M. D. *Selected Readings in Afro-American Anthropology*. Lexington, Mass.: Xerox Publishing Co., 1975.

Williams, M. D. *On the Street Where I Lived*. New York: Holt, Rinehart and Winston, 1981.

Williams, M. D. "Childhood in an Urban Black Ghetto." Unpublished manuscript, Purdue University, n.d.

Williams, W. T. *Pattern Analysis in Agricultural Science*. Amsterdam: Scientific Publishing, 1976.

Williams, W. T., and Clifford, H. T. "On the Comparison of Two Classifications of the Same Set of Elements." *Taxon*, 1971, *20*, 519–522.

Williams, W. T., Clifford, H. T., and Lance, G. N. "Group-Size

Dependence: A Rationale for Choice Between Numerical Classifications." *Computer Journal*, 1971, *14*, 157–162.

Williams, W. T., and Dale, M. B. "Fundamental Problems in Numerical Taxonomy." In R. D. Preston (Ed.), *Botanical Research*. Vol 2. New York: Academic Press, 1965.

Williams, W. T., and others. "Controversy Concerning the Criteria for Taxonometric Strategies." *Computer Journal*, 1971, *14*, 162–165.

Williamson, O. E. *Markets and Hierarchies: Analysis and Antitrust Implications*. New York: Free Press, 1975.

Wish, M., Deutsch, M., and Kaplan, S. J. "Perceived Dimensions of Interpersonal Relations." *Journal of Personality and Social Psychology*, 1976, *33*, 409–420.

Wishart, D. *Clustan 1C User Manual*. London: Computer Centre, University College, 1975.

Wishart, D., and Leach, S. V. "A Multivariate Analysis of Platonic Prose Rhythm." *Computer Studies in the Humanities and Verbal Behavior*, 1970, *3*, 90–99.

Wolfe, J. H. "Pattern Clustering by Multivariate Mixture Analysis." *Multivariate Behavioral Research*, 1970, 5, 329–350.

Wolfe, J. H. "A Monte Carlo Study of the Sampling Distribution of the Likelihood Ratio for Mixtures of Multinormal Distributions." Unpublished manuscript, U.S. Naval Personnel and Training Research Laboratory, San Diego, 1971a.

Wolfe, J. H. "NORMIX 360 Computer Program." Unpublished manuscript, U.S. Naval Personnel and Training Research Laboratory, San Diego, 1971b.

Wright, B., and Evitts, M. S. "Direct Factor Analysis in Sociometry." *Sociometry*, 1961, *24*, 82–98.

Young, F. W. "A New View of Individual Differences in the Weighted Euclidean MDS Model." Paper presented at meetings of the Psychometric Society, Uppsala, Sweden, June 1978.

Young, V. H. "Negro Community." *American Anthropologist*, 1970, *72*, 269–288.

Index